WYM

D1615085

Please return / renew by date shown.
You can renew at: **norlink.norfolk.gov.uk**
or by telephone: **0344 800 8006**
Please have your library card & PIN ready.

NORFOLK LIBRARY
AND INFORMATION SERVICE

ABOUT THE AUTHOR

Lancashire-based writer and photographer Terry Marsh specialises in the outdoors, the countryside, walking and travel worldwide. He has been writing books since the mid-1980s, and is the author or revision author of over 100 books, including the award-winning Cicerone guides *A Northern Coast to Coast Walk* and *The Shropshire Way*, as well as Cicerone guides to the Isle of Skye, the Isle of Mull, the West Pennine Moors, the Forest of Bowland, the Severn Way, the Dales Way and the West Highland Way. More recently he has written and illustrated *Great Mountain Days in Snowdonia*.

Terry has a particular interest in Cumbria and the Lake District, the Yorkshire Dales, Lancashire, the Peak District, the Hebrides and the Isle of Man. Living on the edge of the West Pennine Moors, it was only natural that his interest expanded to embrace the central thrust of the Pennines, and this led to a

book produced in the 1980s – *Great Classic Walks in the Pennines*. Thereafter, he was a frequent visitor to all parts of the Pennines, especially the South Pennines, which have the hearty tang of Lancashire about them.

Terry was born into a Lancashire mining family, but escaped the clutches of the National Coal Board to enter local government, wherein he remained until 1990, by which time his first books had been published. A few years as a driving instructor helped to bolster his earnings as a writer before he went full time and trusted to his pen.

Terry holds an MA in Lake District Studies, and is a Fellow of the Royal Geographical Society (FRGS) and of the Society of Antiquaries of Scotland (FSA Scot), a member of the Society of Authors and the NUJ, and an Honorary Life Member of the Outdoor Writers and Photographers Guild.

Other Cicerone guides by the author

A Northern Coast to Coast Walk
Geocaching in the UK
Great Mountain Days in Snowdonia
The Dales Way
The Isle of Man

The Isle of Mull
The Isle of Skye
The West Highland Way
Walking in the Forest of Bowland and Pendle
Walking on the West Pennine Moors

GREAT MOUNTAIN DAYS
IN
THE PENNINES

by Terry Marsh

CICERONE

2 POLICE SQUARE, MILNTHORPE, CUMBRIA LA7 7PY
www.cicerone.co.uk

Printed by KHL Printing, Singapore
A catalogue record for this book is available from the British Library.
All photographs are by the author unless otherwise stated.

DEDICATION

My son, Martin, and my wife, Vivienne, accompanied me on a number of the walks. But it was my brother-in-law Jonathan Young, who regularly drove over from Abergele in north Wales to accompany me on most of them, and contrived to break his wrist, badly injure his head and lose his watch on one walk in the Peak District. So, I dedicate the book to him, with grateful thanks for his company and unfailing determination to enjoy every last step of the way.

WARNING

Mountain walking can be a dangerous activity carrying a risk of personal injury or death. It should be undertaken only by those with a full understanding of the risks and with the training and experience to evaluate them. While every care and effort has been taken in the preparation of this guide, the user should be aware that conditions can be highly variable and can change quickly, materially affecting the seriousness of a mountain walk. Therefore, except for any liability which cannot be excluded by law, neither Cicerone nor the author accept liability for damage of any nature (including damage to property, personal injury or death) arising directly or indirectly from the information in this book.

To call out the Mountain Rescue, ring 999 or the international emergency number 112: this will connect you via any available network. Once connected to the emergency operator, ask for the police.

INTERNATIONAL DISTRESS SIGNAL

The recognised distress signal is six whistle blasts (or torch flashes in the dark) spread over one minute, followed by a minute's pause. Repeat until an answer is received (which will be three signals per minute followed by a minute's pause).

ADVICE TO READERS

While every effort is made by our authors to ensure the accuracy of guidebooks as they go to print, changes can occur during the lifetime of an edition. If we know of any, there will be an Updates tab on this book's page on the Cicerone website (www.cicerone.co.uk), so please check before planning your trip. We also advise that you check information about such things as transport, accommodation and shops locally. Even rights of way can be altered over time. We are always grateful for information about any discrepancies between a guidebook and the facts on the ground, sent by email to info@cicerone.co.uk or by post to Cicerone, 2 Police Square, Milnthorpe LA7 7PY, United Kingdom.

Front cover: On the summit of Black Hameldon (Walk 36)

CONTENTS

Preface 9

INTRODUCTION 11
About this guide 12
Weather to walk? 17
Before you start 17

NORTH PENNINES 22
1   Thack Moor and Black Fell 23
2   Melmerby Fell and Fiend's Fell 27
3   Cross Fell 31
4   High Cup Nick and Backstone Edge 35
5   Cauldron Snout and Widdybank Fell 40
6   High Force and Cronkley Fell 44
7   Harter Fell and Grassholme 48
8   Bowes Moor 52

NORTH WEST DALES – EDEN VALLEY AND THE HOWGILLS 58
9   Hartley Fell and Nine Standards Rigg 59
10   Lunds Fell, Hugh Seat and High Seat 64
11   Wild Boar Fell and Swarth Fell 69
12   Green Bell 74
13   The Fairmile Circuit 78
14   Cautley Spout and The Calf 82
15   The Calf from Sedbergh 85

YORKSHIRE DALES 91
16   Great Shunner Fell and Lovely Seat 92
17   Upper Swaledale and Rogan's Seat 96
18   Dodd Fell Hill and Drumaldrace 100
19   Gragareth and Great Coum 104
20   Whernside 109
21   Ingleborough 113
22   Giggleswick Scar 119
23   Nappa Cross, Rye Loaf Hill and Victoria Cave 123
24   Pen-y-Ghent and Plover Hill 127
25   Fountains Fell 130

26 Janet's Foss, Gordale Scar and Malham Cove 134

27 Buckden Pike 139

28 Great Whernside 143

29 Cracoe Fell and Thorpe Fell 147

30 Elslack Moor and Pinhaw Beacon 151

31 Rombalds Moor and Ilkley Moor 155

SOUTH PENNINES 160

32 Pendle Hill 161

33 Boulsworth Hill 165

34 Delf Hill and Stanbury Moor 170

35 Wadsworth Moor 174

36 Worsthorne Moor and Black Hameldon 178

37 Thieveley Pike and Cliviger Gorge 182

38 Bride Stones Moor 186

39 Luddenden Dean and Midgeley Moor 190

40 Stoodley Pike 194

41 Langfield Common 199

42 Blackstone Edge 203

43 Rooley Moor and Cowpe Lowe 208

44 White Hill and Piethorne Clough 213

DARK PEAK 218

45 Saddleworth Edges 219

46 Lord's Seat and Mam Tor 223

47 Kinder Downfall 227

48 Rowlee Pasture and Alport Castles 231

49 Back Tor and Derwent Edge 235

50 Stanage Edge 240

Appendix 1   Concise walk reference and personal log 246

Appendix 2   Bibliography 249

Index 250

Route symbols on OS map extracts

(for OS legend see printed OS maps)

route

alternative route

(🧍) start/finish point

◀ route direction

0   1km

0   0.5 mile

The extracts from 1:50,000 OS maps used in this book
have been reproduced at 1:40,000 for greater clarity

Features on the overview map

Urban area

National Park

Area of Outstanding
Natural Beauty

800m
600m
400m
200m
75m
0m

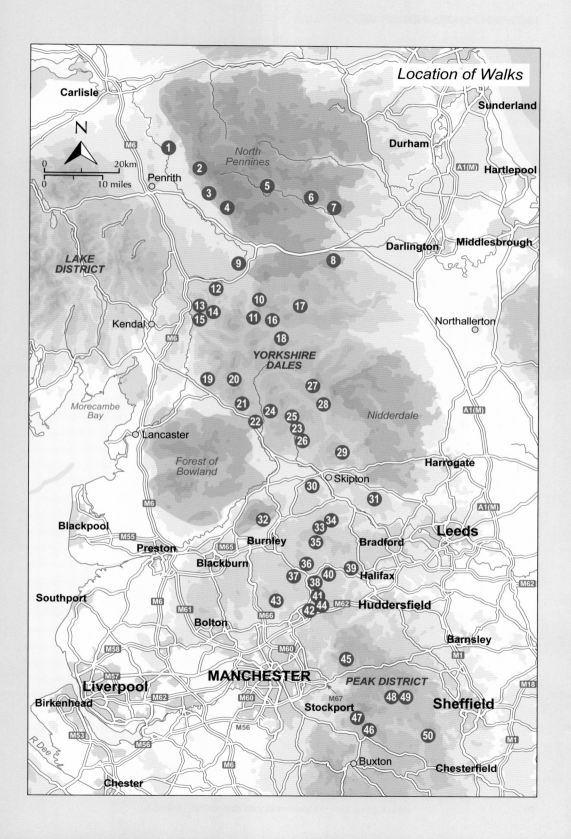

Location of Walks

PREFACE

During the late 1980s, still cutting my writer's teeth, I braved the world of the Pennines to work on *The Pennine Mountains*. It was an eye-opening experience – one that led me into gelatinous peaty folds and across high, airy summits. Raised in industrial Lancashire, what little I knew of the Pennines was to my mind tarred with the same brush of bleak grimness as the towns and villages gathered among the Pennine landscapes.

I soon came to realise that the stereotypical portrait was a chimera, an unfounded legend that betrayed the beauty that I came to discover here. Some years later I visited again, preparing another guide for walkers, but in the meantime had learned how to appreciate these softer, more moulded landscapes, and had realised that absence of the crags that frequent the Lake District and parts of Snowdonia didn't have to mean an absence of a perfect walkers' domain.

The walks in this book are very much personal favourites. There are, of course, the summit routes that one might expect to find, but I've introduced a few that are much less well known. Together they give a taste of the Pennines that should appeal to everyone, and encourage all to try a few new flavours.

Terry Marsh, 2013

INTRODUCTION

The Pennines are a low-rising mountain range, separating the north-west of England from the north-east. Often described as the 'backbone of England', they form a somewhat disjointed range stretching from Derbyshire to the Scottish border. To speak of them as a 'chain' merely serves to draw attention to the weak links, the places where the central spinal mass has been eroded to leave behind distinct groups of hills and moors separated by wide valleys. Geographers would tell you that the Pennines are neither a chain nor a range of mountains, but simply a broad uplift. Moreover, what many would regard as 'Pennine' country means different things in different places. First and foremost, the Pennines are a major water catchment area, with numerous reservoirs in the headstreams of the river valleys. Couple this man-made endeavour with that of Nature, and the result is a region widely considered to be one of the most scenic in Britain.

Although the Pennine Way ends among the Cheviot Hills, they are not part of the Pennines, being separated from them by the Tyne Gap and the Whin Sill, along which runs Hadrian's Wall. Conversely, although the southern end of the Pennines is commonly accepted as somewhere in the High Peak of Derbyshire, often Edale (the start of the Pennine Way), they actually extend further south to the true southern end of the Pennines in the Stoke-on-Trent area, many miles south of Edale.

So, the exact area of the Pennines is difficult to define. In terms of this book they extend no further south than Mam Tor above Edale, and not much further north than Cross Fell, the highest summit of the Pennines, lying on the eastern edge of Cumbria. Within this area is an amazing, and often frustrating, succession of landscapes fashioned from river valleys, moorlands and upland peat bogs, and penned in by a host of cities, towns and villages to form an area that weaves a rich and interesting story of industrial development together with a strong cultural and industrial heritage.

The Pennine Way is often regarded as a strenuous high-level route through predominantly wild country, intended for walkers of some experience, and involving a fair element of physical exertion and a willingness to endure rough going. Those characteristics sum up the Pennines perfectly. But the region is far from the wholly boggy, unremitting, uncompromising, windswept upland desert some might have you believe. The Pennines are not desolate and forlorn, but infinitely varied, rich in wildlife and opportunities for striding out in solitude.

I first explored the Pennines in their entirety more than 20 years ago. I've just done it again with a joyous spring in every step... Well, almost every one!

The view across from Rowlee Pasture to the Kinder plateau (Walk 48)

About this guide

The walks in this guide are grouped into five regions – the North Pennines, the North West Dales, the Yorkshire Dales, the South Pennines and the Dark Peak. At the start of each walk is a box containing key information – distance, height gain, time, grade, start point and maps required, as well as details of where to obtain after-walk refreshments. To compare the walks, refer to Appendix 1, which summarises the route information for every route.

The original intention of including at least one mountain in every route was thwarted, partially by the nature of the terrain, but mainly by a desire to ensure that worthwhile lower-level routes were not pushed out by the need to tick off even the dullest of summits. In any case, the Pennines boast remarkably few 'mountains', with barely 80 summits higher than 600m. The walks in this book do, however, visit 19 of the 32 Marilyns – summits with a relative height of 150m (492ft) in relation to its surroundings, regardless of actual height – in the area covered by this book. There are just two Marilyns in the Dark Peak, two in the Howgills, three in the Southern Pennines, five in the Northern Pennines and 20 in the Yorkshire Dales. Embracing mountain summits in every route in this guide was always going to be difficult but among the

moors and valleys of the Pennines there has been no shortage of terrain with a mountainous feel to explore.

In choosing the walks, the defining criteria was the Pennine watershed. The watershed, if defined literally, is a fine imaginary line that would divide in two a drop of rain falling on it, sending half to the North Sea in the east and the other half to the Irish Sea in the west. The nature of the watershed, which turns out to be nothing like as fine as that dividing line, is admirably described in Andrew Bibby's book *The Backbone of England* (see Appendix 2).

However, since walking the watershed is on many stretches neither enthralling nor inspirational, some sections of the watershed were shunned in favour of other defining criteria, namely the Pennine Way, the Pennine Bridleway and (of equal if not more importance at times) 'clear characteristics of a Pennine landscape'. The Pennine Way is well known and runs from Edale in Derbyshire to Kirk Yetholm just across the Scottish border, following a route that was teased from the landscape under the guidance of Tom Stephenson. The Pennine Bridleway is a relatively new creation, a 320km (200 mile) adventure for walkers, horse riders and mountain bikers, following old packhorse routes, drovers' roads and newly created bridleways.

↑ *Ravenstonedale pastures (Walk 12)*

Looking down on Dove Stone Reservoir (Walk 45)

What makes this approach rather tenuous is the very nature and characteristics of 'Pennine' landscape and 'Pennine' qualities. The gritstone that predominates in the Peak is scarcely evident in the limestone Yorkshire Dales, although it is there. Likewise, the peat bogs and groughs that are hallmarks of the South Pennines are almost nowhere to be found in the Howgills and the Dales. So, it becomes all the more evident that what must, geographically, define the Pennine landscape is whatever happens to flank the Pennine watershed. (It's an argument that would never withstand close scrutiny, but in the context of a book about Pennine walks, it's as useful as anything else.)

Most walks therefore include one of these 'Pennine' criteria, while no walk is more than 16km (10 miles) from the watershed itself. But the author has had no qualms about including a few excellent walks that don't comply with this constraint, such as Rombalds and Ilkley Moor (Walk 31), for example, Pendle Hill (Walk 32) and Ingleborough (Walk 21), in the belief that few would argue that they lacked Pennine qualities.

Walk grades

The grading of walks is a very subjective issue; what is 'easy' for one walker can be a scary experience for someone less experienced. In reality, nothing in the Pennines can safely be regarded as easy; the terrain is often bouldery and complex, marshy and trackless, or, more usually, a mix of all of these conditions. But, in order to convey some notion of the effort and walking skill involved in each route, four grades have been employed to categorise the walks.

- **Moderate**: shorter walks without significant height gain; some occasional issues with route finding or terrain, but generally straightforward
- **Moderately demanding**: devoid of serious hazard in good conditions, but requiring map-reading and compass skills; mainly, but not always, on clear paths
- **Demanding**: similar to 'strenuous', but usually shorter or with less height gain, but still rugged, remote and energetic walks
- **Strenuous**: lengthy, over rough and/or high ground, sometimes in remote locations; there may be long, rugged and/or trackless sections

These grades are no better than a diagrammatic map, not least because almost all the walks in this book contain some stretches that meet each grade criteria; it is possible, indeed likely, that all four grades will be met with on each walk. The grades are therefore no more than a general overview of each entire walk. Within the book the more difficult grades predominate – there are 14 'strenuous' walks, 17 'demanding', 14 'moderately demanding', and 5 'moderate'.

Distances and height gain

This information has been arrived at by a combination of methods, none of which assumes that if the highest point is 500m, and the lowest is 200m, that the amount of height gain is 300m; there are just too many variables to make it that simple. So, precision is not always possible.

The average length of the 50 walks in this book is 15.4km (9.6 miles), and the average height gain is 456m (1495ft).

Times

Timings are subjective, and also depend on the individual's level of fitness. Those given for each walk are the times taken by the author, carrying a day sack, camera and so on, and so they take the nature of the terrain into account. The timings do not include an allowance for any stops.

However, rather than rely on the author's figures, it is far better to learn by experience what your own pace is, and then use the distance and height gain information (in the information box at the start of each walk) to get an idea of how long it will take you, given your personal level of fitness. Then be sure to allow for the terrain, which in the Pennines is renowned for being difficult and boggy, to the extent that minor detours become necessary following wet weather.

Maps

Although the guide contains map extracts, you are strongly advised to take with you the relevant sheet map for the route, not only for safety reasons but also to give a wider picture of the landscapes you are walking through. Note that key landmarks that feature on the maps appear in **bold** in the text to help you plot the route. (The map extracts in this book are taken from these 1:50,000 maps, expanded to 1:40,000 so that 1km is represented by 2.5cm on the map.)

The maps recommended for the walks in this book are Ordnance Survey 1:25,000 **Explorer** maps OL1 (The Peak District: Dark Peak area); OL2 (Yorkshire Dales: Southern and Western areas); OL19 (Howgill Fells and Upper Eden Valley); OL21 (South Pennines); OL30 (Yorkshire Dales: Northern and Central areas); OL31 (North Pennines: Teesdale and Weardale); OL297 (Lower Wharfedale and Washburn valley)

GPS systems

There is an increasing number of satellite-linked GPS systems on the market these days, some of which contain the mapping needed for specific counties or long-distance trails. The precision of these GPS systems significantly reduces the risk of navigational error, and they are very reliable guides in poor visibility. However, they are no substitute for the ability to read conventional mapping or for sound navigational skills, but for some years the author has been confidently using a Satmap Active 10, with appropriate 1:25,000 mapping on SD cards. Satmap Systems also produce mapping specifically for the Pennine Way, which covers many of the walks in this book, particularly where they cross county boundaries.

Bird's-eye primrose

IN CASE OF EMERGENCY

Information about mountain rescue teams operating in the Pennines is detailed at:

- www.mountain.rescue.org.uk.

If you need the services of a mountain rescue team:

- Call 999 or 112 and ask for mountain rescue.
- Tell them where the 'incident' has occurred, by giving an accurate grid reference, and the nature of the incident.
- Give them a contact phone number.
- The messengers may be required to wait by the phone for further instructions, and may be used to guide the team to the exact location of the incident, so they should be the fittest group members if possible.
- Be prepared for a long wait – comprised of the time it takes for your messengers to reach a phone, the team callout and assembly time, and the time required for the team to walk to your location with heavy equipment. You may decide that if there is a danger of hypothermia it is best to evacuate most of the party and leave a small group remaining with the casualty. You may also decide that it is necessary to move the casualty to a more sheltered or safer location (if so, ensure that someone will be on hand to guide the team to your new location).
- Consider how your group members or passers-by can best be deployed, and how the equipment carried by the group can best be redistributed and utilised.
- Consider 'alternative' uses for the equipment you are carrying, for example camera flashes can be used to attract attention in the dark, a rope laid out along the ground will maximise your chances of being located in poor visibility, and a survival bag can be used for attracting attention.
- The standard distress signal is six sharp whistle blasts (or torch flashes) followed by a one-minute silence, repeated.
- Don't lose touch with common sense when coming to any decisions!

Weather to walk?

Mountains everywhere tend to generate their own micro-climate, while remaining subject to whatever is going on nationally. So, while out in the Pennines, whether on the tops or in the valleys, you need always to be aware of what is happening to the weather: is the wind changing direction?; are clouds gathering?; is it getting hotter or colder? Make allowance for the fact that conditions on the tops are generally more severe than in the valleys.

Some indication of what might be happening can be obtained by checking the weather forecast both the day before you go and again on the morning you intend to walk. There are reliable sources of weather information on the internet, notably:

- www.bbc.co.uk/weather (this site allows you to set your favourite locations in order to obtain a more specific forecast)

- www.metoffice.gov.uk (the Met Office's own website) – this is also available as a free app for use on iPhones, iPads and hybrid smartphones.

Most other sites draw information from these two.

Before you start

What to wear

Someone once said: 'There's no such thing as bad weather, just inadequate clothing.' Well, as everyone knows, there is such a thing as bad weather, sometimes so bad that no amount of clothing will prove adequate. But the comment makes a fair point, and, unless you aspire to being no more than a fair weather walker, going adequately and suitably clothed facilitates walking regardless of all but the most severe weather conditions. Let's face it, if you have to wait for the sun to shine before venturing out, you may never begin.

Being adequately clothed makes all the difference, and well-prepared walkers, who will always be equipped with wind- and water-proof garments and a stout pair of waterproof walking boots for a day in the Pennines in any season, have nothing to fear from an inclement day.

The question of what to wear can only be answered in such general terms, however, for the simple reason that each of us is physically different

At the Aiggin Stone, Blackstone Edge (Walk 42)

– we have different metabolisms, our bodies function in different ways when exercising, and the way, and amount, we perspire varies, too. All these factors generate bodily conditions that are specific to each of us and which require personalised solutions.

To complicate things even further, there are numerous clothing and equipment manufacturers clamouring to sell you their own brand, but without the certainty that one brand is any more suitable for you than another. It is purely a process of trial and error, often over a period of time, sometimes years. But eventually, you find a combination that works best for you. When you do, stick with it. Just as important, when you settle on the type of clothing that suits you and decide to kit yourself out, go for the most expensive you can afford. Quality really does count when it comes to outdoor clothing.

What to carry

So, what is considered essential? It is not intended that this list should be slavishly followed in every detail, by every person in a group, but it is suggested as a guide or checklist. Small groups may manage

without some items, but if the group is such that it may become fragmented, then it pays to have the key items throughout the group.

- **Map** – everyone should carry a map for the area of the walk, and know how to read it. If you are using maps on a GPS device, do ensure that you have more than one set of replacement batteries.

- **Compass** – much the same; map and compass are essential.

- **Whistle** – every individual should carry a whistle; it is vital as a means of communication in the event of an emergency. There are numerous inexpensive mountain and survival whistles available, but any whistle will do.

- **Torch** – you may not intend to be out after dark, but a torch will prove useful if you are. Make sure that every individual carries their own torch, even if there are only two of you. There are many samples of suitable pocket or head torches on the market these days, but be sure

Gordale Scar – the route lies up the brown-coloured boulder in the centre (Walk 26) →

to carry spare batteries. A torch is also useful for signalling in an emergency.

- **First aid kit** – there is nothing worse than a developing blister or getting a bad scratch from a bramble. Even the smallest of first aid kits contain plasters or skin compounds like Dr Scholl's® Moleskin or Compede Blister Packs that can ease the irritation. The kit does not need to be huge, but should include a good cross-section of contemporary first aid products, including ointments and creams suitable for easing insect stings and bites. Today's outdoor market offers plastic first aid 'bottle' kits containing everything you are likely to need for minor emergencies.

- **Food** – it is important to carry day rations sufficient both for the walk you are planning to follow and for emergencies. Every rucksack should contain some emergency foods, such as Kendal Mint Cake, chocolate bars or glucose tablets, that remain forever in your pack – although it is a good idea to replenish them at regular intervals.

- **Drink** – liquids are vital, especially in hot conditions, and in winter a stainless steel thermos of hot drink goes down a treat. Cold liquids can be carried in water bottles or in pliable water containers that fit into your rucksack and have a plastic suction tube that leads over the shoulder and allows water to be drunk as required.

- **Spare clothing** – there is no need to duplicate everything you wear or would normally carry, but some extras permanently embedded in your rucksack will prove beneficial – T-shirt, sweater, scarf, spare socks (to double as gloves, if necessary) and spare laces.

- **Other bits and pieces** – strong string (can double as emergency laces), small towel (for drying post-paddling feet during summer months), notebook, pencil, pocket knife and a thermal blanket or survival bag for emergencies. Hopefully you will never use it, but half a roll of toilet tissue in a sealable plastic bag has eased many an embarrassing moment.

The route up to Hag Dyke, and Great Whernside beyond (Walk 28)

NORTH PENNINES

Looking up to the summit of Cross Fell (Walk 3)

NORTH PENNINES

The mountain uplands that rise between Hadrian's Wall and the Yorkshire Dales spread themselves across too broad a landscape to have acquired any true generic name. Most walkers know of Cross Fell, Cauldron Snout, High Cup Nick, High Force and similar honey pots, but the region is almost 50km (30 miles) wide in places, and much the same from its most northerly summit, Cold Fell, to the Stainmore Gap, which runs either side of Brough – 2500 square kilometres (900 square miles) of wild, windy and beautiful moorland where the Pennines rise to their greatest height.

Within this comparatively unknown area lies the largest concentration of hills in England outside the Lake District, and while it does not boast the status of a national park (although there are many who think it should), a sizeable chunk has been designated as the North Pennines Area of Outstanding Natural Beauty. Here, in these bleak moorland heights, it has been suggested that the valleys rather than the hills form the attraction. Certainly, no walker keen on broadening his or her horizons should turn aside

from a skirmish or two with the hills of the northern moors; there are grand days out to be had up here.

Some parts (AONB notwithstanding) are affected by access controls: Mickle Fell, for example, forms part of the Warcop military training area, and vast areas of the region are actively managed grouse moors with all the attendant obligations such conditions impose on walkers. But there is ample room for everyone, and anyone venturing there will find the northern moors too big to ignore, too wild to take for granted.

For this book, the North Pennines provide a useful counterbalance to the Dark Peak of Derbyshire, but are considerably less frequented by walkers and enjoy much greater altitude, in Cross Fell reaching to 893m (almost 3000ft). It may be tempting to dismiss these moors as unappetising fare enriched occasionally by the taste of something more spicy. In the right mood, on the right day, the North Pennines will be seen in their true colours: a place of ever-changing hues and with a subtlety of flavour that will please all but the most jaded of palates.

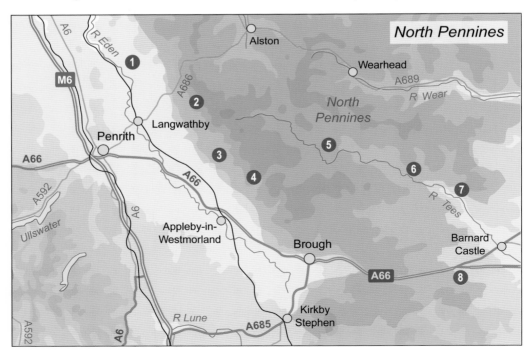

Thack Moor and Black Fell

*T*he soft, moulded grassy fells that gather to the north of the A686 trans-Pennine Penrith to Alston *road are only rarely visited by walkers. Solitude, peace and tranquillity are therefore found here in abundance, along pathways seldom trodden and below massive skies. The Hartside Pass is well known and popular with bikers in particular, but the East Fellside village of Renwick knows no such fame – a small, close-knit community going quietly about its business.*

The Route

The ascent to Thack Moor, also known as Renwick Fell, is very direct, barely wavering from a straight line once the open fell is gained. Start off along the road for Outhwaite, a steep little pull. The gradient soon eases, and when the road swings to the right, leave it by going forward onto a stony track. Where the ascending track divides (NY604441), keep left, and continue along a wall-enclosed track. About 100m after the left-hand wall ends, go forward through a metal gate onto Access Land and continue beside a fence.

Setting off up the track from Renwick

↑ Bothy cottage just below Hartside summit, looking across to Thack Moor   23

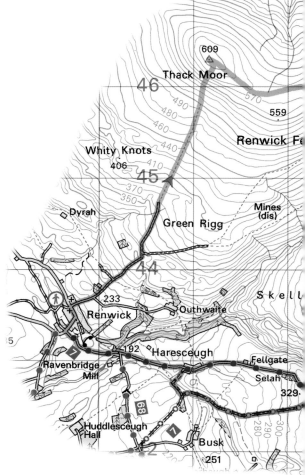

ROUTE INFORMATION

Distance	18km (11¼ miles)
Height gain	525m (1725ft)
Time	6–7hrs
Grade	strenuous
Start point	Renwick NY596436

Getting there
Roadside parking at Townhead in Renwick, near the church

Maps
Ordnance Survey OL31 (North Pennines: Teesdale and Weardale)

After-walk refreshment
Pubs in Kirkoswald

When the accompanying fence veers away and is left behind, maintain the same direction, briefly and steeply uphill onto the grassy top of **Thack Moor**, climbing through reeds for a while before moving onto the sloping summit plateau, the highest point of which is marked by a trig pillar at a meeting point between a wall and fence. The view embraces most of the northern and eastern Lakeland fells that lie to the

On the summit of Watch Hill

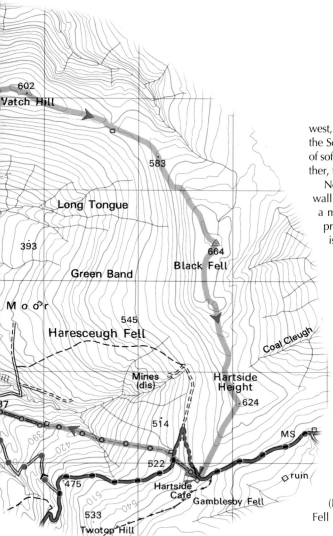

west, while northwards the dome of Criffel beyond the Solway Firth is visible. But it is the nearer display of soft-shaped hills running to Cold Fell and, even further, to the Cheviot that really commands attention.

Now turn south-east alongside the wall. When the wall changes direction, it's time to leave it; but take a moment to inspect the nearby sheepfold, which proves to be a useful shelter, if needed, since there is no shelter on Thack Moor. Cross tussock moorland to a stile in a fence (NY616459), beyond which a broad quad-bike track is joined, heading for **Watch Hill**.

There are two summits on **Watch Hill**, the first occupied by a pile of stones, a currick, and the other by a ladder-stile spanning a wall, with a 602m spot height just beyond. The former is slightly higher, at 604m.

Cross the ladder-stile, which has a small gate with a formidable spring. Over the stile, now head in a south-easterly direction, keeping to the high ground, devoid of useful tracks, but not unduly difficult to cross. In the distance, a ruined sheepfold and bothy cottage stand out and serve as a useful target. Nearby, another ladder-stile crosses a trans-ridge wall (NY636457), now with the whale-back of Black Fell looming in the distance. Once over the stile,

Retrospective view to Black Fell, Watch Hill and distant Thack Moor

keep beside the wall to a gate, where the wall ends and a fence takes over. Pass through the gate and follow a quad-bike track beside the fence, and ever onwards, since it leads all the way to the top of **Black Fell**, where the Pennine watershed is joined. It is a sobering thought, but Black Fell actually marks only the half-way point of the walk; the rest, however, is almost entirely downhill.

The onward route now follows the watershed down to the Hartside Pass, variously accompanied by a fence or a wall and climbing onto **Hartside Height**, where a through-stile takes the route over the wall, and then down beside a fence to a kissing-gate just above Hartside summit, with **Hartside Top Café** (the highest café in England) directly opposite.

Turn right at the road, but leave it almost immediately for a broad stony track that takes a shortcut, crossing the A-road again, lower down. Go through a gate and forward to pass a bothy cottage with a fabulous view across the Eden valley to the Lake District fells, after which a splendid cross-fell track

ensues, gradually descending to cross Ricker Gill Bridge and then on to a derelict farmhouse, just after which a gate gives onto a fenced track leading down to a surfaced lane. A short way on, cross Selah Bridge and make a short ascent.

At the top of the ascent, an **alternative** section of track saves about 1 mile of road walking, rejoining the road just past the cluster of buildings at Haresceugh.

Stroll along the road, which is generally quiet, largely traffic free and a delight to walk, with a fine view northwards to the summit tackled at the start of the walk.

From **Raven Bridge**, where Raven Beck eases through a dark ravine, a rough path offers a variant finish across fields back to **Renwick**, but stay on the road to a T-junction. Turn right and walk towards the village centre, and at another T-junction turn left (for Croglin) to complete the walk.

Thack Moor from below Hartside summit

Melmerby Fell and Fiend's Fell

*M*elmerby is a pleasing red-sandstone village tucked into the area known as East Fellside, and it proves to be a perfect starting point for this assault on the Northern Pennines. There is a tranquillity about both the village and the fells to the east, and while navigational skills may well be needed in poor visibility, on a good day the sense of well-being that comes from striding out across spacious fell moors will refresh most souls.

The attractive village of **Melmerby** is thought by some to have Danish origins, being named after a certain Melmor, who lived nearby in the ninth century. A person called Melmor, however, also appears in Gospatric's charter in the 11th century as a landowner in Allerdale. The likelihood is that there was more than one Melmor, although the name Melmor is believed to be Gaelic rather than Danish. In the 14th century, John de Denum of Melmerby Hall petitioned Edward II for 'help

in the form of wages or otherwise until times change, because all the country around would suffer great loss peril and loss if it were taken through lack of garrison'.

The Route
Leave the village on the Ousby road, passing the Shepherd's Inn, and turn into the first lane branching on the left (signed for Melmerby Fell and Gale Hall). Continue up the lane until it swings to the

↑ Melmerby Fell from the stony track above the village

The route as it heads towards the high fells after leaving the plantation

ROUTE INFORMATION

Distance	16.5km (10¼ miles)
Height gain	546m (1790ft)
Time	6hrs
Grade	demanding
Start point	Melmerby NY616373

Getting there
Limited off-road parking near Shepherd's Inn

Maps
Ordnance Survey OL31 (North Pennines: Teesdale and Weardale)

After-walk refreshment
Shepherd's Inn pub, Melmerby

Land, and then makes a circling loop to the north to gain a gently rising track onto **Melmerby Low Scar**. Here, the track passes between the scar and higher rocks to the east, and eventually runs up to a gate in a wall giving onto open moorland.

Beyond the wall, the route passes through spreads of small boulders, initially as a green trod and heading up towards a large cairn. From the cairn, continue in an easterly direction. There is an indistinct

right, and there leave it on the apex, going forward onto a stony track between walls and along the edge of a **plantation**.

The track leads up to enter the plantation and crosses a stream at a footbridge. On leaving the plantation, the route continues towards the high fells, bounded by fences. At another gate, it reaches Access

Looking north from the top of Knapside Hill

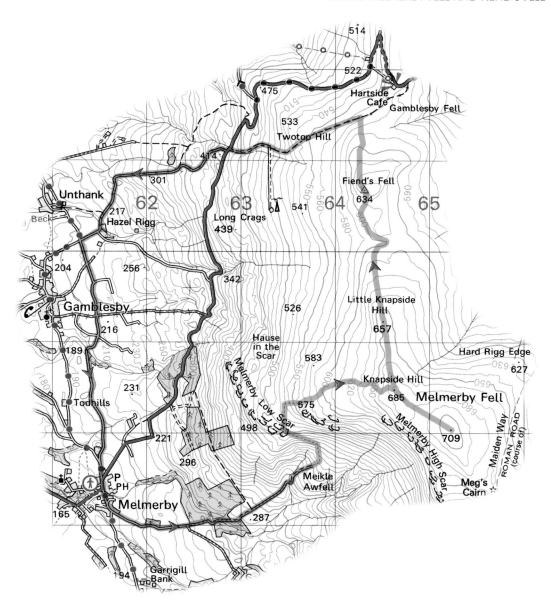

path, but choice of route will be determined by how wet the ground is underfoot. The target is another prominent cairn on the eastern skyline; this is the location of **Knapside Hill**, the summit of which is marked by a substantial shelter-cairn.

Melmerby Fell rises to the south-east as an unpromising moorland mound, easily reached and barely 1km distant; its top is marked by a large cairn. Return from Melmerby Fell to Knapside Hill, from where a narrow but distinct path leads northwards to **Little Knapside Hill**.

Pass through a kissing-gate in a fence (NY645392). Another narrow, grassy path then runs on across surprisingly firm turf (for a while). Continue down to another gate (NY644399) and fence (new, and in the middle of a quagmire in 2012). From it cross rough ground towards Fiend's Fell, crossing an shallow ravine to gain a quad-bike track that circles around a low shoulder and leads to one final gate (NY642404), from where it is a short pull up onto **Fiend's Fell**, marked by both a low shelter and a trig pillar.

29

Fiend's Fell was the original name for Cross Fell, some 5 miles away, which seems possible since the name Cross Fell derives from the erection of a cross there to ward off evil spirits. That, however, does not explain why the name was transferred to an otherwise innocent location nearby.

From the top of Fiend's Fell, a solitary stone pillar is in sight, as is the café at Hartside Pass (the highest café in England). Head down to the pillar following quad-bike tracks, and gradually the return route, a clear stony track, comes into view. Walk forward towards a fence, and then bear left to a kissing-gate when it comes into view, beyond which a short section of rough ground leads to the track. Turn left.

Simple walking now ensues, following the stony track down to cross the A686 and continuing into a walled track opposite (signed for Hazel Rigg Farm). Just after passing **Hazel Rigg**, join a surfaced lane at a bend. Bear right for a short distance and then, opposite a side road to Unthank, turn left onto a stony track enclosed between walls. Over a distance of about 2.75km (1¾ miles), and keeping forward at all track junctions, this track leads unerringly and agreeably, if in places muddily, all the way back to **Melmerby** – a remarkably pleasant concluding stretch of the walk.

The way north to Fiend's Fell

Cross Fell

*A*lthough its summit plateau is largely devoid of features, Cross Fell remains the highest summit in the Pennines, and is worthy of a visit on that count alone. Moreover, there is a calming, pastoral beauty about the Eden valley; the villages, built from lovely red sandstone are small and isolated, and the general ambiance is quite at odds with the proximity of mountains that reach almost to 3000ft.

The Route

Drawing to their greatest height at the very spot where the River Tees begins its long journey to the North Sea, and overlooking the massively broad Eden valley, the Pennines form a seemingly impenetrable barrier between the Lake District and the moorlands of Cumberland and Westmorland, and what used to be the North Riding of Yorkshire.

The ascent route uses an old corpse road linking the church and graveyard at Kirkland with the distant community of Garrigill. In the 17th century, one funeral party, caught in a blizzard high on the mountainside, abandoned its burden, scurrying back to Garrigill and returning only two weeks later for the coffin when it was finally considered safe to retrieve it. The mourners then brought the coffin back to Garrigill, where it was buried in a piece of glebe land. The land was subsequently consecrated by the Bishop of Durham as a burial ground, and thus the need for the corpse road came to an end.

↑ Cross Fell from the upper part of the corpse road

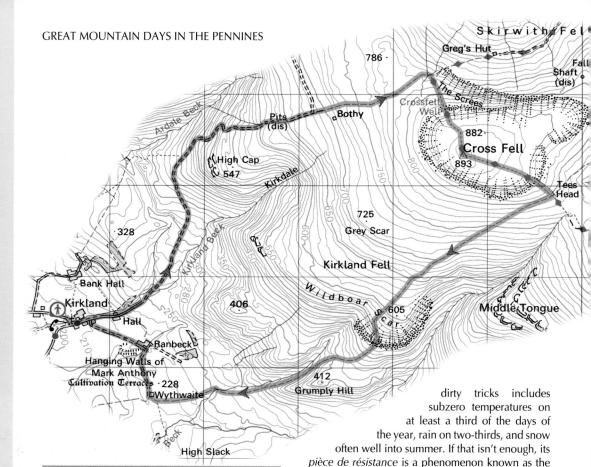

ROUTE INFORMATION

Distance	15km (9¼ miles)
Height gain	683m (2240ft)
Time	5–6hrs
Grade	strenuous
Start point	Kirkland NY645325

Getting there
Limited off-road parking near the church at Kirkland

Maps
Ordnance Survey OL31 (North Pennines: Teesdale and Weardale)

After-walk refreshment
Pubs and cafés in Langwathby and Penrith

In fine weather, the mountain has an avuncular appearance, and seems a calm, endearing place to visit. Alas, all is not as it seems, for its repertoire of dirty tricks includes subzero temperatures on at least a third of the days of the year, rain on two-thirds, and snow often well into summer. If that isn't enough, its *pièce de résistance* is a phenomenon known as the Helm Wind, a remarkably ferocious and localised gusting of the wind.

The precise nature of the **Helm Wind** is neatly summarised in *Legends and Historical Notes of North Westmoreland* by Thomas Gibson: 'the air or wind from the east, ascends the gradual slope of the western (sic) side of the Pennine chain... to the summit of Cross Fell, where it enters the helm or cap, and is cooled to a less temperature; it then rushes forcibly down the abrupt declivity of the western side of the mountain into the valley beneath, in consequence of the valley being of a warmer temperature, and this constitutes the Helm-Wind. The sudden and violent rushing of the wind down the ravines and crevices of the mountain, occasions the loud noise that is heard.' As for its force, Thomas Wilkinson of Yanwath, a Quaker friend of Wordsworth, describes in his *Tour to the British Mountains* (1824) how 'if I advanced it was with my head inclined to the ground, and at a slow pace; it I retreated and leaned against it with all my might, I could hardly keep erect; if I did not resist it, I was blown over'.

In spite of its unappealing summit and the high incidence of clouds which bedevil the mountain, Cross Fell is a superb viewpoint, taking in the fells of Lakeland, dotting the horizon beyond the Eden valley, and extending far across the northern countryside into Scotland, and east to the North York Moors.

From the church at **Kirkland**, walk to the nearby road junction and turn left to follow a road and later a good track along Kirkland Beck, leading out onto the moors and gradually curving north to skirt **High Cap**, a prominent bump due west of Cross Fell's summit. A little further on the route swings eastwards above Ardale Beck and starts the climb to the plateau above. The gradient, nowhere unduly steep, is eased by a few bends, and on reaching gentler ground a few old pits might be found.

Within sight of the summit plateau, the corpse road bears sharply left. Here leave it and continue ascending eastwards on a cairned and grassy path, passing ultimately around the northern scree slopes of Cross Fell to intercept the Pennine Way (NY684352) on its descent to Garrigill. On a clear day it is possible to make for the summit as soon as you feel happy about it, although this entails negotiating a broad stretch of loose scree and some wet ground. But the line taken by the Pennine Way to the summit is clear enough, although very wet underfoot as it climbs away from the descent to Garrigill. It soon dries out, and a line of cairns leads uneventfully to the summit of **Cross Fell**, with its shelter-cairn and trig point.

Having ascended to the highest point of the Pennines, press on across the summit plateau aiming for the summit of Great Dun Fell and its conspicuous masts and globular radar station. In poor visibility this will call for good navigation, although the line of the Pennine Way is marked by low cairns. Near the edge of the plateau a couple of larger cairns indicate the way down to Tees Head. This proves to be the key to the completion of quite a pleasant round-trip.

Brown Hill and the upper reaches of Ardale Beck

From **Tees Head** (NY697339), a cairned path (not immediately obvious, narrow in places and crossing numerous spring streams) heads south-west across what is initially bouldery terrain to the edge of **Wildboar Scar** (NY679326). This stretch is open moorland, and there is an invigorating sense of freedom, with the whole place to yourself (more than likely), the Eden valley rolling away ahead, and the Lakeland fells sitting like a frieze on the western skyline.

Wildboar Scar is nothing more than an abrupt escarpment, grassy, rounded and sporting a much clearer path curving below it. Ahead lies the mound of **Grumply Hill**, and the path keeps north of it (right) to enter Littledale, one of the tributaries of Crowdundle Beck. At the right time of year this enchanting section of moorland resounds to the piping call of the golden plover, as white-rumped wheatears dart about and chatter busily, and curlews bubble a constant accompaniment.

Onwards the path descends easily to and through a sheepfold and across a wide, walled tract of rough ground, scented in spring and early summer with gorse, to a large ruined barn and farm building at **Wythwaite** (NY654317), from where there is a fine retrospective view of Great Dun Fell in particular. Once at Wythwaite, turn through a gate and follow a surfaced lane to pass a curious feature marked on the map as the **Hanging Walls of Mark Antony**.

Precisely what are, or were, the Hanging Walls of Mark Antony is open to question, but the generally accepted view is that they are cultivation terraces, possibly as much as 3500 years old. There is a contrary view, however, which suggests that while they are indeed agricultural terraces, they date only from the seventh century, and that the naming of them on maps is a mistake, which ought to place them nearer to Culgaith. William Camden in *Britannia* refers to 'the river Blencarne' and 'the confused ruins of a castle called the Hanging walls of Marcantoniby'.

From this enigmatic place it is only a short walk along the access lane, and back to the church at **Kirkland**.

The stone shelter on Cross Fell, looking north to Scotland

High Cup Nick and Backstone Edge

*H*igh Cup Nick will be no stranger to those who have walked the Pennine Way, and its dramatic and sudden appearance for those travelling south to north on that route is a memorable moment. For walkers ascending from Dufton, however, this remarkable geological phenomenon eases into view gradually, but reserves its full impact for those who continue to its head, where sometimes a river cascades down the shattered rocks of the Whin Sill.

The Route

Unlike many mountain ranges, the Pennines, being gentle, moulded moorland hills, offer few dramatic, sharp-edged profiles to catch the eye and lodge in the mind. One of the few exceptions to this is the impressive sculpted escarpment of High Cup Nick, formed by forces cold, wet and windy, where outcrops of igneous Whin Sill dolerite have intruded into the thick layers of mountain limestone and gritstone.

The walk starts from the rural cluster of cottages that forms **Dufton**, a charming, friendly oasis,

Pennine Way signpost

↑ *High Cup Gill*

35

ROUTE INFORMATION

Distance	15.5km (9½ miles)
Height gain	592m (1940ft)
Time	5–6hrs
Grade	strenuous
Start point	Dufton NY689249

Getting there
Dufton village car park (toilets)

Maps
Ordnance Survey OL19 (Howgill Fells and Upper Eden Valley)

After-walk refreshment
Stag Inn in Dufton; pubs, cafés, snack bars and restaurants in Appleby

contrasting sharply with the mountain wilderness high above it, and owing its place on the walkers' map to an idiosyncratic kink in the Pennine Way, which here quits the high ground for an overnight halt before pressing on to the highest Pennine summit, Cross Fell. Ironically, the day which transports Pennine Wayfarers heading north from Teesdale to Dufton lands them further removed from their destination, Kirk Yetholm, than when they began the day.

From the small car park, turn right and follow the road through the village. At the bottom of a dip, the Pennine Way is signposted and leads up along the lane to **Bow Hall Farm**, set on gently sloping pastures. There is invariably a red flag mounted at the entrance to Bow Hall Lane, signifying activity

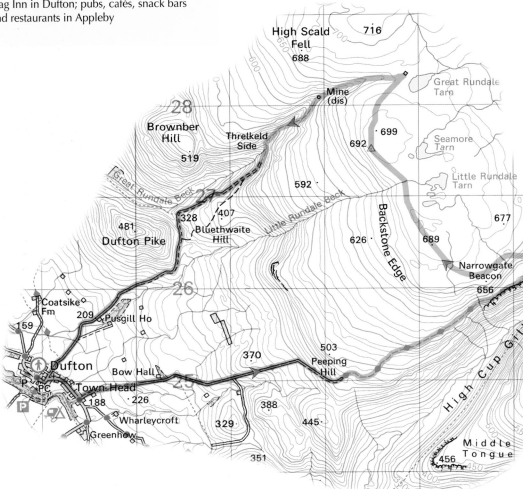

on the Warcop Artillery Range, part of the Warcop Principal Training Area.

Firing on the **artillery range** is unlikely to affect anyone ascending to High Cup Nick, but walkers tempted to stray onto Murton Fell could be walking into trouble. Activity, with no concession to walkers, occurs every day except Mondays.

The onward route beyond Bow Hall lies along a walled green lane, and beyond climbs high onto the hillside. On passing through the intake wall, the views open up across the Eden valley to the fells of Lakeland and southwards to the Howgills. The path eases up to a sheepfold. Pass through this, and a short way on enter a natural hollow with a large cairn at its centre, just below **Peeping Hill**. From here, take the high route up to a cairn, from where the ongoing Pennine Way route is clear throughout.

Continue easily along the edge of a developing escarpment, which drops in precipitous green slopes to unseen High Cup Gill. As the gill narrows, so the scenery assumes a more inspiring

and dramatic aspect, and the Pennine Way, crossing a couple of cascading streams, then relaxes to form a gentle greenway around the craggy amphitheatre to the Pennine watershed ahead. The path, as if possessing no head for heights, maintains a respectable distance from the escarpment, but as the crags become more evident a cautious diversion will reveal an architecture of shattered pinnacles and precarious columns of basalt.

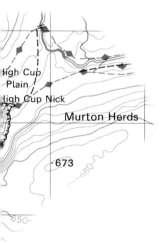

Nichol's Chair

High Cup Head

The most notable of these pinnacles and columns, **Nichol's Chair**, is named after a cobbler who used to live in Dufton, and who not only climbed the pillar but is reputed to have repaired a pair of boots while on its top. Any ascent now runs the risk of precipitating the collapse of the whole column.

For all its comparative lack of stature, the stream that flows (sometimes) lemming-like over High Cup Nick will, when caught by a westerly wind, often plume high into the air, reminiscent of Kinder Downfall in the Peak District, and nearby folds in the grassy shoulder of the escarpment offer lunch-time shelter. While recovering from the effort required to reach this point, it's worth bearing in mind that the best fell-runners start in Dufton and come up to High Cup Nick, and back down, in just a fraction over one hour!

High Cup Nick is a classic U-shaped valley on the western flanks of the North Pennines Area of Outstanding Natural Beauty. A deep chasm on the Pennine fellside, this famous geological formation at the top of High Cup Gill is part of the Whin Sill and overlooks the best glaciated valley in northern England, displaying grey-blue dolerite crags of the type that also form High Force and Cauldron Snout.

Here the walk leaves the Pennine Way, which presses on eastwards to Cauldron Snout and into Teesdale. To continue to Backstone Edge, about-face to ascend the easy grassy slopes north-east of **Narrowgate Beacon**, which has overlooked much of the route thus far and is crowned by a large cairn.

From the beacon there are two choices: one (shown on the map) to pursue an intermittent gritstone edge around the lip of the high moors; the other to tackle a section of bogs, giving way eventually to heather and tussock grass. A clear day in winter, when the ground underfoot is frozen in its grip, may well be the best time to tackle these featureless moors; following prolonged rain is certainly the worst.

The immediate objective of both routes is the trig pillar west of **Seamore Tarn**, a lonely sentinel in an austere landscape made auspicious by its position on the watershed of Britain, for here the waters of Little Rundale Tarn gush westwards to the Eden and on to the Solway, while those of nearby Seamore and Great Rundale tarns empty to the North Sea. The highest point of Backstone Edge lies a short way north-east of the trig, marked by a cairn of large boulders.

Hidden from the summit, the return route follows the deep valley of Rundale, which sports a broad track that descends from the col with High Scald Fell along the line of **Great Rundale Beck** to Dufton. Quarry workings are shortly encountered, relics of the search for barytes.

Wild and rugged, and despoiled by man, **Great Rundale** is less open than High Cup Gill, the

view westwards restricted by the pyramid of Dufton Pike, one of a number of distinctly different little summits dotted along the western side of the Pennines here. These are actually formed from older, Ordovician (formed 495–440 million years ago) and Silurian (440–415 million years) Lake District rocks, which elsewhere have been overlaid with those of the Carboniferous period (350–290 million years old).

But for all the damage that has been done in Great Rundale's upper reaches, the lower valley is quite a charming end to the day. On approaching Dufton Pike, pass south of it on a broad track, finally to regain **Dufton** not far from the starting point.

Dufton Pike: the walk concludes along the track across its base

Cauldron Snout and Widdybank Fell

A nyone who visualises the Pennines as dark, gritstone-bound uplands of peat bog and bleakness will be heartily surprised by this circuit of Widdybank Fell. It lies within a spectacular National Nature Reserve, one of great importance, and is a delight to explore. The walk takes in the powerful falls at Cauldron Snout, and then uses the Pennine Way alongside the River Tees, and these treats offset the hard-surface walking that concludes the walk.

The Route

Once a remote corner of the North Riding of Yorkshire and part of the ancient Forest of Teesdale in which deer roamed freely, the landscape this walk crosses is now embraced within the Moor House–Upper Teesdale National Nature Reserve. Apart from a little awkwardness scrambling down beside Cauldron Snout and a few short sections crossing boulders, the walking is easy throughout.

From the car park overlooking **Cow Green Reservoir**, way up on the moorland of Widdybank Fell, an undistinguished summit that the walk encircles, walk back along the road to a signed path on

the right for Cauldron Snout (NY813308) and here leave the road. When the path intercepts a track, turn left briefly to a gate on the right giving into the Nature Reserve.

Stretching across the upper reaches of the River Tees, the **Moor House – Upper Teesdale National Nature Reserve** comprises 8800 ha and embraces an extensive range of upland habitats typical of the North Pennines. These include hay meadows, rough grazing and juniper woods, as well as limestone grassland, blanket bogs and summit heaths on the high fells. What makes

ROUTE INFORMATION

Distance	13km (8 miles)
Height gain	145m (475ft)
Time	4–5hrs
Grade	moderate
Start point	Cow Green Reservoir NY811309

Getting there
Weelhead Sike car park

Maps
Ordnance Survey OL31 (North Pennines: Teesdale and Weardale)

After-walk refreshment
Pub at Langdon Beck and along the B6277 to Middleton-in-Teesdale, where there are also cafés

Upper Teesdale so important is that nowhere else in Britain is there such a diversity of rare habitats in one setting.

The reserve is renowned for the plants that originally colonised the high Pennines after the last Ice Age (about 10,000 years ago) and have survived here ever since. There are also rare rock formations, such as outcropping sugar limestone and the Great Whin Sill.

The diversity of wildlife and plantlife is quite remarkable. Spring gentian grows here, the only place in England, while the country's largest juniper woodland is here, too, in great abundance near High Force (see Walk 6), but also growing alongside the River Tees in a few places. An early morning visit is necessary to spot the black grouse, but at any other time there is a wealth of birdlife – skylark, lapwing, curlew, snipe, red grouse, redshank, common sandpiper, dipper, golden plover, pied and yellow wagtails, and ring ouzel – all of which tends to contribute to slow progress.

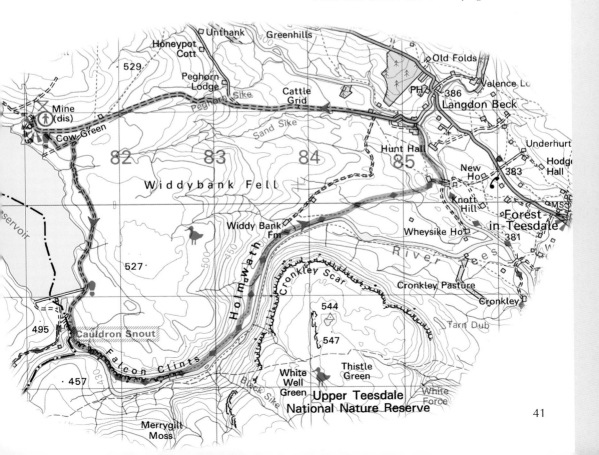

41

The ongoing track (surfaced) speeds on towards the **dam** of the reservoir.

Cow Green Reservoir is 3km (2 miles) long and was built between 1967 and 1971 to supply the industries of Teesside. The reservoir acts as a river regulation reservoir, releasing water into the River Tees during dry conditions so that it can be abstracted further downstream.

The reservoir, which rests against a backdrop of Dufton Fell and, further to the north-west, Cross Fell and the two Dun Fells, lies within the North Pennines AONB and European Geopark. The AONB was designated in 1988, and it became Britain's first European Geopark in 2004.

Walk down from the dam to the bridge spanning the Tees as it gushes from the base of the dam wall. Now, joining the southbound Pennine Way, take care descending the eastern side of the river for a fine view of Cauldron Snout, more a long cataract than a waterfall, and at 180m reckoned to be the longest waterfall in England. The awkwardness is short-lived, but care is needed while traversing slippery rocks until the level ground beside the river is reached.

Once below the falls, at the confluence of the Tees and Maize Beck, turn eastwards below the impressive crags of **Falcon Clints**, the southern escarpment of Widdybank Fell. A clear path leads on, parallel with the river, the worst ground spanned by boardwalks, but with a few sections where care is needed traversing boulder downfall. Cronkley Scar on the other side of the river combines with Falcon Clints to create the narrow defile known as **Holmwath**.

At the approach to **Widdy Bank Farm**, a gated stile gives into an enclosure, then go shortly left at another stile, beyond which a grassy path runs on above the river. As the river swings to the southeast, the path bears away across rough pasture and a few walled fields before heading down to Sayer Hill Farm.

Here, turn right, using the farm access to walk to Saur Hill Bridge, which spans **Harwood Beck**. On reaching the bridge, turn left before it, leaving the Pennine Way and taking to a path alongside the beck, and follow this beckside path to a crossing point on the road from Langdon Beck. Now, turn left, and simply follow the gently rising road across undulating pastures for 4km (2½ miles) back to the car park overlooking **Cow Green**. There is an air of openness about this return section, enlivened throughout by bird song and, in spring especially, a wealth of wild flowers, both of which combine to speed the return journey.

← *The River Tees below Falcon Clints* ↑ *The River Tees below Cronkley Scar*

High Force and Cronkley Fell

F or much of its long journey the Pennine Way is charted across desolate acres, the preserve of experienced walkers. But for a while, as it progresses northwards from Middleton-in-Teesdale, it relaxes its challenge and injects a soft, pastoral interlude of riverside meadows before heading for the highest ground of all on Cross Fell. In this gentler stretch, the River Tees holds sway, just a few miles from its source. In places it meanders smoothly over a wide bed of rock; elsewhere it cascades forcefully with all the might of a major river over rocky downfalls.

The Route

Once a remote corner of the North Riding of Yorkshire and part of the ancient Forest of Teesdale in which deer roamed freely, the area that the walk passes through now lies entirely within the county of Durham. Middleton-in-Teesdale is the largest town hereabouts, formerly a local centre of lead-mining activities.

From a long trail of boulders, it is possible to chart the course of the glacier that fashioned this region more than 10,000 years ago. It swept over gaps from the Eden valley, the Lake District and even the south of Scotland, carrying Shap granite and Borrowdale lava as far as the mouth of the Tees, where an accumulation of granite pinpoints what must have been the terminal moraine of the Tees glacier.

The walk begins from a parking and picnic area at **Bowlees**. From here take a nearby footbridge and walk through Bowlees to the main road. There,

↑ *High Force*

ROUTE INFORMATION

Distance   20.5km (12¾ miles)
Height gain   372m (1220ft)
Time   6hrs
Grade   demanding
Start point   Bowlees NY908283

Getting there
Bowlees picnic area car park

Maps
Ordnance Survey OL31 (North Pennines:
Teesdale and Weardale)

After-walk refreshment
Pubs, cafés and restaurants in
Middleton-in-Teesdale

opposite the telephone box, take to a clear path towards woodland flanking the unseen River Tees. Once in the woodland, a clear path leads down to cross the river by **Wynch Suspension Bridge**. The original Wynch Bridge was built in 1704 for miners, but it collapsed in 1820 and had to be rebuilt 10 years later.

Immediately, the Tees puts on a show in the form of **Low Force**, a place where the riverbed is wide and punctuated by islands of dolerite. Set against a backdrop of dark woodlands, this is the Tees at its most beautiful.

Climb the steps beyond the bridge and set off beside the Tees. This is a delightful stretch of the Pennine Way, which, at the right time of year, produces a display of plants that has given Teesdale an international reputation among botanists. Globe flower seems to grow everywhere, while among the rocks shrubby and alpine cinquefoil have found root. The most famous of Teesdale's plants is the spring gentian, making its home here among other rarities, the alpine forget-me-not, bitter milkwort, bog sandwort, bird's-eye primrose and others.

Why such great **plant diversity** should appear here seems a puzzle – but the answer lies in the study of geology and early land formations. Teesdale (and parts of Scotland) were grassy islands in a vast forest, fragments of the carpet of tundra that covered Britain after the Ice Age. Later, when the climate improved, these areas were shaded out by trees. Carbon dating of pollen remains in the underlying peat reveals a history going back to the last Ice Age.

Further on, juniper bushes cloak the slopes of Keedholm Scar. Juniper wood was once gathered to make high-quality charcoal, and the berries to flavour London gin.

Looking along the Pennine Way to Cronkley Fell

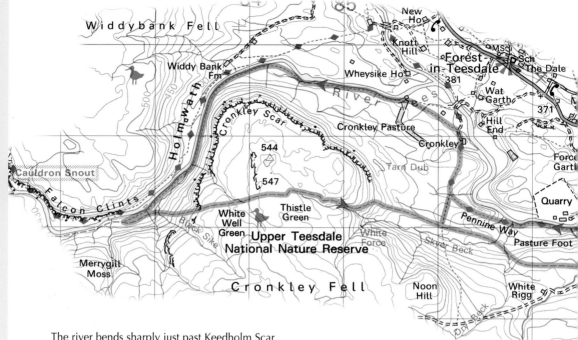

The river bends sharply just past Keedholm Scar, and suddenly the air is filled with a distant rumbling, the sound of the most famous of Pennine waterfalls, **High Force**. A slight diversion at metal railings is necessary to get a decent view from this side of the river, but care is needed this close to the edge. The Force is a dramatic plunge over a shelf of dolerite and shale of some 21 metres (70ft), dark brown and peaty, often lost in a fine mist of spray. This is not the highest waterfall in the country by any means, but it is the biggest, and a sight everyone should see.

Upstream, the sound of the falls soon dies away and the Tees resumes a more docile air, rising in restless moorland wandering to its source high on the southern flanks of Cross Fell. The double falls of **Bleabeck Force** are nothing by comparison, a mere ripple. Ahead the route follows the Pennine Way as it climbs onto the shoulder of Bracken Rigg to an old Pennine Way marker post. From here it descends to a step-stile near a wall corner, beyond which the Way is paved for a while before reaching **Cronkley Farm**.

Anyone looking for a **short-cut** can leave the route at the high point of Bracken Rigg and take a path down (left) to pass through a wall. A short distance further on, the later stages of the walk are joined. Turn left towards Skyer Beck, and pick up the route from there.

Now continue north along the Pennine Way to a farm-access bridge, but remain on the south bank of the river following a good path that circumnavigates **Cronkley Scar** and squeezes through a relatively narrow valley. Continue until almost level with the cliffs of **Falcon Clints** on the north side of the Tees. At (or just before) NY825281 turn sharply back on yourself to take an ascending bridleway up onto and across **Cronkley Fell** (a diversion is necessary to reach the trig pillar to the north).

Press on across the fell, with the view down Teesdale improving with every step. The bridleway drops as a broad grassy track through bracken (and heather lower down), but is less pronounced as it parallels Bracken Rigg, passed earlier in the walk. Ford **Skyer Beck** (stepping stones if needed), and then climb beside a wall. When the wall changes direction, keep climbing a little further to a clear track, now striking eastwards. The track runs on to pass through a line of shooting butts and climbs to pass a large cairn, from which the route crosses rough pasture to a gate and stile in a fence. More wet, rough pasture lies beyond, along with another stream crossing.

Press on to a gate giving onto a gravel vehicle track, and now follow this to a point where it circles round to descend to **Holwick Lodge**. Here, leave the track by branching right at a couple of stone sheep to a track that descends through a disused quarry area below Holwick Scars. The ongoing track leads out to a surfaced lane. Walk past cottages and turn left at the first road junction.

Stone sheep on boundary of Strathmore Estate

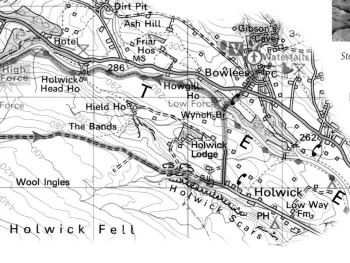

Follow the lane to a cattle grid at the boundary of Strathmore Estate, and just after the grid leave the lane at a signpost for a waymarked route across a flower meadow.

The path is waymarked across a number of fields and leads back to **Wynch Bridge**, from where the outward route is retraced to complete the walk.

Crossing Skyer Beck

Harter Fell and Grassholme

*T*here is a soothing gentleness about this walk, which in its first half follows the route of the *Pennine Way. Few Pennine Wayfarers visit Harter Fell itself, even though it is only a short, easy pull up from their route, but the wide landscapes of Teesdale that embrace gently rolling moors in all directions, rippling away to distant horizons, make it worthwhile.*

The small market town of **Middleton-in-Teesdale** is clearly comfortable with itself, possessing neither airs nor graces, or needing to. It expanded in the early 19th century, when the London Lead Company moved its northern headquarters here from Blanchland in Northumberland, and much of the architecture from its days as a company town is still clearly visible. This includes Middleton House, formerly the headquarters of the company, the school (which is now an outdoor centre, and part-time car parking area) and some company houses.

The Route

From the centre of town, walk down Bridge Street and cross the lovely bridge spanning the Tees. Walk up the road until it bends to the left, and there leave it for a side-lane on the right, for Holwick. Almost immediately, leave this lane for the Pennine Way, on the left, climbing initially on a gravel track up a field to a gate. Beyond this, just after the gate, as the track divides at a small cairn, bear right.

Higher up, after the next gate and stile, bear right along a broad grassy track towards the lower slopes of Harter Fell. Off to the left is a conspicuous

↑ Looking back from the Pennine Way towards Middleton-in-Teesdale

Distance	13.5km (8½ miles)
Height gain	317m (1040ft)
Time	4–5hrs
Grade	moderately demanding
Start point	Middleton-in-Teesdale NY948254

Getting there
Large long-stay car park at the old school on Bridge Street, Middleton-in-Teesdale, and a smaller car park just beyond the bridge over Hudeshope Beck at the northern end of town

Maps
Ordnance Survey OL31 (North Pennines: Teesdale and Weardale)

After-walk refreshment
Pubs, cafés and tearooms in Middleton-in-Teesdale

knoll topped by a stand of trees; this is Kirkcarrion, a Bronze Age tumulus said to be the burial place of a chieftain called Caryn.

The route lies across the eastern and southern slopes of Harter Fell, traversing wall-enclosed pastures. Eventually, Grassholme Reservoir comes into view, and then Selset. On entering a large pasture with a group of three trees off to the right, turn up towards the trees, which are found to be within a collapsed enclosure known as Pin Gate. From here it is an easy walk up grassy slopes to the trig pillar at a collapsed wall corner on the summit of **Harter Fell**. Return to Pin Gate and rejoin the Pennine Way, now heading towards a derelict barn nearby.

Carry on across a gated pasture, after which there is a stony track. Within a few strides, turn left at a through-stile and gate. Walk for less than 100m, and then leave the track by branching right on an indistinct path to a wall-gap and stile. Press on across a low ridge, descend obliquely right to a wall corner at the bottom of the pasture and cross a stone stile. Go across the ensuing field diagonally left towards a walled track. Pass through a dip, and walk up the

Kirkcarrion: Bronze Age tumulus

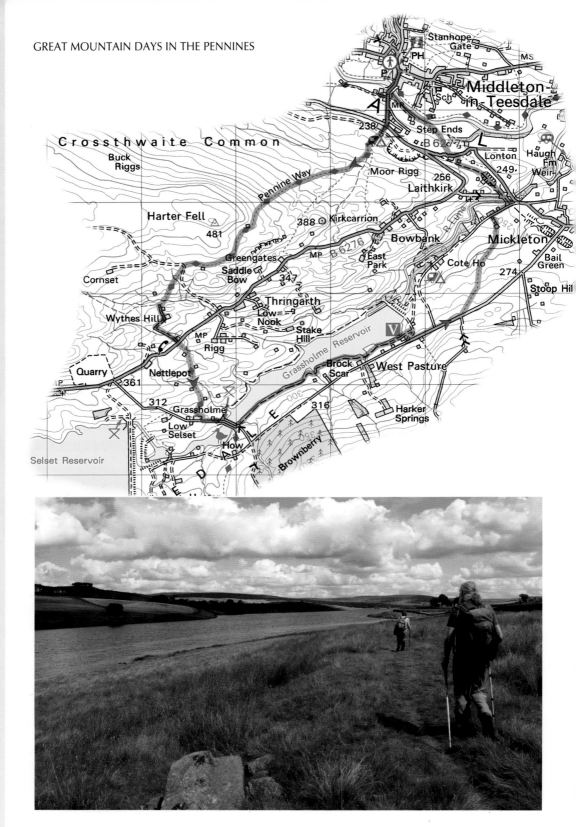

Walking beside Grassholme Reservoir

The final climb of the day

track to pass **Wythes Hill Farm**, then take its access track out to the **B6276**.

Cross the road and go over a stone stile. In the next field bear half-right, through a dip, and then climb beyond to a stile at a wall corner. Now keep forward on a clear descending, grassy path not far from a wall on the right. Press on across two more pastures towards **Grassholme Farm**, beyond which the route joins a lane running down to **Grassholme Reservoir**.

Continue across the end of the reservoir, climbing briefly, then leaving the lane to pass through a metal gate onto the South Shore Path. Now enjoy the waterside path that continues until it meets a surfaced lane near the visitor centre, which is worth visiting (exhibition, refreshments and toilets).

Continue across the centre car park and follow the lane up to meet a quiet back lane. Follow this, left, for about 600m, as far as a footpath signpost opposite a lane on the right. Leave the lane here and head diagonally right, down-pasture, towards a wall and a waymarked stile. Through the stile, keep left beside the wall and walk down to the bottom of the field, crossing a couple of step-stiles on the way.

At the bottom of the field, cross a stile and the bottom corner of a sloping pasture. On the other side, from a gate climb a clear path and then pause for a moment at the high point to enjoy a retrospective view of the route followed. A field-margin path now leads out to a lane at West Field Cottage. Turn right and walk as far as a gate on the left giving onto the Tees Railway Walk. Cross the viaduct ahead, spanning the River Lune, and then make the most of a delightful, tree-shaded railway trackbed, bright in spring and summer with wild flowers, including purple vetch, field scabious and foxglove.

Continue as far as a concrete ladder-stile on the right, and from it move half-left across a farm enclosure to a gate and stile giving onto a lane at **Lonton South Farm**. Walk briefly along the lane, then leave it at a signpost and gated gap-stile. Cross a meadow (diagonally left to a stile by a gate) and the corner of the next field to pursue a clear route across more fields eventually to reach the Tees. Now follow the river, upstream, but before the broad farm track underfoot reaches the Middleton road, bear right with the river to Bridge End Steps. Turn right up into **Middleton** to complete the walk.

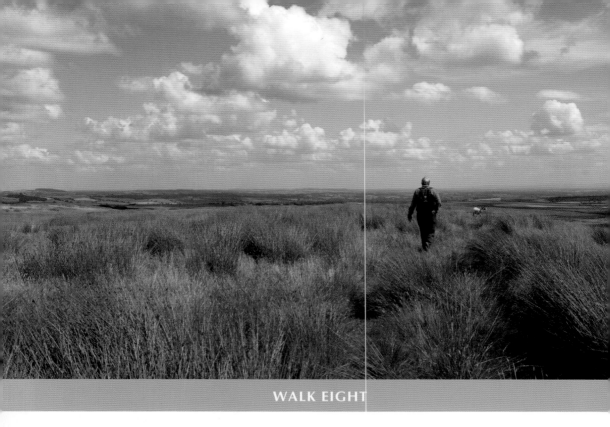

Bowes Moor

*M*aking use of both the Pennine Way and the Bowes (Pennine Way) Loop, this walk starts out in the agreeable company of the River Greta before heading up onto the grass and heather moors to the north, known locally as Bowes Moor. There is an openness about the moors that allows extensive views, which in turn bring a great sense of freedom, while the grassy ridge that links the two arms of the Pennine Way is a joy to follow.

Bowes has long served travellers crossing the Pennines; it sits at an obvious gap (Stainmore) that facilitates an east–west link. The Romans had a fort here (Lavatrae), although all its masonry went into building Bowes Castle in the 12th century. This was a lawless and unsettled region, and the castle was intended to bring some form of regulation.

The only pub in the village, The Ancient Unicorn, is said to be haunted. This 17th-century coaching inn was visited by Charles Dickens, who found inspiration in the village academy (Shaws), which he immortalised as Dotheboys Hall in *Nicholas Nickleby*. In the north-east corner of the churchyard is the grave of William Shaw, headmaster of Shaws Academy. Dickens met Shaw, who is generally accepted to be the prototype of Wackford Squeers, the brutal headmaster at Dotheboys Hall. In the south-east part of the churchyard is the grave of George Ashton Taylor, who died while a pupil at Shaws Academy. Dickens said that he thought it was on this spot that he conceived the idea of Smike, the boy who ran away from Dotheboys Hall.

↑ *Striding out across the top of Bowes Moor*

ROUTE INFORMATION

Distance	16.7km (10½ miles)
Height gain	205m (675ft)
Time	5+hrs
Grade	moderately demanding
Start point	Bowes NY996134

Getting there
Parking opposite Bowes village hall, and roadside parking on nearby road to Scotch Corner

Maps
Ordnance Survey OL31 (North Pennines: Teesdale and Weardale)

After-walk refreshment
Ancient Unicorn pub in Bowes

The Route
Walk up through the village street as far as the church, and then turn left into Back Lane (signed for Bowes Castle). The castle, which soon appears, stands in the north-west corner of the Roman fort.

Immediately on passing the castle, leave the lane and turn right at a gate/stile, and then go through another gate onto a signed path for the Pennine Way. Follow this as it runs around the castle boundary, through a dip and over a wall-gap stile and on across two fields to a narrow stile beside an ash tree. Keep on alongside a wall at a field boundary, cross another stile, press on beside a fence and shortly cross the top end of a sunken track and the field beyond to a lane at a Pennine Way signpost.

Turn left, up the lane, and then keep on past **Swinholme Farm**, beyond which the route descends to cross the River Greta by a footbridge. On the other side, cross a meadow to a gate, and just after this join a lane to go past **Lady Myres Farm**. The route then continues as a rough track, and runs around **West Charity Farm** to a footbridge spanning Sleightholme Beck. A good path now leads round towards **East Mellwaters**, which conceals a considerable history of farming in the area, probably going back as much as 5500 years, but today offers specialist accommodation and holidays for

Bowes Castle

less-abled people, for whom a network of trails has been constructed. Follow one such as it runs from a lane near a single-arch bridge and follows the River Greta all the way to the limestone feature known as **God's Bridge**.

God's Bridge, a Site of Special Scientific Interest (SSSI), is a natural limestone bridge formed by a process of cave development in the limestone beneath the river bed. It is the best example in Britain of a natural bridge formed in this way. The SSSI covers a portion of the river above and below the bridge where shallow cave development by water erosion is still taking place.

Cross the bridge and walk up through obsolete railway abutments (the line closed in the 1960s) to pass a nearby cottage. Follow a track up to the **A66**, where a path diverts left to an underpass. On the other side, turn right through a metal gate and walk across to **Pasture End Farm**. On reaching the farm, turn left along its boundary (Pennine Way sign for Clove Lodge) and walk up onto the moor. When the boundary wall changes direction, leave it and strike across open moorland.

Initially the way is not abundantly clear, but a path soon materialises and now leads northwards

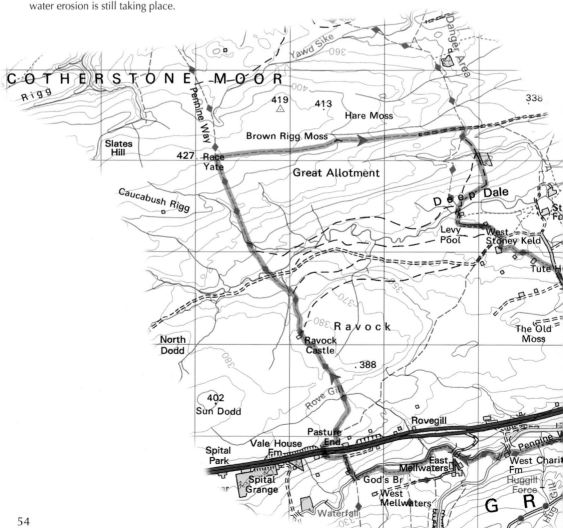

God's Bridge

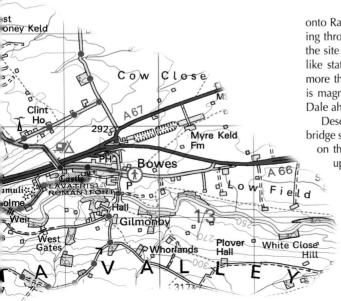

onto Ravock Moor, crossing **Rove Gill** and continuing through heather to the pile of stones that marks the site of **Ravock Castle**. Any aspirations to castle-like status are misplaced; this was probably never more than a hut or sheep enclosure, but its setting is magnificent, with the broad depression of Deep Dale ahead and the onward moor rising easily.

Descend to a prominent hut/shelter and a footbridge spanning **Deepdale Beck**. Pass through a gate on the other side, and then simply walk straight up the moor, parallel with a wall on the right.

Just before reaching the high point of **Cotherstone Moor**, turn right through a field gate that gives onto a broad track running eastwards, initially through reeds. To the north-east, a trig pillar marks the top of West Hare Crag, which can be reached by continuing first with the Pennine Way to a stile at **Race Yate Rigg**, and then crossing

Ravock Castle and Deep Dale

rough ground. Return the same way. The crag marks the highest point hereabouts.

Continue eastwards across the moor on an improving track that eventually leads to a gate at a wall-end. Here, the Pennine Way moves away in a south-westerly direction, but is not always clear underfoot. A surer guide is to turn right at the gate (do not pass through it) and pick up a clear, narrow path descending to cross Hazelgill Beck. When the accompanying wall changes direction, move to a south-westerly direction and aim across reedy ground for the conspicuous, isolated farm at **Levy Pool**, set in the middle of a stand of trees. A footbridge gives onto a track around the building and then out along a stony track.

The ongoing track passes through a gate near the end of a surfaced lane. Here, branch right on the Pennine Way at **West Stoney Keld Farm**. Just before reaching the farm buildings, turn left through a field gate and walk alongside a wall. Turn with the wall when it changes direction, but then drop obliquely left across a low slope to cross a corner of rough pasture towards a fence. Walk up beside the fence to a gated gap-stile. Cross the ensuing field towards the left-hand side of a barn; a short way on, another wall-stile gives into a field, across which a path leads out to join a lane.

Turn right to follow the lane, and when it ultimately divides near a compound of radio masts, bear right, descending, towards **Bowes**. The lane feeds into the western end of the village street, which is now followed back to the start.

NORTH WEST DALES –
EDEN VALLEY AND THE HOWGILLS

'Watercut' on the High Way above the Eden valley (Walk 11)

NORTH WEST DALES –
EDEN VALLEY AND THE HOWGILLS

Possessing a geological affinity with the low fells around Windermere in Lakeland, and owning little of the moorland bog usually associated with the high summits of the Pennines, the Howgills are unique, a diversion from the main thrust of the north–south Pennines. Yet they lie just a short distance west of the Pennine watershed, with only the bulk of Baugh Fell to intervene.

Their name comes from a small hamlet in the Lune valley, which was supplanted by Ordnance Survey cartographers to give to a fairly well-defined group of hills a collective name; and quite fortuitously, too, for neither 'the Sedbergh Fells' nor 'the Lune Hills' has quite the same ring. 'Howgill' derives from two old Scandinavian words – one from Old Norse (*haugr*, meaning 'hill' or 'mound'); the other from Old West Scandinavian (*gil*, meaning 'ravine'). Combine the two meanings and it becomes easy to see why 'fells', as in 'Howgill Fells', is surplus to requirements – tautology, in fact.

Walkers in the Howgills are certain to encounter springy turf underfoot almost everywhere, outcrops of rock being few and occurring only at Cautley Spout and in the confines of Carlin Gill. This is free-range country, where bosomy fells, unrestricted by walls and fences, and sporting surprisingly few trees, rise abruptly from glaciated valleys, their sides moulded into deep, shadowy gullies, and their tops a series of gentle undulations that shimmer in the evening light like burnished gold. This is a region inhabited by free-roaming cows, black-faced Rough Fell sheep and long-haired wild fell ponies, and is a delight to travel.

Three of the walks in this section (Walks 13–15) head for the highest point, The Calf, each by completely differing routes that reveal the best the Howgills have to offer, and encourage further independent exploration. Included, too, are three excellent walks that are neither truly Howgills nor wholly within the Yorkshire Dales National Park. Flanking the Eden valley are two outstanding and much neglected walks, including one that visits the source of both the River Ure and the Eden. Further north, Nine Standards Rigg is plumb on the Pennine watershed and enjoyably ascended from the market town of Kirkby Stephen.

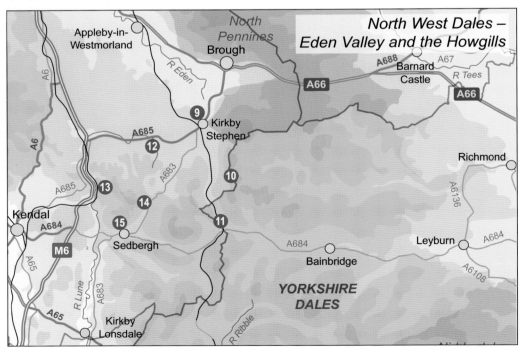

Hartley Fell and Nine Standards Rigg

'*R*igg' means 'ridge', and so Nine Standards Rigg is the ridged summit of Hartley Fell, a short distance south-east of Kirkby Stephen and marginally outside the Yorkshire Dales National Park boundary. You can get bogged down, literally as well as metaphorically, if you try to shoehorn Hartley Fell into a 'Pennine' or 'Dales' category. It's much more agreeable to ignore all that and to enjoy this airy saunter for its own merits. The whole of the ascent takes the line of the northern Coast to Coast walk; the onward route from Nine Standards Rigg lures you into the boggy clutches at the head of Whitsundale. But you don't have to be drawn; you can simply go back the way you came.

The Route

Opposite the Pennine Hotel in **Kirkby Stephen** leave the Market Place by a short lane to the right of the churchyard and enter Stoneshot, bearing right and then left down steps to meet the River Eden at Frank's Bridge. Cross the bridge and turn right to follow the river until it swings away to the right. From a gate, take to a surfaced path beside a wall and later a hedgerow, and continue to another gate in the top left corner of a field. Through this, go forward to arrive at the hamlet of **Hartley**.

Frank's Bridge, Kirkby Stephen

↑ *Long Rigg on the lower slopes of Hartley Fell*

ROUTE INFORMATION

Distance	14.5km (9 miles)
Height gain	540m (1770ft)
Time	4–5hrs
Grade	demanding
Start point	Kirkby Stephen NY775087

Getting there
Plenty of parking in Kirkby Stephen

Maps
Ordnance Survey OL19 (Howgill Fells and Upper Eden Valley)

After-walk refreshment
Kirkby Stephen is well endowed with pubs and cafés

On reaching a minor road, cross diagonally left to a narrow path leading to a small bridge across Hartley Beck. A short way on, on joining another road, turn right. When the road shortly swings left, leave it on the apex for a brief path that remains with Hartley Beck a little longer before rejoining the road. Turn right again, and now climb easily to the entrance to Hartley Quarry.

The route passes close by the site of **Hartley Castle**, a medieval fortified house built in the 14th century and extended at the start of the 17th. There's virtually nothing there now; by the late 18th century most of the original structure had been used to repair Eden Hall.

On passing the quarry, keep climbing and stick with the fell road, which gives fine retrospective views across the Vale of Eden to the high summits of the Pennines. A short descent leads past the entrance to **Fell House Farm**, and beyond this climb once more to the road end.

Just after the road end, branch left (for Rollinson Haggs) and soon pass through a gate. Go forward past the crags of Long Rigg and onto **Hartley Fell**. A broad track now leads on, and with the increasing

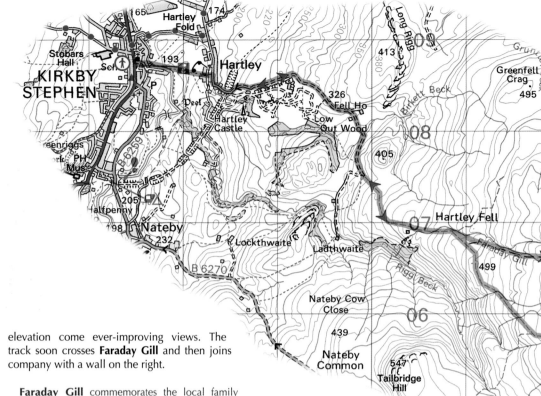

elevation come ever-improving views. The track soon crosses **Faraday Gill** and then joins company with a wall on the right.

> **Faraday Gill** commemorates the local family whose offspring, Michael, was the English chemist and physicist who discovered electromagnetic induction and other important electrical and magnetic phenomena. Such was the regard in which Faraday was held, that it is said Albert Einstein kept a photograph of him on his study wall alongside Isaac Newton.

Continue as far as a branching path on the left that leads unerringly up to the conspicuous cairns on the summit ridge. Arrival here is quite special, not just for the views, but because the ridge lies along the Pennine and British watershed.

> No one has yet come up with a valid explanation for the **Nine Standards** – the monoliths found on the summit. They stand on the former county boundary between Westmorland and the North Riding of Yorkshire, and that may be explanation enough, but unlikely given the effort involved. Happily, after a prolonged period of neglect, the cairns have seen much restoration in recent years and are worthy of heritage protection.
>
> The cairns have long been dismissed as late medieval at best, but recent research has shown that the nine cairns appear on old maps, and reference has been found in documents from the Brough Court indicating their existence as early as 1507, and possibly much earlier. Low-level oblique aerial photographs of the summit reveal the possible outline of a rectangular enclosure with the cairns running diagonally through it, and this may indicate some underlying archaeology.
>
> On a fine day there are few vantage points that provide a wider or more inspiring panorama over wild moorlands. The highest point of the summit ridge is actually at the nearby trig pillar, but the view from there is nothing like so impressive.

The onward route continues past the trig pillar into conflict with rough, boggy, heathery, tussocky moorland, with many variable peat bogs to circumnavigate. If you don't fancy this, then simply retrace your outward route.

Otherwise continue past the trig pillar, descending to an extended boggy area on the very edge of the national park (NY827057). Here the Coast to Coast route turns east, heading down into Whitsundale, but this walk turns west (right), although there is no path for a while. Maintain a westerly direction and soon a large cairn is seen off to the south-west. It is important to keep north of this; don't be drawn towards it. Eventually pass scattered rocky outcrops and a wide grassy channel through peat. These are **Rollinson Haggs**, beyond which a signpost is encountered on the line of a bad-weather route for the Coast to Coast (NY817058).

Keep ahead now, crossing a moorland shoulder in a north-westerly direction. The path, sketchy at first, improves and becomes a wide grassy track running alongside a wall. Turn right along it and stride out, away from the bogs and mire, and rejoin the outward route at **Faraday Gill**.

On Nine Standards Rigg

Lunds Fell,
Hugh Seat and High Seat

*T*he Eden valley is a delight, and any walk here is graced with stunning landscapes. The hills on
the east of the valley fall gently in that direction over the moors of Birkdale Common and Angram
Common. To the west they present what seems like a formidable array of cliffs, known as Mallerstang
Edge; it is through these cliffs that the final descent needs to be made, thereby introducing a severe
sting in the tail of the walk. By way of compensation, the walking is fairly straightforward throughout
and passes close by the source springs of two rivers, the Ure and the Eden itself.

The Route

A journey along the length of the River Eden is admirably described by Neil Hanson in *Walking through
Eden* (see Appendix 2). It takes readers on a wonderful
and inspirational journey, which begins here above
the scattered houses of **Thrang**. Set off up the Pennine
Bridleway (signed for Hell Gill Bridge), immediately
engaging the course of a green road that has probably
been in use since Bronze Age times. Today, the road
is known as the High Way, but also as Lady Anne's
Way, in memory of Lady Anne Clifford, the Countess
of Pembroke, who used the route in her journeys
between her castles in Yorkshire and Westmorland.

↑ *Mallerstang Edge and High Seat from the Eden valley*

The **High Way** has been a trade route for thousands of years, and provided marauding Scots with an invasion route through the Pennines to Skipton, Richmond and beyond. Long after these troubled times ended, the High Way remained in use by pack-horse trains, drovers, pedlars and travellers well into the 19th century, and in preference to the turnpike that later ran along the valley bottom, on which a toll was charged.

The High Way makes the most of well-drained limestone plateaux, which offered much easier going than the swampy valley bottom; not without good reason is the area known as Mallerstang – 'the marsh, or pool, of the wild duck'.

Gradually, the High Way rises to encounter a large and unexpected artwork, known as 'Watercut', that has been in view for some time.

Watercut is one of a number of art works, known as the **Eden Benchmarks**, by the East Cumbria Countryside Project, which was commissioned to create a series of 10 site-specific, carved stone sculptures which also functioned as seats. They are located on public paths along the length of the River Eden from its source at Mallerstang to where it joins the sea at Rockcliffe, just north of Carlisle. The project involved 10 different artists and was commissioned to mark the millennium. 'Watercut' was created by Mary Bourne from Cumbrian Salterwath limestone.

Press on beyond 'Watercut', now on level ground, as far as **Hell Gill Bridge**. The gill rises in the landscape folds west of Hugh Seat, and is the source of the Eden.

Cross the bridge and turn immediately left, leaving the High Way for a quad-bike track that rises initially alongside the wooded Hell Gill ravine. Later, it bears away, targeting a solitary stone pillar, known as Outer Pike, on the edge of Lunds Fell. Off to the right, the course of Jingling Sike (not named on the 1:50,000 map) is a boundary that guides the route upwards, although the quad-bike track is continuous all the way onto Lunds Fell, even though there are places where that may be doubted from time to time.

Outer Pike is a good intermediate target, but the top of **Lunds Fell** lies another 600m to the east, with a modest cairn and pole. The final approach to the

ROUTE INFORMATION

Distance	16km (10 miles)
Height gain	535m (1755ft)
Time	6hrs
Grade	strenuous
Start point	Thrang NY783004

Getting there
Roadside pull-in for a few cars at Thrang; Outhgill is an alternative starting point, but with little parking opportunity

Maps
Ordnance Survey OL19 (Howgill Fells and Upper Eden Valley)

After-walk refreshment
Moorcock Inn, Garsdale, or pubs, cafés and restaurants in Kirkby Stephen

'Watercut', one of the Eden Benchmarks, Eden valley

On the summit of Lunds Fell, looking north to Hugh Seat and High Seat

summit is bedevilled by numerous lateral drainage ditches that can be trip-hazards for the unwary, and especially so in winter conditions.

Lunds Fell has a second summit, 1m lower, to the south, and between the two lies Ure Head, the source of the river that goes on to flow through Wensleydale. Further to the south, Yorkshire's 'Three Peaks' poke into the landscape, while to the east rises Great Shunner Fell (Walk 16), the parent fell hereabouts, at least so far as Marilyns are concerned.

From the top of Lunds Fell, set off northwards, keeping as much as possible to the high ground, where a clear path soon materialises. Cross a fence at SD808975, after which an indistinct path leads on. Head for a fence corner at SD807979, and then keep to the right of the fence, rising steadily through the most boggy stretch of the entire walk and being funnelled into a fence junction. Just beyond a gate, use a step-stile to cross the ensuing fence, and then walk beside it up onto **Hugh Seat**, the highest point of which is marked simply by fences, although there is a large cairn nearby.

The grassy dome of **Hugh Seat**, with its fine view, is said to be named after Hugh de Morville, one of the knights who murdered Thomas à Becket in Canterbury Cathedral in 1170. He and his accomplices are believed to have spent a year in hiding in his castle at Knaresborough 64km (40 miles) away.

Close by Hugh Seat the River Eden rises, at Eden Springs, flowing down Red Gill, described by Camden in *Britannica* as a 'stygian rivulet flowing through a horrid silent wilderness': something of a jaundiced outlook; this is the most soothing of landscapes.

Gregory Chapel, looking over to High Seat

From Hugh Seat follow the fence north-eastwards until it changes direction at a large cairn, and then head for a waymark pole and a brief line of cairns, now targeting a prominent stone pillar. This section of the walk is along the Pennine watershed, and so, while Hugh Seat sends the waters on its western flanks to the Eden and the Irish Sea, those to the east flow down into the Swale, and ultimately to the North Sea.

Press on past the pillar to follow a path up to **Gregory Chapel**, marked by a cairn and rough shelter. A clear path now leads across to **High Seat**, although the highest top along the ridge is marked by nothing more than lowly cairns.

Now comes the sting in the tail, because the descent is via very steep grassy slopes, with boulders and low cliffs to avoid. There is a clear way down,

67

but crossing through **Mallerstang Edge** demands total and sustained concentration; there is no path until much lower down.

Move to the west from the top of High Seat. At first, the slope is easy and grassy, but gradually the steep edge appears, dropping 115m (375ft) in less than 250m horizontal distance. The target is Sloe Brae Gill (not named on the 1:50,000 map, but the southerly stream of two to the west of High Seat). There are gullies to cross and recross, but slow and careful progress is needed at all times.

The path shown on maps is barely discernible, and once lower ground is reached it is fairly straight-forward to walk down beside the gill, changing sides as necessary. Eventually, the route does join the marked right of way (at NY790012) and starts to improve, passing through reeds and then tussock grass before finally descending to a gate on the edge of **Outhgill**. Walk down into the hamlet and bear left towards the telephone box.

Outhgill is the main hamlet in the dale of Mallerstang and retains the Norse pattern of its original settlement, one of isolated houses, with no distinct village centre. In the 19th century, Outhgill had an inn, a post office, a smithy, the parish church and a Methodist chapel. Of these, only the church survives. In the churchyard there are the unmarked graves of 25 of the builders of the Mallerstang section of the Settle–Carlisle railway, who died during the construction of the line.

By the side of the village green is a replica of the so-called 'Jews Stone', a monument set up in 1850 by the eccentric William Mounsey, and which got its name from the inscriptions in Greek and Hebrew.

James Faraday, father of Michael Faraday (1791–1869), the scientist, was for many years a blacksmith in Outhgill, moving to London when Michael was born.

Turn left and walk along the valley road to the church, entering the churchyard and walking through to a meadow flanking the river; the stile at the rear of the churchyard is a very tight fit. Go diagonally left towards the river and stay with the river to a stile giving onto a stony track. Turn left, and shortly bear right along an access track for Sycamore Farm.

When the access track divides, branch left towards the farm and walk past cattle sheds to join a broad farm track, once more walking beside the river. Keep an eye open for a through-stile and waymark on the left before reaching the end of the field. Cross here, and continue beside the dipper-favoured river, crossing it at Thrang Bridge and walking up the ensuing track back to the valley road to complete the walk.

Wild Boar Fell and Swarth Fell

*W*ild Boar Fell (so name because here in the 15th century Sir Richard Musgrave is said to have chased and killed the last wild boar in England) rises majestically from the beautiful Vale of Eden, a perfect counterpart to the long escarpment of Mallerstang Edge across the valley. Also across the valley is the so-called Lady Anne's Way, and this is used at the start of the route before it descends to tackle the climb onto Wild Boar Fell. The high ground turns out to be easy walking on springy turf and limestone. Some untracked sections are included, but these should deter no one.

The Route

The walk begins at **Shaw Paddock Farm**, where the B6259 passes beneath the Settle–Carlisle railway line. Leave the road here for a broad track (signed for Hell Gill Bridge) that runs on to a single-arch bridge spanning the infant River Ure, which rises on the slopes of Lunds Fell to the east. The track is a pleasure to walk and rises gently to intercept an old road, now no more than a track, which is known variously as the High Way, Hellgill Wold and Lady

Anne's Way. The latter is a reference to its use by the redoubtable Lady Anne Clifford, later Countess of Pembroke, the only surviving child of the third Earl of Cumberland; she was famed throughout Westmorland during the 17th century for her extensive programme of castle renovations.

The path leads up to **Hell Gill Bridge**, a place with a number of distinctions – being on the county boundary between Cumbria and North Yorkshire

Stanier LMS 'Princess Coronation' Class No. 46233
'Duchess of Sutherland', on the Settle–Carlisle railway line, July 2012

ROUTE INFORMATION

Distance	16.5km (10¼ miles)
Height gain	570m (1870ft)
Time	6+hrs
Grade	demanding
Start point	Shaw Paddock SD784952

Getting there
Roadside parking north and south of the point where the road passes beneath the railway line at Shaw Paddock

Maps
Ordnance Survey OL19 (Howgill Fells and Upper Eden Valley)

After-walk refreshment
Pubs at Garsdale Head; pubs, cafés and restaurants aplenty in Kirkby Stephen

as well as the Yorkshire Dales National Park. Hell Gill Beck is also the source of the River Eden, and, with the River Ure only a few hundred metres to the south, it follows that in the final approach to Hell Gill Bridge, the Pennine watershed is crossed.

Press on now northwards from the bridge, crossing an almost level limestone landscape to reach a

most unusual and unexpected structure (SD785985), known as 'Watercut', one of a series of Eden Benchmarks (see Walk 10).

At 'Watercut', the High Way is now left by descending steeply in a north-westerly direction, parallel with a wall. There is no significant path on this descent. At the bottom, a bridleway is encountered close by a ruined barn, but it is far from evident, and this passes as an indistinct way (occasionally waymarked) through rushes and across rough pasture eventually to reach a metal gate (SD783993) just above **Elmgill Farm**. Walk down to the farm, and from there out to the B-road. Turn right along the road as far as a track on the left that is both the route of the Pennine Bridleway and the way to **Hazelgill Farm** (signed for High Dolphinsty).

Follow a waymarked route to the left of the farm, and soon climb to pass beneath the Settle-Carlisle railway line, which, especially at weekends, carries steam trains. The Pennine Bridleway now follows a clear route onto the northern ridge of Wild Boar Fell. Double back above the railway line, then walk on beside a wall until the bridleway changes direction, heading west. The onward route is clear throughout and in its upper section waymarked to lead into a narrow gully that rises to the ridge at **High Dolphinsty**.

Now turn southwards and, starting easily, head for the upper slopes of Wild Boar Fell, which near the top are steeper for a short while as **The Nab** is reached. From here a broad grassy path leads across to the shelter and trig on the summit. This is the generally favoured summit of **Wild Boar Fell**. But Wild Boar Fell infuriates, for there are two more spots of equal height, each with equal claim to the summit crown. One, barely discernible, lies due east of the trig (SD761988), on the edge of the escarpment, while the third is among the conspicuous stone pillars a short distance further south, also overlooking the sharp drop to Mallerstang Common. A diversion to inspect these pillars, which seem to increase in number each year, demands hardly any additional expenditure of energy and provides a convenient and sheltered spot for a short halt.

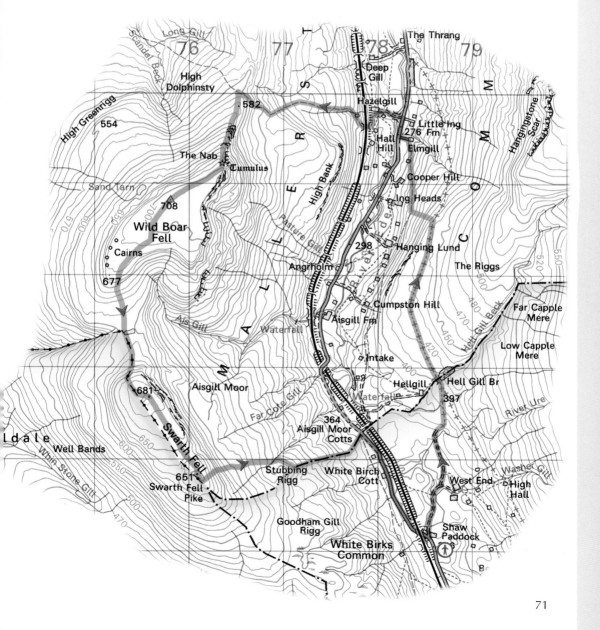

The last section up onto The Nab at the northern end of Wild Boar Fell

Wild Boar Fell from the High Way

Whether the last wild boar really was killed on **Wild Boar Fell** is debatable, not least because wild boar tended to favour wooded areas. But, it is argued, there is credence in Sir Richard's claim, for when the chancel and side chapels of Kirkby Stephen Parish Church were restored in 1847–1851, Sir Richard was found to have been buried with his wife – together with the tusk of a wild boar. Which of the two he valued more is not recorded. This, then, is the generally accepted view, but the presence of a Wild Boar Inn at Crook, near Windermere, and a Wild Boar Scar on the shoulders of Cross Fell suggests other possibilities.

In *Legends and Historical Notes of North Westmoreland* by Thomas Gibson of Orton, however, there is a story in verse penned by a Mr Joseph Steel of the legend of the death of a wild boar at the hands of a giant:

> *The giant with one stroke on loins*
> *Deprived the boar of life,*
> *Which gave a title to the hill*
> *That ne'er will pass away,*
> *For it is called Wild Boar Fell*
> *E'en to this very day.*

Whatever the derivation of its name, Wild Boar Fell is a fine lofty mountain, having a large and fairly level summit on which in former times there used to be horse-racing, wrestling and other athletic sports, just as on High Street above Kentmere in the Lake District.

The route then continues to Swarth Fell circles around Aisgill Head. There is a fence across the top of **Ais Gill**, and this can be intercepted simply by walking south across the fell's grassy top and then crossing the low fence at some convenient point, without causing damage or injury. A path descends on both sides of the fence to the broad col between the two mountains, on which nestles a shallow tarn. The fence is a good guide in poor visibility and finally abuts a wall ascending from Uldale to the southwest. Now simply follow the wallside path to the top of **Swarth Fell**. The summit, marked by a large cairn, is easily located to the east of the wall amid a scattering of boulders. All along this stretch from Wild Boar Fell to Swarth Fell the sprawling mass of Baugh Fell is a dominant feature to the south, with the top of Whernside beyond, while to the west rise the inviting domes of the Howgills.

There is a broad path linking Swarth Fell and its lower sibling, Swarth Fell Pike, escorted at a distance by a wall and then a fenceline. On the top of **Swarth Fell Pike** there are two large cairns. From a large boulder near the higher of these, a grassy path strikes eastwards, descending steeply at first, but then easing and more or less parallel with the county boundary. Quad-bike tracks help for some of the way, but the target ultimately becomes the white **Aisgill Moor Cottages**, where a gate gives onto the road. Now simply turn right and follow the road for 1km to complete the walk.

Green Bell

*T*he grassy summit of Green Bell, high on Ravenstonedale Common, drains into streams, Dale Gill in particular, that are commonly regarded as the source of the River Lune. These bosomy hills are a pleasure to wander, a place where solitude reigns supreme, disturbed only by the call of moorland birds and the occasional passage of feral fell ponies.

This is traditional Westmorland, even though the administrative county has long gone, and **Ravenstonedale** (known locally by some as 'Rassendel') is one of the most exquisite Westmorland villages, an agreeable cluster of ancient houses and cottages with a village green and a couple of pubs, all immersed in pleasant beck scenery.

Field barn, Ravenstonedale Common

↑ *Thornthwaite and Green Bell*

ROUTE INFORMATION

Distance	10.5km (6½ miles)
Height gain	430m (1410ft)
Time	4hrs
Grade	moderately demanding
Start point	Ravenstonedale NY722042

Getting there
Room to park a few cars near a road junction south of the church at Ravenstonedale

Maps
Ordnance Survey OL19 (Howgill Fells and Upper Eden Valley)

After-walk refreshment
Pubs in Ravenstonedale

The Route
Leave the village by walking along the road for Sedbergh, soon passing the Black Swan pub and village shop, and turning right to walk up to Town Head. Walk all the way through the village, and then, as the main road for Sedbergh bends to the left, leave it at a junction with the lane to Artlegarth; but shun this, too, in favour of another lane leading to a single-arch bridge spanning Artlegarth Beck.

Over the bridge, go forward onto a gravel track (signposted for Green Bell) leading to **Kilnmire Farm**. Just beyond the farm, a metal gate gives onto a broad track that climbs easily beside a wall, with ever-improving views. Once above the intake walls, the

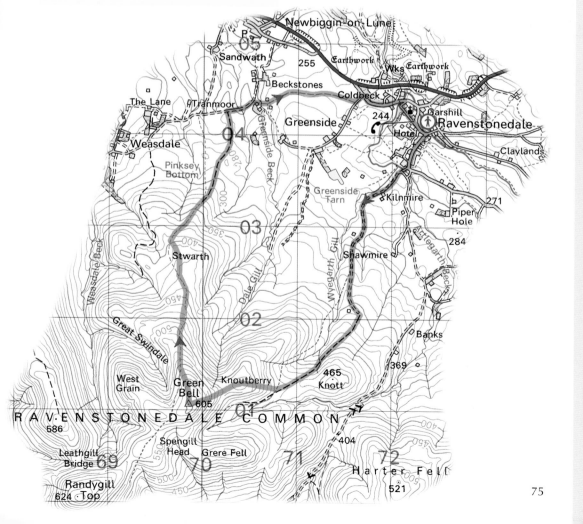

Take the path rising onto Knoutberry and Green Bell

route continues as a broad and clear grassy track up onto the moorland. The initial target is a walled enclosure at Thornthwaite. Aim to pass to the left of the enclosure, abandoning the track that heads into Wyegarth Gill.

On rounding the enclosure, an improving path leads across the slopes of Knott, while another rambles off to tackle its slopes head on. Go this way to include **Knott** in the walk – its summit is marked by a small cairn – or continue across its slopes. Both routes combine on the broad col between Knott and Knoutberry.

Yarlside and Cautley Crags from the summit of Green Bell

Now tackle the steep slope of Knoutberry and continue with a clear path – this, however, passes below the summit of **Knoutberry**, to which a diversion is necessary to find the small pile of stones that mark its highest point. Press on beyond Knoutberry for more uphill work on a clear path that rises to the summit of **Green Bell**, marked by an S-series trig pillar; these were introduced in 1920.

The summit of **Green Bell**, bare save for its trig pillar, is one of the finest viewpoints in England below 610m (2000ft). It embraces much of the distant Lakeland skyline, the trio of summits – Cross Fell and the two Dun Fells – that are the highest in the Pennines, and a host of lower summits that ripple southwards into the Yorkshire Dales. Most captivating, however, are the nearby summits of the Howgills themselves, a shapely gathering of largely grassy hills, the nearest of which, Randygill Top, might easily be tacked on to this walk (an out-and-back extension), adding 1.6km (1 mile) in each direction. (If this is added, there is no need to reascend Green Bell on the way back; a clear track runs northwards from the narrow col just south-west of the trig, and later joins that descending from the summit.)

From the top of Green Bell, a clear grassy path descends northwards, targeting distant Cross Fell. It is an easy and speedy descent, crossing the shoulder of Hunthoof Pike, which bears a decent cairn but is otherwise uninteresting except for its view over Swindale. Stick with the descending path as far as a waymark pole (NY696028). Here, bear right, with the ongoing path now becoming narrower and in places less distinct.

On passing a small reedy area, there is another path junction (NY701034), even less clear, just where the right of way on the map bears left. At this junction, branch right along a narrow trod through grass that eventually is seen to run parallel with the course of an old vehicle track. The path does continue to finally intercept a more pronounced vehicle track and descend to a surfaced lane.

Turn right, and follow the lane to the first building on the right, and there (signposted bridleway for Low Greenside) pass through two gates to gain a sloping pasture with a barn ahead. Keep to the right of the barn to locate and ascend an enclosed track, and at the top pass through a bridle-gate. Cross the ensuing field to enter a brief continuation of the enclosed lane. Another gate gives into the edge of a meadow. Keep right, parallel with a wall, and on the far side of the field join another walled continuation.

The track runs out through more pastures, eventually to meet a lane. Turn left down the lane to a T-junction, and there turn right to walk back into **Ravenstonedale**. On entering the village, turn sharply right in front of the King's Head, and then follow the road, left, to return to the start.

Ravenstonedale pastures, with the central Pennines in the distance

The Fairmile circuit

*T*his circuit is an unashamed attempt to cram as many of the western Howgill delights as possible into the shortest distance. Inevitably that means a fair amount of ascent, which begins from the very start, and virtually all of it is concentrated into the first 4km (2½ miles). So, be prepared for a strenuous start, but one followed by some of the most agreeable high-level wandering the Howgills have to offer. The going underfoot is easy throughout, but keen navigation could be vital in poor visibility.

The defining line between the Pennines to the east and the easier landscapes of the Lakeland fringe, the **Lune valley** has long been a key access route. For the Romans, who had a fort at Low Borrow Bridge, it was of strategic importance – their western way northwards – eventually linking with the Eden valley at Kirkby Thore. Between Sedbergh and Fairmile Gate the ancient road is these days known as Howgill Lane. But

on reaching Fairmile Beck, where the enclosed fields and pastures of this rich and fertile neck of land finally retreat, it becomes Fairmile Road (sometimes Fair Mile Lane). Here, little more than 500m distant, modern man's access routes, the M6 motorway and the Glasgow–London railway line, squeeze through a narrow gap carved thousands of years ago by glaciers and the infant River Lune.

↑ *Looking up to White Head from Chapel Beck*

ROUTE INFORMATION

Distance	13.8km (8½ miles)
Height gain	900m (2955ft)
Time	5hrs
Grade	strenuous
Start point	Fairmile Gate SD629981

Getting there

Informal parking area, north of Fairmile Gate, along minor road between Sedbergh and Tebay

Map

Ordnance Survey OL19 (Howgill Fells and Upper Eden Valley)

After-walk refreshment

Pubs in Tebay or Sedbergh

The Route

From the parking just north of **Fairmile Gate** begin by following a grassy path through bracken – roughly on the line, and to the north, of Dry Gill. The path climbs steeply until, as the gradient eases, it enters a shallow gully, from the top of which a path swings right towards the tussocky summit of Linghaw.

Looking towards the Lake District, the far horizon captures the bulk of Black Combe, the Coniston Fells and the Scafells, with High Street and the eastern fells rippling across the skyline to the right of Grayrigg Forest. When you arrive at the summit of **Linghaw**, Great and Green Gable have also muscled in on the scene.

A narrow path leads on and descends to a neat col, crossed by a good path ascending from Beck Houses, and then climbs again to **Fell Head**, visiting the western summit, marked by a small cairn, before crossing to the slightly higher main summit, also crowned by a cairn.

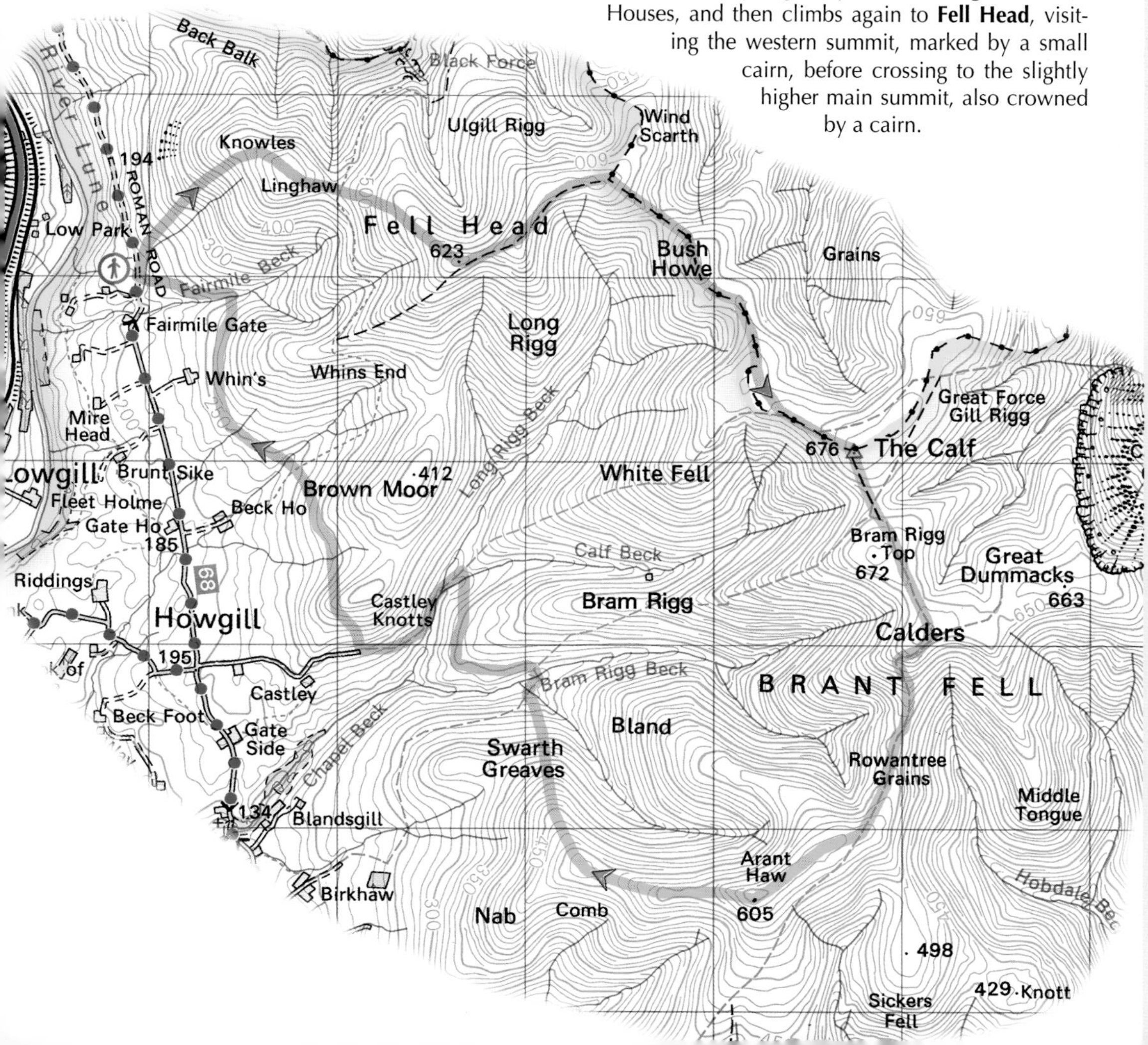

A simple and delightful ridge walk follows, curving lazily round the head of Long Rigg Gill, Crooked Ashmere Gills and Long Rigg Beck to descend to another col, Windscarth Wyke. Yet more ascent follows, this time steadily to the top of **Bush Howe**, to be greeted by the first real view of The Calf.

Heading for the highest point now involves little ascent. Just north-east of White Fell, the path divides, with the main path continuing clearly to The Calf and its prominent trig pillar. There are tremendous views along this broad and lofty ridge, west to the Lakeland fells, south-west to the Kent estuary, and south-east into Dales country.

From **The Calf**, a broad path presses on east of south to **Calders**, although on a clear day a slight diversion to take in Bram Rigg Top will reward with a splendid

vantage point on which to stop for lunch, gazing down on Chapel Beck and the distant Crook of Lune.

Once across the summit of Calders stay with the path beside a fence to the narrow col,

The two summits of Fell Head

View northwards from the summit of The Calf, showing the long line of ascent from distant Fell Head

The final stages of the descent from Arant Haw to Chapel Beck

Rowantree Grains, from where the route starts climbing again, more or less for the last time. A cairn marks the diversion (right) of a grassy track leading to the summit of **Arant Haw** (better known locally as Higher Winder)– the left fork eventually descends to Lockbank Farm on the outskirts of Sedbergh, so ignore it.

Continue across the summit of Arant Haw, and descend at first west then, no longer on a path, north-west, aiming for the confluence of Bram Rigg Beck and Chapel Beck, below the minor top of Castley Knotts. In times of spate conditions the becks may look impassable, but Bram Rigg Beck can usually be forded above its confluence with Swarth Greaves Beck (at SD650958) or near Chapel Beck (SD645958).

From the point where Chapel Beck and Bram Rigg Beck meet (SD644958), go northwards on a narrow path just above the beck to the confluence of Long Rigg Beck, Calf Beck and Chapel Beck

(SD646963), and there swing left along a rising vehicle track around the flanks of Castley Knotts. From here the return to Fairmile Gate is a delightful stroll. Initially it takes to a grooved path, ascending parallel with an intake wall on the left, to pass around **Castley Knotts**. As the wall and path change direction and start to descend, look for a narrow grassy trod that contours around Castley Knotts, later descending rough ground to rejoin the wall. All that then remains is to follow the intake wall back to Fairmile Beck.

At Beck Houses Gate, where nothing but trouble seems to loom ahead, keep to a narrow path that descends into and crosses a ravine before returning to the wall. Another bout of ravine crossing is met at **Fairmile Beck**, where the choice lies in keeping left, following the beck to Howgill Lane, or crossing the ravine, climbing steeply out on the other side, and then following a narrow path through bracken back to the start.

Cautley Spout and The Calf

*C*autley Spout is a natural draw – its great white gash, set against the backdrop of the rounded slopes of the Howgills, is both provocative and inviting, and sooner or later everyone gets drawn in for a closer look. Although there is a route that passes tantalisingly close to the falls, this walk bypasses them and curves high above to head for the airy summit of The Calf. A long, panoramic descent follows from Great Dummacks, plunging to the Rawthey valley, and a steady conclusion above the Rawthey Farm fields.

The **Cross Keys Inn** dates from the early 17th century and was originally a farmhouse known as High Haygarth, and probably an alehouse, which converted to an inn in the early 19th century to provide hospitality for travellers along the rerouted highway that formerly ran over Bluecaster Fell.

With the rise of the Temperance Movement in the 19th century, it became an alcohol-free establishment. In 1948, the inn was bequeathed to the National Trust by its last owner, Mrs Edith Bunney, on the condition that it remained temperance.

↑ *Cautley Crag and the upper falls of Cautley Spout*

ROUTE INFORMATION

Distance	11.5km (7 miles)
Height gain	603m (1980ft)
Time	5hrs
Grade	demanding
Start point	Cross Keys Inn SD698969

Getting there
Roadside parking on the A683, just north of
the Cross Keys Inn

Maps
Ordnance Survey OL19 (Howgill Fells and
Upper Eden Valley)

After-walk refreshment
Cross Keys Inn at start (temperance); more
pubs and cafés in Sedbergh

Bowderdale Head

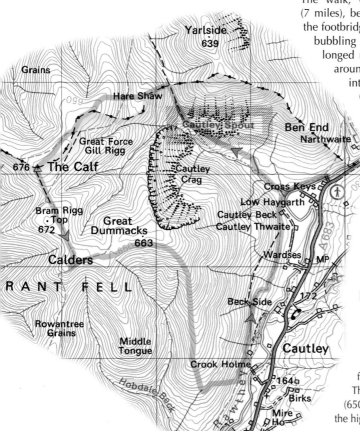

The route

The walk, which crams a lot into its 11.5km
(7 miles), begins with instant delight as it crosses
the footbridge spanning the Rawthey, a bright and
bubbling watercourse, turbulent only after prolonged rain. On the other side, a path leads
around the base of **Ben End** and later curves
into a north-westerly direction, now with
Cautley Spout in view.

Follow the track as it ascends the
valley of Cautley Holme Beck (not
named on 1:50,000 maps) steadily towards the waterfall, which
improves visually almost with every
step. Continue as far as two prominent medium-sized boulders, one
either side of the track. Here, leave
the main track and bear right onto
a grassy path that swings across the
scree slopes of Yarlside's southern top.
The path is narrow in places and the
cross-slope steep, but there are plenty of
places to pause and admire the improving view of the falls.

Cautley Spout is England's highest
waterfall above ground – Gaping Gill
(below Ingleborough – see Walk 21)
falls a greater distance into a pothole.
The tiered cascade tumbles almost 200m
(650ft) down a narrow ravine that spills from
the high plateau topped by The Calf.

83

Eventually, the ascent eases and runs on across marshy ground to the boundary of the Yorkshire Dales National Park, overlooking long and lonely Bowderdale. But just before reaching the obvious col, the path forks. Branch left for a short distance and then turn abruptly westwards, climbing steeply on grass to the peaty top of **Hare Shaw**.

A dip separates Hare Shaw from the north-easterly extension of The Calf. Cross this and use an obvious green ramp to ascend to a north–south track. Now, turn left along this and follow it as it rises steadily all the way to the summit of **The Calf**, one of only two Marilyns in the Howgills.

From The Calf, head roughly southwards, following a constructed path that bypasses Bram Rigg Top to reach a large cairn on **Calders**, with a fence, something of a rarity in the Howgills, close by. Turn eastwards, following a broad grassy path alongside the fence, heading for the mound of Great Dummacks. When the fence changes direction to strike down the ridge of Middle Tongue, leave it and take to a grassy and narrowing path onto **Great Dummacks**.

An obvious fork marks the point at which an easy ascent onto the summit of Great Dummacks is possible. But otherwise, continue on the traversing path. On a clear day it is worth diverting across the top of Great Dummacks for a fine view of Cautley Crag.

A long descent of Fawcett Bank Rigg now follows, swooping downwards in great undulations, always following the course of a quad-bike track and eventually leading towards a wall. As the wall is approached, bear left to a wall corner, which marks the boundary of Access Land. Turn left with the wall, following a parallel path until the wall abruptly changes direction and drops steeply towards the Rawthey. At this point, maintain the original direction for a short distance to gain easier ground and then descend steep grassy slopes, eventually through stands of gorse, to find the course of a bridleway just above the valley intake wall.

Now, turn northwards (left) along the bridleway, and follow this through a few undulations until finally, near a ruined farmhouse, it passes through the right-hand one of two gates and runs on to cross a footbridge and rejoin the outward route. Now simply retrace the first few minutes of the walk to return to the start.

Rawthey Gill and the distant Cross Keys Inn

The Calf from Sedbergh

*S*erving as a geological stepping-stone between the main line of the gritty Pennines and the limestone fells of Cumbria, the Howgills rise immediately to the north of Sedbergh. These smooth, grassy, rounded domes provide both excellent walking and dramatic scenery, as this walk reveals. It begins by a long haul across the slopes of lower fells before striking for the top, and then finding a delightful way down past the popular Cautley Spout to conclude with a long and satisfying romp down the Rawthey valley.

From almost any point in the narrow streets of **Sedbergh**, the Howgills are visible, their steep slopes presenting a theatrical backdrop to the small, stone-built town. Formerly in the West Riding of Yorkshire, Sedbergh became part of Cumbria only in 1974, even though it remains in the Yorkshire Dales National Park (just), and clearly has many 'Dales' affinities. Sedbergh is largely one long main street, an ancient market town with a charter dating from 1251, and is mentioned in the Domesday Book as among the manors held by Earl Tostig of Northumbria. Today, the fame of the town rests on the laurels of its school, set in parkland on the edge of town; it was founded in 1525 and has grown steadily to earn a national reputation.

↑ *The descending bridleway above Swere Gill*

ROUTE INFORMATION

Distance   17.5km (11 miles)
Height gain   675m (2215ft)
Time   6+hrs
Grade   strenuous
Start point   Sedbergh SD658919

Getting there
Loftus Hill car park, Sedbergh

Maps
Ordnance Survey OL19 (Howgill Fells and
Upper Eden Valley)

After-walk refreshment
Pubs and cafés in Sedbergh

The Route

Start from the car park in **Sedbergh** and turn right, walking up to a bend near the Old Reading Room. Turn left, and take the first on the right, after the post office, into Howgill Lane. The road rises gently and passes round a playing field. Keep on, towards a small housing estate on the upper edge of Sedbergh. Just past the houses, leave the road by turning right on a narrow hedgerowed lane leading up to **Lockbank Farm**.

Go through a gate onto a broad walled track to a fell-gate. Through this, turn left, climbing beside a wall. Almost immediately, leave the wallside path by ascending on the right along a clear path crossing the hillside, climbing steeply. This shortly bears right and rises through bracken, in due course closing in on a small stream, where it intercepts a broader, grassy path.

Turn right towards a shallow col ahead, beyond which the path continues rising at an easier angle across the southern slopes of **Winder**. Eventually, it climbs to a small cairn, beyond which it contours around the head of a valley on the right to reach another col linking Winder with Arant Haw. Now, although it can be bypassed, climb up onto **Arant Haw** (Higher Winder) for a fine view northwards along the western fringe of the Howgills.

On the summit of The Calf – the route follows the curving path around the pond

Head on in a north-easterly direction across the narrow **Rowantree Grains** and follow a fenceline up onto **Calders**, the summit of which is marked by a large cairn.

Now a wide and clear path runs on across the shoulder of **Bram Rigg Top** to the summit of **The Calf**, marked by a trig pillar, and not much else, except a nearby pond.

Move on from The Calf by taking a clear path that heads in a north-easterly direction to encounter another shallow pond. The route, above Swere Gill, is now following a clear bridleway that ultimately heads down into Bowderdale, while Swere Gill shortly becomes the white-water dash of Cautley Spout.

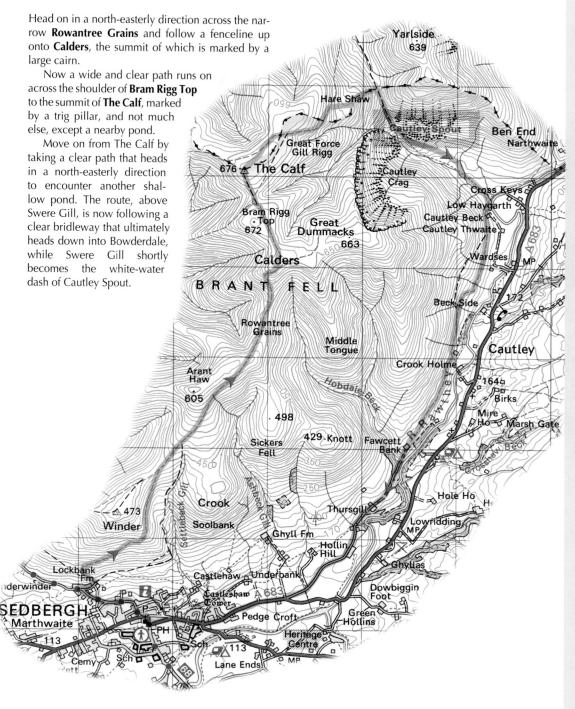

As the bridleway swings to a more northerly direction, look for an opportunity to leave it roughly eastwards and across peaty ground to **Hare Shaw**, from where there is a trackless descent of steep grass slopes to the obvious broad col of Bowderdale Head not far from a ruined sheepfold and on the boundary of the Yorkshire Dales National Park.

Once on the col, turn right (south) and follow a path across the scree slopes that spill from Yarlside's southern top. There is an alternative lower, but steeper descent from just below Bowderdale Head. Both paths provide fine views of Cautley Spout (see Walk 14 for details) and come together once beside Cautley Holme Beck (not named on the 1:50,000 map) in the valley bottom. The setting here is quite splendid, with Cautley Crag dominating the western skyline and Cautley Spout doing its best to put on a fine display.

Now walk out on a broad path roughly parallel with the beck until a footbridge appears on the right. Cross this and follow a wall to a gate, beyond which a long and straightforward return to Sedbergh begins along a bridleway that dips in and out of Access Land at gates, but remains clear throughout. It leads ultimately to **Fawcett Bank Farm**, crosses Hobdale Beck and continues to **Thursgill**, where road surfacing is encountered. This quiet access lane leads on, and about 1.6km (1 mile) further on finally joins the A683. Turn right and follow the A-road back to **Sedbergh**.

YORKSHIRE DALES

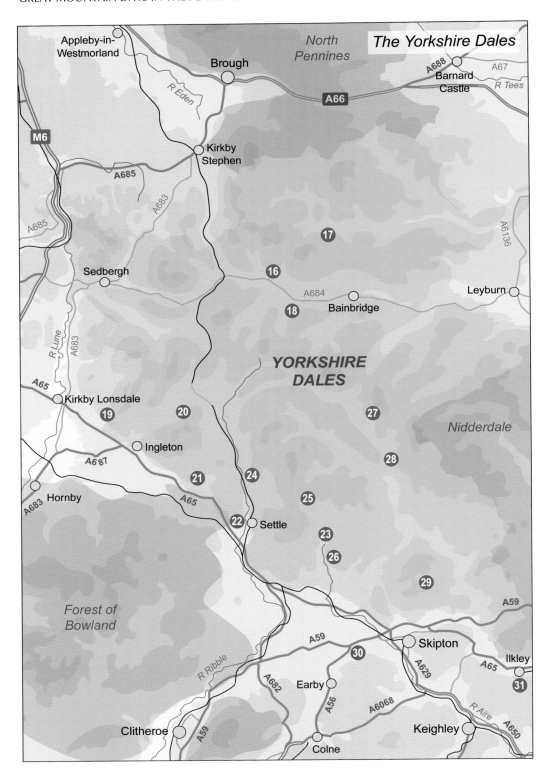

The Yorkshire Dales

Appleby-in-Westmorland

Brough

North Pennines

Barnard Castle

A688

A67

R Tees

A66

M6

A685

Kirkby Stephen

A685

A683

17

16

Sedbergh

A684

A6136

Leyburn

18

Bainbridge

YORKSHIRE DALES

R Lune

A683

Nidderdale

A65

Kirkby Lonsdale

19

20

27

Ingleton

A687

28

21

24

A683

Hornby

A65

25

22

Settle

23

26

Forest of Bowland

29

A59

A59

Skipton

Ilkley

R Ribble

30

A629

A65

31

A682

Earby

A56

A6068

R Aire

A650

Clitheroe

A59

Keighley

Colne

YORKSHIRE DALES

The Yorkshire Dales are arguably the best known part of the Pennines, and yet they are probably not everyone's stereotypical image of a Pennine landscape. Here it is limestone that predominates – fashioning the scenery, sketching the fine detail of the countryside, and shaping fine towering cliffs and extensive beds of limestone pavement. Even out of sight, underground, the influence is still there, in the form of tortuous labyrinths that extend over great distances and underpin the very foundations that support this unique and irreplaceable beauty.

The greater part of the Dales has been embraced within the jurisdiction of the Yorkshire Dales National Park, although the boundaries seem to have been arbitrarily drawn in places and exclude the whole of Nidderdale, the upper Eden valley between the heights of Mallerstang Edge and Wild Boar Fell, Middleton and half of the Howgills, all of which have unmistakeable 'Dales' characteristics, although the Eden valley and the Howgills have been united in this book to create a separate but very distinct section.

In spite of the preponderance of limestone, other rocks do occur and provide a frequently changing scene – limestone gives way in places to the gritstone, craggy escarpments relax into soft-shouldered fells, and high mountains surrender benignly to rolling moorland. All around lies evidence of the titanic struggle between land and the elements – ravines, steep-sided gills and waterfalls all testify to the power of glaciers and water; water with the capacity, it seems, to disappear and reappear almost at will as the age-old underground plumbing pursues an ambiguous course that few understand.

But perhaps the most prominent feature of the Dales are the ubiquitous stone walls, fashioned often by the hands of men dispossessed under the Enclosure Acts of the 18th and 19th centuries, and now mute testimony to a dying skill and bureaucratic skulduggery. Later, the Industrial Revolution brought mills and mines and quarries, some of which still scar the landscape, but provide a treasure trove of delight for the industrial archaeologist.

↑ Stainforth Force (Walk 22)

Great Shunner Fell and Lovely Seat

*A*part from walkers tackling the Pennine Way, Great Shunner Fell is likely to prove a place of *solitude; certainly it can be turned into such a place simply by making a slight digression from the line of the Way into one of the numerous nooks and crannies overlooking Cotterdale to the west and Swaledale to the east. The ascent is quite long, but nowhere difficult, and is a generally relaxing experience. The climb onto Lovely Seat is not as steep as it appears and is fairly short-lived. Hardly anyone ever comes here or takes the long moorland descent to Sedbusk to complete the walk.*

The Route

From Hardraw to the summit of Great Shunner Fell, the route follows the Pennine Way. In days past, erosion had created an unsightly swathe across the southern ridge of the fell, but paving work in the 1990s brought a welcome improvement, as a result of which there are very few stretches where dancing with bogs is necessary. In fact, the whole ascent is most pleasurable, but with hardly any respite – every step of the way is uphill.

Start along the walled lane leaving **Hardraw** to the west of the bridge. For about 3km (2 miles) the route is enclosed between walls. The track is here called Pen Lane and linked coal pits in Cotterdale with Hardraw. Coal was used as a fuel from the earliest times in the Dales, and although it was not of the best quality, often being shaley, it was used domestically to heat homes and for cooking, and was also used in lime kilns. The dominating rock

↑ Heading up the start of the Pennine Way at Hardraw onto Great Shunner Fell

ROUTE INFORMATION

Distance	19.5km (12 miles)
Height gain	615m (2020ft)
Time	6–7hrs
Grade	strenuous
Start point	Hardraw SD866917

Getting there
Roadside parking to the west of the bridge at
Hardraw

Maps
Ordnance Survey OL30 (Yorkshire Dales:
Northern and Central areas)

After-walk refreshment
Pub and tearoom in Hardraw; numerous pubs,
cafés and restaurants in Hawes

type, however, is limestone, although millstone grit
forms outcrops extensively on Great Shunner Fell.

Continue up the lane to a gate at its end, beyond
which lies Access Land and open moorland. A short
way on, when the track divides, branch left and
remain on the signed Pennine Way, which later
reaches the large expanse of moorland known as High
Abbotside at another gate. Now all that is needed is to
plod steadily up to the summit of **Great Shunner Fell**.
A final, brief pull leads onto a sloping plateau crossed
by a fence. The top is marked by a stone cross-shelter,
into which the trig pillar has been absorbed.

> **Great Shunner Fell**, at 716m (2349ft), is the
> third highest mountain in the Yorkshire Dales
> and the highest point in Wensleydale. Its north-
> ern slopes feed waters down into the River Swale,
> while those to the south are bound for the River
> Ure. The view northwards reaches over Swaledale
> and north to the high Pennines.

From the summit shelter, now abandon the
Pennine Way and take to a broad grassy path,
roughly eastwards, heading towards a fence. Follow
the fenceline down to a corner, and cross it at a
low step-stile. The way now lies over Little Shunner
Fell, a fairly undistinguished summit. In dry conditions a direct line is possible, but there is a path/
track alongside the fence that is mostly dry, and the

The summit shelter (with trig pillar built in) on Great Shunner Fell

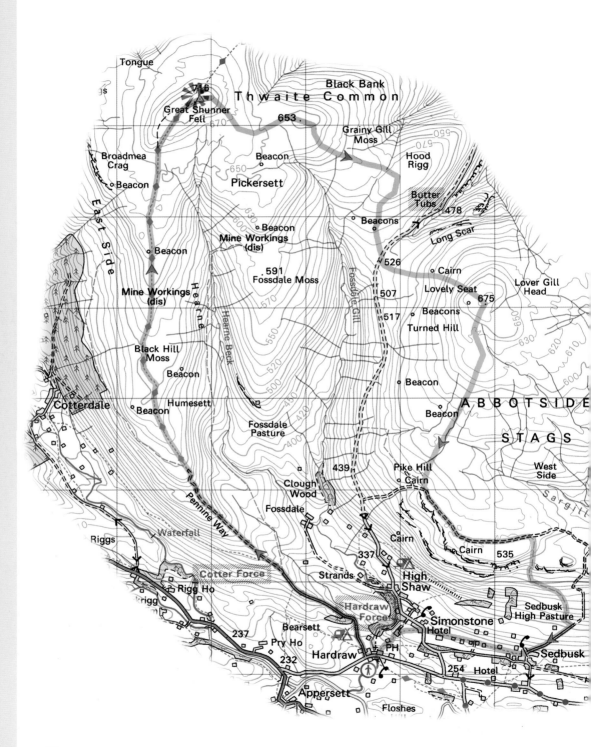

Lovely Seat from the Buttertubs road

fence is a sure guide in poor visibility. (In fact, the fence takes the onward route all the way to the Buttertubs pass – reassuring knowledge should mist roll in.) Most of the way is generally dry, although there is one potentially boggy passage through aptly named Grimy Gutter Hags. Once this is passed, then keep closely parallel with the fence as it leads down past a solitary tall cairn, and then to the road.

To make a **short-cut** that avoids the ascent of Lovely Seat, saving about 3km (2 miles), there is the option at this point to simply walk down the road. It is pleasant enough, with fine views over Hawes to Dodd Fell Hill and Widdale Fell, but quite steep (17 per cent) in places. It rejoins the walk just past Simonstone Hall.

Cross a cattle grid, and walk on a short distance further, until a fence on the left changes direction. Here simply leave the road and follow the fence up a few gentle rises all the way to the top of **Lovely Seat** – little more than 1km, with 149m (489ft) of ascent. The summit, much like Great Shunner Fell, has extensive views, particularly of the Yorkshire Three Peaks.

From the summit of Lovely Seat the concluding part of the walks heads almost due south across open and largely trackless moorland to the twin edges of High and Low Millstones (neither shown on the 1:50,000 map). Here, the geology changes from millstone grit to limestone again, and below Bleak Haw most of the streams disappear into swallow holes.

The target is a wide track that runs east–west above High Clint. On reaching this, turn left and head east to North Rakes Hill (SD884924). Now turn sharply to the right and descend steeply to leave Access Land at Shutt Gate and then continue by sloping pastures to join Shutt Lane, which is followed down to the village of **Sedbusk**.

In Sedbusk, a narrow path runs between the houses opposite a phone box and feeds into a long series of stiles and fields across to **Simonstone**. Here, on reaching the road, turn briefly left, and then leave the road for a signed footpath on the right that leads to the rear of Simonstone Hall. On reaching the hall, go left through a gated gap-stile and walk along a field edge to another. Cross the ensuing field towards a farm, where one final gap-stile gives into a steeply sloping pasture. Follow the path across it, which leads down to emerge in **Hardraw** next to the pub.

95

Upper Swaledale and Rogan's Seat

*T*he climb to the summit of Rogan's Seat is almost incidental to this walk; the interest, especially for industrial archaeologists, lies on the lower slopes of the hill. A start beside the lovely River Swale leads to scenes of man's industry before the walk climbs high onto the moors, where the views are extensive and inspiring. The contrast between the relics of an industrial age and lovely lush, green landscape makes this walk especially worthwhile.

The Route

Everywhere empty moorlands and derelict mine workings are a reminder of the demise of a great industry that found its centre here, and of the community it sustained. Throughout the valley, allotments, smallholdings and small farmsteads proliferate, kept long ago by men who worked the mines and managed the farms to supplement their income.

Upper Swaledale, in particular, is very much a place for the walker rather than the motorist; its many side-valleys, all of them beautiful, may only be reached on foot – their secrets accessible only to the pedestrian. Once a busy industrial valley, Swaledale is a favourite of many walkers. Its rich beauty, especially in the higher reaches of the dale, has acquired for it the epithet 'Herriot Country', a distinction it shares with Wensleydale through the books and television films of James Herriot.

The walk begins from **Muker**, a huddle of cottages around a church, everything just where it should be. From the car park turn left towards the village and

↑ *Approaching Swinner Gill at the head of Swaledale*

ROUTE INFORMATION

Distance	20km (12½ miles)
Height gain	485m (1590ft)
Time	5–6hrs
Grade	demanding
Start point	Muker SD910978

Getting there
Pay and display car park, adjacent to bridge in Muker

Maps
Ordnance Survey OL30 (Yorkshire Dales: Northern and Central areas)

After-walk refreshment
Pub and tearoom in Muker; pub in Gunnerside; tearoom in Thwaite

soon branch right to pass the Literary Institute and walk up into the village. Follow the village road to a signpost (for Gunnerside and Keld), pointing the way through a gate and onto a paved pathway through numerous enclosures of meadowland, rich in springtime with wild flowers. Eventually, the path passes through one final gap-stile to continue directly above the Swale. Turn right and cross nearby Rampsholme

Bridge, and then go left, following a broad trail (part of the northern Coast to Coast walk low-level route).

The track leads all the way up the valley towards the conspicuous gash of **Swinner Gill**, crossed by a sturdy footbridge. On the other side, a short pull leads through a gate and up to a path junction (NY904008). Turn sharply to the right here, and walk up to the ruined buildings at **Crackpot Hall**. Press on, initially on a gently rising terraced path, and then, once through a gate, on a narrower, rugged path high above Swinner Gill. This leads on to cross another stream, **Hind Hole Beck**.

If Hind Hole Beck isn't flowing excessively, it's worth a short detour into the **ravine**, a place of fascinating geology that terminates in front of a fine waterfall, a place of water-loving ferns and plants, where some of the water doubles back on itself and disappears into a low cave at the foot of the waterfall. Some maps show this to be Swinner Gill Kirk, said to refer to a place where, in less tolerant times, people gathered to worship. Another, more pragmatic view, suggests that 'kirk' is Yorkshire dialect for a limestone gorge. The cave is very low and doesn't look as though it could conceal many people.

Mine buildings at Crackpot Hall

From the miners' bridge at the foot of Hind Hole Beck, climb briefly to more derelict lead mine buildings, beyond which a narrow path climbs steadily above **East Grain** eventually to join a broad vehicle track. Turn left along this, the gradient easing, and shortly after a gate reach the junction with the track (NY926012) that leads up to Rogan's Seat. The track is maintained for the benefit of shooting parties that make use of these active grouse moors and heads north to **Rogan's Seat**, a desolate spot. The summit is broad, flat and featureless, and the highest point, if you can locate it, marked by a small cairn on a broad peaty uplift. A larger cairn nearby is marginally lower.

The trek to Rogan's Seat is simple enough, if lacking in interest, and needs now to be retraced to the junction of the tracks. From here, continue eastwards, the broad track leading unerringly to a fine traverse high above **Gunnerside Gill**.

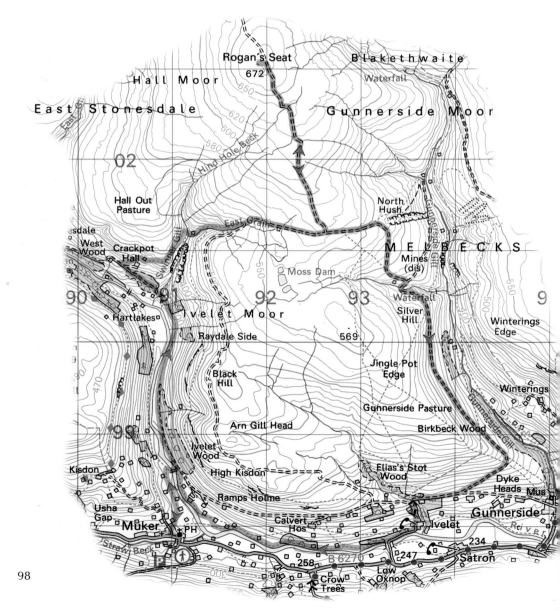

East Grain at the head of Swinner Gill

The view across **Gunnerside Gill** is impressive. This is an evocative place of ruinous smelt mills, adits, chimneys, water-wheel pits, spoil heaps and, grooving the hillsides, artificially created 'hushes', great channels formed by the scouring action of water as it coursed the steep slopes to expose the lead ores. Nature is now taking back much of the landscape, and the scarring is far less evident than of old.

Ivelet Bridge

Now simply follow the gently descending track to reach a road midway between Gunnerside and Ivelet. Turn right and walk the road as it descends to cross a stream (Shore Gill); climb on the other side to a road junction at a high point, and then go forward, descending steeply to the hamlet of **Ivelet**. Keep following the road down through Ivelet and then on to rejoin the Swale at Ivelet Bridge. The bridge at Ivelet is an attractive single-arch construction on the old corpse road used by communities higher up the dale to access Grinton, near Reeth, at one time the only place with hallowed grounds.

On reaching the bridge, turn right through a gated gap-stile, and now follow a clear path across meadowland, never far from the Swale. On reaching a stile and gate on the left, cross and walk alongside the river for a short distance, and then follow a clear path across enclosed meadows back to Rampsholme Bridge, and from there retrace the outward route to **Muker**.

Dodd Fell Hill
and Drumaldrace

*L*ike a pair of slumbering sentinels, Dodd Fell Hill and the more evident Drumaldrace rise above the market town of Hawes, inviting attention. Dodd Fell Hill is the less obvious of the two, leaning far back at the head of Sleddale and remote from view, while Drumaldrace, which also goes by the name Wether Fell, poses a sharp-edged escarpment that culminates in shapely Yorburgh. Combining the two in one long circuit is a delight and, in spite of some surfaced walking along the course of a Roman road, very satisfying.

The Route

The walk is essentially in three parts: the long ascent via the Pennine Way to Dodd Fell Hill, the gently undulating transition across the head of Wharfedale following the course of a Roman road, and the final stretch over Drumaldrace and down to Burtersett. The complete round-trip involves a modest amount of ascent, all accommodated gradually, and most of that on the ascent of Dodd Fell Hill. In poor visibility the vistas that so characterise the Yorkshire Pennines, and are the main reason for doing this walk, are obscured. But the walk has considerable merit in its own right, and there are no navigational difficulties of any note other than on the short stretch from the summit of Drumaldrace.

↑ *Patterned field enclosures above Hawes*

ROUTE INFORMATION

Distance   20.8km (13 miles)
Height gain   512m (1680ft)
Time   6+hrs
Grade   strenuous
Start point   Hawes SD876899

Getting there
Car park adjoining National Park Information
Centre in the old station yard, Hawes

Maps
Ordnance Survey OL2 (Yorkshire Dales:
Southern and Western areas) and OL30
(Yorkshire Dales: Northern and Central areas).
These two maps overlap to cover this walk; if
you want to take only one map use OL30.

After-walk refreshment
Numerous pubs and cafés in Hawes

The market town of **Hawes** is an appealing cluster of alleyways and cottages, concealed nooks
and crannies, giving the illusion of mellowed old
age, a stalwart settlement with credentials that
must at least date back to the Domesday Book. If
it were so, the town might be forgiven its eccen-
tricity, its seeming indifference to planning law
and order, as if buildings had tumbled haphazardly from a toy box.

But it's nothing of the sort – the town is a mere
stripling, unable to trace its pedigree beyond the
14th century. In fact, when the Domesday Book
was compiled, Hawes and the surrounding countryside was forest land, and, as Camden saw it, 'a
dreary waste and horrid silent wilderness among
the mountains'. The region above and around the
town is still wild. But perceptions change, and the
conditioned opinions of ancient chroniclers, drifting lazily from the pages of history, serve only as
peepholes into the past.

From the station car park walk back into town,
and just after passing the church look for a narrow
ginnel (signed for Gayle road and the Pennine Way)
that runs up beside the churchyard and, as a paved
route, across fields above Gayle Beck to the village of
Gayle. On reaching Gayle Road, turn left for a short
distance, crossing the road and walking as far as a bus
stop, and there squeezing onto a narrow path through
a housing estate. Cross fields by a paved pathway to
West End, there passing cottages and farm buildings
and following the lane to a T-junction. Turn briefly
right, and then cross a stile to enter a field. Continue
ahead, crossing an intermediate stile, and walk on a
short distance to another stile, at which a change of
direction is called for to head for Gaudy Lane. Turn
briefly right along Gaudy Lane, and then left on the
access to **Gaudy House Farm**. Just before reaching the

The view from the Pennine Way across Sleddale to Ingleborough and Whernside   101

The summit of Dodd Fell Hill

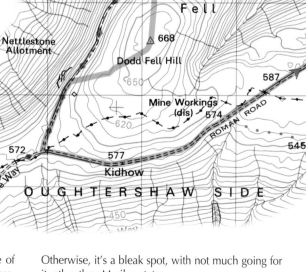

farm, cross a stile on the left and climb steadily, parallel with a wall, to begin the long but gradual ascent to Kidhow Gate.

This stretch is little more than pleasant strolling along an old packhorse route, known as West Cam Road. For a while, the modest gradient eases as the path swings right round the base of **Ten End**, where in days gone by peat was gathered as commoners exercised their ancient right of turbary. Away to the right the profiles of Swarth Fell and Wild Boar Fell rise above the hollow of Mallerstang, while to the left the bulk of Drumaldrace blocks all views in that direction, for the moment. Just beyond Ten End, the Pennine Way merges with a track ascending from the right, after which the onward route is more pronounced.

Walkers making for the summit of **Dodd Fell Hill** should leave West Cam Road after the last intake wall ascending on the left (at about SD841858) and head across rough, peaty ground to the summit, marked by a trig. (An alternative line is to stay on the Pennine Way until due west of the trig, and then ascend grassy slopes to the summit.) As might be expected, the view is extensive, reaching to Cross Fell, Blencathra in the northern Lake District, the Scafells, and round to Morecambe Bay; all three of Yorkshire 'Three Peaks' are on display from up here.

Otherwise, it's a bleak spot, with not much going for it, other than Marilyn status.

The long stroll from Kidhow Gate to Drumaldrace (also known as Wether Fell), along the Roman road, is an easy and tranquil traverse high above Langstrothdale at the head of Wharfedale. Follow this gated road for more than 4km (2¾ miles), and then, at the start of the descent into Sleddale, the Roman road branches right as an enclosed track that climbs for a while. Stay with this track until the wall on the left ends, and from here an easy jaunt leads up to the large cairn which marks the summit of **Drumaldrace**.

Now aim for a gate in a wall at SD880874, beyond which a green path winds downwards, around the knobble of **Yorburgh**, towards the hamlet of Burtersett. Ignore a signpost pointing the way to Gayle, and continue following lanes that lead through the village towards the A684.

The quiet hamlet of **Burtersett** is a charming place, one of many in the Dales with names ending in 'sett', a clear indication that this was formerly a Norse settlement, for the ending comes from *saetr*, meaning 'shieling' or 'hill village'. There was a settlement here during the reign of Edward I (1272–1307), too, when the hamlet had a forest lodge.

Before reaching the main road, take a footpath striking westwards across fields that makes a safer return to **Hawes**, emerging on the A-road a short distance east of the starting point.

On leaving the summit, take a narrow trod in a south-westerly direction that targets a gate at SD832841, near a ruined cottage (Rock Edge Cottage, shown but not named on the 1:50,000 map), where the Pennine Way is rejoined for the final section to **Kidhow Gate** (SD829834).

At Kidhow Gate the route meets the Roman road from Ribblehead to Bainbridge (Virosidum), and this is the onward direction. But Kidhow Gate is a convenient place to halt for a while, and to reflect how the ill-defined slope to the south-east separates the waters ultimately destined for the Wharfe and the Ribble, a distinction more apparent on the map than on the ground. To the north-west the streams feed Snaizeholme Beck and in due course the Ure.

Looking down from Cam High Road into the head of Wharfedale 103

Gragareth and Great Coum

*T*ucked away out of sight (and for many walkers out of mind, too) in the top right-hand corner of *Lancashire lies a wild stretch of moorland that is a delight to wander – a stubby finger of ground prodding into Cumbria and North Yorkshire, but once flanked by Westmorland and the West Riding of Yorkshire. It rises easily to a moorland fell with a strange name, Gragareth, and continues over Green Hill, wholly insignificant in the scheme of things, except that by just 1m it is the highest point in Lancashire.*

The Route

Gragareth is part of a ridge that forms the boundary of the Yorkshire Dales National Park and culminates at its northernmost end with an even higher summit, Great Coum, in Cumbria (just) and overlooking Dentdale. The whole ridge is an excellent vantage point, with splendid views over the Yorkshire Dales, the coastal plain of Lancashire, Morecambe Bay, and most of the Lakeland fell summits. Yet this is an area seldom visited – a truly wild, massive, sprawling amphitheatre of burbling becks, drystone walls and some of the finest pot-holes in the Pennines. Few trees grow here, with the tussock grass bending low as it cowers from prevailing winds, and the numerous bogs and peat channels are a challenge for even the toughest walkers, although most of this is confined to the drainage grounds of Ease Gill, which can be avoided.

↑ *The Three Men of Gragareth*

ROUTE INFORMATION

Distance	13km (8 miles)
Height gain	435m (1425ft)
Time	4–5hrs
Grade	moderately demanding
Start point	Near Leck Fell House SD674791

Getting there

Cowan Bridge and Ireby both afford access to Leck. From there drive up a gated lane that leads to Leck Fell House and park just below the house (a working farm).

Maps

Ordnance Survey OL2 (Yorkshire Dales: Southern and Western areas)

After-walk refreshment

Pubs in Kirkby Lonsdale and Nether Burrow

The most direct approach is from Leck, a small and quiet village lying just off the A65, a short distance south-east of Kirkby Lonsdale, and accessed from Cowan Bridge. The village owns a certain notoriety, for here is the school for clergymen's daughters attended by the Brontë sisters. The original school, immortalised in Mrs Gaskell's biography of Charlotte and as Lowood in *Jane Eyre*, although altered and now a row of terraced cottages, is still there, with a plaque commemorating its place in history. The school was moved to Casterton, 5km (3 miles) away, in 1833. Looking at the old school's present-day setting, with the main road and the constant flow of traffic hurrying by, it is difficult to imagine how harsh and isolated a place it could have seemed in the 1820s.

From the parking areas just to the south of **Leck Fell House** set off along the road to a gate on the right, just as the road dips towards Leck Fell House. Through the gate, a broad track heads out across the lower slopes of Gragareth. Follow this track for a short distance or take immediately to the hillside. Either way the immediate objective is the stand of three stone pillars, the Three Men of Gragareth, prominent from the starting point, but not from directly below them. It is presumed the pillars were constructed by the men who built the stone wall along the summit ridge. There is no upward

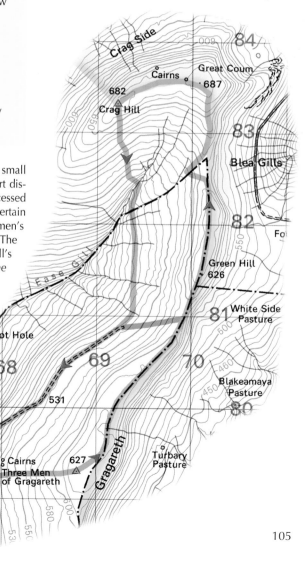

Looking across from the summit of Gragareth to Great Coum and Crag Hill

path, just a grassy slope spread with rocks through which a route needs to be fashioned. At the first 'lip' a number of cairns are reached, among them the **Three Men of Gragareth**.

From the Three Men, follow a gently rising path eastwards over easily sloping ground. The distance is just 850m, but it seems further. The path leads directly to the trig point marking the highest point of **Gragareth**. If this is missed in poor visibility, then a wall 200m further on, which marks the county boundary, acts as a backstop.

The modest summit of Green Hill, the highest point in Lancashire

The view is superb! Barbondale and the Howgills are close to hand, while also visible are Kirkby Lonsdale and the winding River Lune, Lancaster, the great mud flats of Morecambe Bay glinting in the sun, the high fells of Lakeland, the Forest of Bowland, and the broad sweep of the Yorkshire fells and dales. Quite one of the best.

To continue to Great Coum take a clear grassy path from the trig pillar, roughly east-of-north, which gradually closes in on the wall, a remarkably well-constructed and unusually high affair that might have been intended to keep Lancastrians and Yorkshiremen apart in days gone by. The path reaches the wall at a gated through-stile. Ignore this, and instead cross a nearby fence to remain on the western side of the wall. On the eastern side many more walls ascend from Kingsdale, but the western side is free of these impediments to progress, although sections of the path closest to the wall are

106

boggy and call for diversionary tactics. That aside, it is an easy stroll over **Green Hill**, which actually is green compared to adjacent fells.

> The top of **Green Hill** is marked by a low cairn, significant in being the highest point in Lancashire, by just 1m. But neither Green Hill nor Gragareth are wholly in Lancashire; the distinction of the highest summit entirely in the county goes to Ward's Stone in the Forest of Bowland.

The ongoing wall leads all the way to Great Coum, interrupted by only one other wall, which has a convenient gate a short way down the hill slope to the south-west. Just beyond the gate climb right, up to where the wall and ridge wall meet, to find the County Stone, a large primeval boulder where the old counties of Lancashire, Westmorland and West Riding met.

Further on, up a slight rise, the top of **Great Coum** is adorned by an impressive and large cairn. It stands

on the north side of the ridge wall, and there is no easy way to it. The cairn does not mark the highest point of the hill, although it is commonly regarded as such. The true summit is a spot height, 687m, at SD700835, impossible to reach without climbing walls and not worth the dilemma.

Continue along the wall to **Crag Hill**. Like Great Coum, its highest point, a trig pillar, lies across the wall, but nearby the wall ends, and stones piled against a fence give easy access without damaging the fence.

The return to Leck Fell House tackles 2.5km (1½ miles) of strenuous terrain, mostly tussock grass, spring-sodden oases, and numerous stream and peat channels, all of which have to be crossed. Descending from Crag Hill, **Ease Gill** is crossed at or just above Long Gill Foot (SD692821). Beyond that the going becomes considerably more trying and tiring. The target objective is a shooting hut on the skyline (it looks like a large boulder from this distance). The hut sits beside a track, the end of which is at SD692808; aim for this point. Contouring will help, but it is a good idea not to drop too low down the course of Ease Gill.

> **Alternative route** The difficulties of the Great Coum hollow can be avoided by the simple expedient of returning from Crag Hill all the way to Green Hill and then, from the shallow col south of Green Hill, descending rough ground to the track end.

Once the end of the track is reached, all difficulties are over, and a simple stroll along the track leads back to the start.

The County Stone

Whernside

This is a splendid and lofty walk on an elongated ridge, with views reaching deep into Yorkshire. The route concludes by descending to the Ribblehead Viaduct before returning easily through pastureland to the start.

The Route

Whernside has none of the dramatic Yoredale Facies cragginess of neighbouring Ingleborough and Pen-y-ghent, but retains the distinction of being the highest mountain in the Yorkshire Dales. Looking rather lumpish from every angle, Whernside is an elongated ridge (few people realise just how long), narrow and undulating, rising from the distant village gardens of Ingleton and descending gently northwards into Dentdale some 14km (9 miles) away.

Head down the B6255, passing the Old Inn, but almost immediately turn right onto a farm access lane (Philpin Lane) which leads pleasantly and easily across farm pastures to **Bruntscar Farm** (SD739791). At Bruntscar the access lane reaches a T-junction. Here, turn right and walk a short distance to a gate giving access to wide grassy pastureland. (Note at this point a narrow gate on the right, the path signed for Winterscales. The return leg will come back to this point.)

Crossing the lower part of the pasture is easy, and leads to a couple of gates and a stile, beyond which the going becomes a little steeper, climbing to the intake wall. A pause for breath will allow you to take in the Ribblehead Viaduct and the long

↑ Whernside from the Winterscales pastures

Distance	15.2km (9½ miles)
Height gain	550m (1805ft)
Time	5hrs
Grade	demanding
Start point	north-east of the Old Inn SD745777

Getting there
Roadside parking area just north-east of the Old Inn on B6255; otherwise start at Ribblehead

Maps
Ordnance Survey OL2 (Yorkshire Dales: Southern and Western areas)

After-walk refreshment
Pubs at Chapel-le-Dale and Ribblehead

The summit trig on Whernside, one of only a small number of Second Geodetic Levelling trigs dating from pre-1921

drystone wall on the south side of the dale that extends from the distinctive top of Ingleborough across Simon Fell to Park Fell, overlooking the Ribble valley.

The long ridge leading up to the summit of Whernside

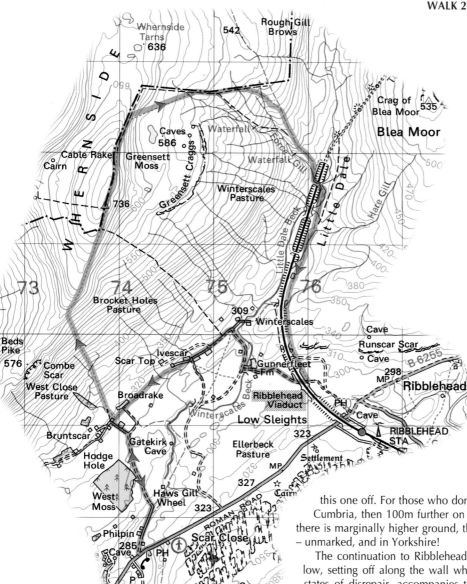

Beyond the intake gate a flight of steps awaits, largely fashioned from old cobble sets, no doubt transported from some distant city. It is a short, brutal pull now to gain the ridge above. Thankfully, the end of this leg-wearying wonder brings the end of all significant ascent: only minor ups remain, and these follow the ridge wall all the way to the summit of **Whernside**. The summit is marked by a trig on the other side of the wall, in Cumbria, so you will have to step into Cumbria if you want to tick

this one off. For those who don't want to visit Cumbria, then 100m further on along the wall there is marginally higher ground, the true summit – unmarked, and in Yorkshire!

The continuation to Ribblehead is easy to follow, setting off along the wall which, in varying states of disrepair, accompanies the path across Whernside's highest ground, a splendid, narrow romp, for just under 1.5km (about 1 mile). The path then leaves the wall, and the fence that follows it, to drop sharply at first towards **Little Dale** and later ease downwards as a paved path to join an ancient track, the Craven Way, at a stile and signpost. Cross the stile and continue descending until the valley bottom is reached near the entrance to Blea Moor **railway tunnel**, a remarkable feat of engineering on the Settle–Carlisle line, which was for many years threatened with closure. The tunnel burrows for 2km (almost 1.5 miles) under the moors and was constructed in the 1870s.

At the same point stands another remarkable feat of ingenuity, for the bridge spanning the railway line is also an aqueduct carrying the waters of Force Gill. The crossing of Little Dale Beck, just after the railway bridge, is accomplished by a narrow footbridge, but it necessary to resort to the bridge only when the beck is in spate.

The hard work is now over, and all that remains is a steady amble back to the starting point. A broad path continues from the bridge to Blea Moor Sidings. Just beyond this it is possible to pass, right, beneath the railway line (signpost) to make for Winterscales Farm. However, this walk continues to the **Ribblehead Viaduct** (it would be a pity to have come this far and not visit it), a place where everyone will stand in wonder at the skills of those hardy engineers who in the early 1870s constructed this giant monument.

The **Settle–Carlisle railway**, a stark reminder of the Midland Railway's determination to construct its own route to Scotland, was built at enormous cost both in terms of finance and of human life. In recent times, affected by the ravages of time and the sheer inhospitability of the climate, the future of the railway was called into question as the spectre of financial viability reared its ugly head. During this time a vigorous campaign was waged against closure, which was at last vindicated in April 1989, when the government announced that the line was to remain open. It will long stand as a proud testament to Victorian endeavour and achievement. From 1989 into the early 1990s, the viaduct saw massive repair work, funded by a consortium comprising British Rail, English Heritage, local authorities and other interested bodies, and designed to resolve a problem of water seepage and falling masonry.

A clear track branches right to pass under the viaduct, beyond which an access road leads to **Gunnerfleet Farm**. Here, just after crossing Winterscales Beck, turn right on a surfaced lane and walk up to intercept the track from **Winterscales Farm** (SD752800).

At the track junction turn left (south-west), following the ongoing track to **Ivescar** and Scar End. Then head across farm pastures to return to **Bruntscar Farm**, and from there retrace the outward route back to the **Old Inn**.

For a **variant finish** turn left at Gunnerfleet Farm and follow a surfaced lane, recrossing Winterscales Beck and finally emerging onto the B-road a short distance north-east of the start.

The long descent from the summit of Whernside

Ingleborough

A superb walk of no inherent difficulty (although falling into Gaping Gill is not a good move) beginning in the charming village of Clapham and taking in meltwater ravines, potholes, wild moorland wandering, a high mountain summit and dramatic limestone scenery. There are other ascents of Ingleborough, but this is undoubtedly the most satisfying, rising gradually in geological steps to the plateau-like summit.

The Route

Viewed from a distance, Ingleborough rises from a plateau of limestone, culminating in a fine series of scars overlooking Chapel-le-Dale. Its comparative isolation meant that it was once thought to be the highest mountain in England. In spite of its everlasting association with Whernside and Pen-y-ghent, as Yorkshire's 'Three Peaks', Ingleborough retains unique appeal, its diverse nooks and crannies an immense store of botanical and archaeological surprises, and its geological infrastructure a honeycomb of delight that few get to see.

Bridge in the village of Clapham

↑ *Ingleborough from the vicinity of Bar Pot*

Distance	17.5km (11 miles)
Height gain	593m (1945ft)
Time	6hrs
Grade	strenuous
Start point	Clapham SD746692

Getting there
Clapham village car park (pay and display; toilets)

Maps
Ordnance Survey OL2 (Yorkshire Dales: Southern and Western areas)

After-walk refreshment
Pubs and cafés in Clapham

Clapham is a delightful place of old bridges, waterfalls, white cottages, old stone houses and stands of ancient trees, a place not so much of clichéd charm as rural contentment, a place at ease with itself and its popularity.

Leave the car park and cross Clapham Beck by an old stone bridge, turning right past ancient cottages fronting the beck, which is a favourite haunt of dippers and grey wagtails.

There is an option, soon encountered, of visiting the landscaped grounds of **Ingleborough Hall Estate** (an attractive proposition, for which there is a fee – 65p per person in 2012). Just follow the obvious path and eventually emerge at a gate not far from the entrance to Ingleborough Cave. Ingleborough Hall was formerly the home of Reginald Farrer (1880–1920), a renowned botanist who, during the second half of his brief life, made repeated journeys across the world in pursuit of his passion and brought many foreign plant specimens to Clapham to decorate the grounds of his home.

The main route continues past the entrance to the estate and turn right into Clapdale Lane (signposted: 'Ingleborough; Gaping Gill: Ingleborough Cave') and stroll easily as far as **Clapdale Farm**, where a sharp descent, right, leads down to join the path from the estate grounds.

↑ *Heading into Trow Gill*

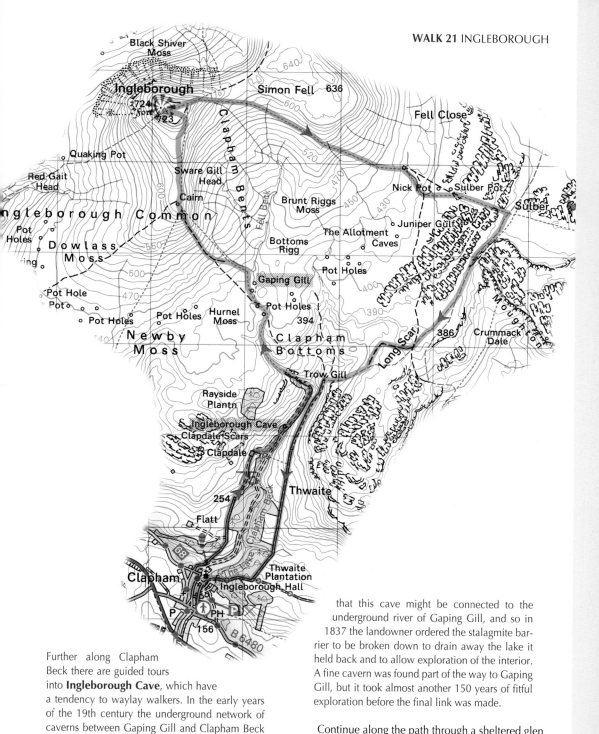

Further along Clapham Beck there are guided tours into **Ingleborough Cave**, which have a tendency to waylay walkers. In the early years of the 19th century the underground network of caverns between Gaping Gill and Clapham Beck Head was largely unknown. Ingleborough Cave, the obvious entrance, was blocked after only a few metres by a wall of stalagmite, beyond which a tiny space of air stretched above a pool of water into the darkness. Occasional floods suggested that this cave might be connected to the underground river of Gaping Gill, and so in 1837 the landowner ordered the stalagmite barrier to be broken down to drain away the lake it held back and to allow exploration of the interior. A fine cavern was found part of the way to Gaping Gill, but it took almost another 150 years of fitful exploration before the final link was made.

Continue along the path through a sheltered glen between low scars of limestone. Ahead the main valley curves left to a stile/gate that gives into the rocky jaws of **Trow Gill** that has suddenly appeared.

Rising steadily the gorge is overlooked by slopes, popular with rock climbers, which become higher

115

and steeper until the gorge narrows dramatically between vertical rock walls more than 25m high on each side containing a spill of boulders, over which the onward route clambers to the dry, grassy valley beyond. Trow Gill is a classic example of a limestone gorge, created by a surface stream of meltwater flowing off the limestone plateau above as the glaciers retreated at the end of the last Ice Age.

The path follows the line of a wall to a couple of adjacent stiles, beyond which lies the broad limestone plinth of Ingleborough. Only a few metres ahead, on the left, a sizeable pothole, Bar Pot, provides the easiest access for cavers into the Gaping Gill system, whose network of caverns underlies all this stretch of moorland. Bar Pot is not a place for walkers; the entrance is obvious enough, but the deep shaft immediately inside is not.

Ahead rises the broad slope of Little Ingleborough (not named on the 1:50,000 map), with the main summit overtopping that. The onward route is obvious, shortly dividing to enable visits to the most famous of all potholes, **Gaping Gill**, away to the right and surrounded by a fence.

Gaping Gill takes its name from its great entrance, which swallows the waters of Fell Beck as they gather from the high grounds of Ingleborough. This wide, open hole, of evident great depth, was an irresistible challenge to the explorers of the 19th century, but it was not until the last decade of the century that a Frenchman, Edouard Martel, in August 1895, finally reached the floor of the shaft, more than 100m down.

The main chamber of Gaping Gill is the largest cavern in Britain, 140m long and almost 30m high and wide. The shaft was the deepest known in Britain until 'Titan' in Derbyshire was discovered in 1999. Gaping Gill still retains the record for the tallest unbroken waterfall in England and the largest underground chamber naturally open to the surface.

Because of the alternative entrances into the Gaping Gill system, a descent of the main shaft is now rarely undertaken. But on May and August bank holidays Bradford and Craven caving clubs divert the flow of Fell Beck and rig up a winch chair so that visitors may descend in comfort.

Alongside Clapham Beck →

From Gaping Gill a path heads north-west for the base of Little Ingleborough, gained by a steep pull to a multitude of shelter-cairns on its upper edge, from where there is a fine prospect across Ribblesdale to Pen-y-ghent and Fountains Fell. The path leads onwards to begin a slanting ascent to the rim of Ingleborough's main summit.

On reaching the rim, the route passes through the remains of a hill-fort wall, a massive encircling wall, now collapsed, around the edge of a summit plateau. The plateau also contains the foundations, still traceable in the peaty summit, of 19 circular huts believed to be a settlement of early Iron Age settlers in this district.

The continuation to the summit of **Ingleborough** follows a line of small cairns to a massive cairn beside a trig point and a crossed-wall shelter surmounted by a view indicator erected by the Ingleton Fell and Rescue Team to commemorate the coronation of Queen Elizabeth in 1953. The highest point, the true summit, is marked by another cairn on a rocky plinth a few metres north-west of the trig, overlooking the Doe valley.

The onward descent leaves the north-east corner of the summit plateau to gain a path along the southern flank of **Simon Fell** to a derelict shooting hut. Beyond lies a weird landscape known as Sulber Scars, a massive desert of fissured white limestone through which a path picks its way to a lonely signpost (SD778735). Horton-in-Ribblesdale lies not far ahead, but at the signpost turn right on a grassy path to a stile at Sulber Gate.

Continue ahead, keeping to the right of a wall, and when the path forks at a cairn a short distance further on, keep right, making for the conspicuous cairn atop **Long Scar**. Later, before reaching Long Scar, another cairn marks a change of direction, again right, to enter a wide grassy amphitheatre known as **Clapham Bottoms**. The path is clear enough and leads via one gate to another at the head of Long Lane, an old bridleway connecting Clapham and Selside in Ribblesdale.

A short way down Long Lane there is a fine view of Trow Gill, its naked limestone walls contrasting with the moulded grassy slopes of glacial moraine to its right. There are splendid views, too, across woodlands below, in which shelters the village of Clapham, while a conspicuous dip in the lane marks the line of the North Craven Fault. Long Lane in due course meets Thwaite Lane at a T-junction; this ancient route is a continuation of Mastiles Lane above Kilnsey, a monastic highway that crossed the southern Dales to link the lands of Fountains Abbey.

Turn right into Thwaite Lane and descend towards **Clapham**, passing through two tunnels built by the Farrers to protect the privacy of their estate. This tunnelled lane ends near Clapham church at the top end of the village, from where, left, the car park is only a short distance away.

Welsh poppies, Clapham

Giggleswick Scar

*G**iggleswick Scar, running along the boundary of the Yorkshire Dales National Park, is famous for its many archaeological caves (it contains the highest proportion of such caves in the Yorkshire Dales). This circular walk begins in Settle, and from there heads to the village of Giggleswick before climbing steadily onto the limestone plateau above the scar and continuing in splendid fashion for the hamlet of Feizor. A long, steady descent leads to Stainforth, where the Force usually puts on a white-water display. After that the walk follows the River Ribble all the way back to Settle.*

The Route

From the centre of **Settle**, turn down a narrow lane (Kirkgate) opposite the town hall (signed for the Friends' Meeting House). Go beneath a railway bridge and past a supermarket, shortly turning left just before the fire station to head towards the Ribble. Follow the road, right, around Kingsmill to reach the pedestrian bridge spanning the river.

Today's attractive market town of **Settle** is thought to date from the seventh century, its name being the Saxon word for 'settlement'. After the so-called 'Harrying of the North' – a series of campaigns waged by William the Conqueror between 1069 and 1071 – the area was left in poor condition. A market charter was granted to Henry de Percy (1228–1272) by Henry III in 1248. The first bridge over the River Ribble, linking Settle with the church at Giggleswick, was mentioned in 1498.

↑ *Heading across the limestone moorland above Feizor*

Below Giggleswick Scar

ROUTE INFORMATION

Distance	14.5km (9 miles)
Height gain	310m (1015ft)
Time	5hrs
Grade	moderately demanding
Start point	Settle SD819638

Getting there
Car park near petrol station at northern end of Settle

Maps
Ordnance Survey OL41 (Forest of Bowland and Ribblesdale)

After-walk refreshment
Pubs and cafés in Settle (plus tearoom at Feizor)

Over today's bridge, bear half-left onto an ascending path (signed for Giggleswick) to enter a walled walkway that emerges on the edge of the village. Turn right and continue to the end of Bankwell Road, and there turn right and climb to meet the B6480 at the top of Belle Hill. Cross into The Mains opposite.

Follow The Mains up to its end at Woodlands, and here move onto a broad track through light woodland cover to a gate giving onto rough pasture. Follow the broad track ahead, which shortly swings round as it climbs to run alongside a limestone wall along the boundary of an active quarry, with views of Pen-y-ghent and Fountains Fell off to the right. Stay with the path and climb to the edge of a limestone plateau above, there bearing left to a prominent cairn. From this cross to another nearby.

Now the route continues by an obvious grassy path through bracken and along the rim of **Giggleswick Scar**, both above and below crags. After cresting a high point, the path gradually descends, eventually intercepts a bridleway (SD797661), and then swings northwards up to gate in a drystone wall. The path continues rising gently, following a clear route across a wide, grassy limestone plateau, targeting the distant summit of Smearsett Scar.

Keep on across the plateau, with Ingleborough now in view, to a field gate, and beyond this keep left beside a wall to a signpost. Now keep ahead along a bridleway for **Feizor**, steadily descending to reach the village lane. Turn right for a short distance to a ladder-stile on the right signed for Stainforth (there is a tearoom nearby), and go ahead through two narrow gates, passing around a farm to a field gate.

Now parallel a wall and shallow gully on the right, climbing steadily to another ladder-stile. The path rises gradually to a high point from which, below the crags of **Smearsett Scar**, it strikes across limestone moorland on a clear route linked by

Smearsett Scar from just above Feizor

ladder-stiles. For a moment, there is fine glimpse of Pen-y-ghent through a gap to the east of Smearsett Scar, a view that becomes better as the descent is made towards Stainforth and the view of Ribblesdale opens out.

The track eventually drops to a gated stile near a field gate just above **Little Stainforth**. Head down through the village and along the lane leading to the 17th-century Stainforth Bridge. Leave the road here by squeezing through a gap-stile on the right to gain the true right bank of the Ribble, with the spectacular **Stainforth Force** just a short way ahead.

A clear path now courts the river at varying distances from it, and continues easily as far as a weir east of Stackhouse. Here, turn right to walk up a walled track to the lane at **Stackhouse**, and there turn left. Follow the lane as far as a signpost on the left for the Ribble Way and Settle Bridge. Cross a field diagonally to resume a course near the river once more, gradually losing height to reach the edge of a sports field. A path now runs around the field and emerges onto the B6480 at the northern edge of **Settle**. Turn left to complete the walk, recrossing the Ribble in the process.

Stainforth Bridge

Nappa Cross,
Rye Loaf Hill and Victoria Cave

In the overall scheme of things, Rye Loaf Hill is comparatively insignificant, a minor summit on the edge of the Yorkshire Dales National Park. Yet it commands a view of immense proportions, not least across the nearby limestone plateaux and escarpments of Langcliffe. It also lies directly on the Pennine watershed, and its inclusion in this walk, a modest deviation that should deter no one, will reward in more ways than one.

The Route

From the car park head west along the road, immediately crossing the outflow from Malham Tarn and, a few strides further on, turning left through a gate onto the Pennine Way. Follow the Pennine Way, soon passing a spot known as **Water Sinks**, where the stream from Malham Tarn disappears sullenly into stream-bed debris. Keep forward, following a path into a deepening dry valley until it

makes a pronounced curve to the right to avoid a dry waterfall (Comb Scar). Here, the path twists about to reach the head of a tributary valley known as Watlowes that leads south to Malham Cove. But, instead of turning down into this, keep right beside a wall until you can cross it and follow another wall-side path up to the road at Langscar Gate (SD888649).

↑ *Rye Loaf Hill*

Cross the road and pass through a field gate onto a Byway Open to All Traffic (BOAT), signed for Cow Close and Langcliffe. Continue up the track as far as a signpost (SD881649) and here turn left onto the Pennine Bridleway, a gently rising path, for Stockdale Lane. Clear tracks now lead across hill pastures, finally reaching the wall-mounted Nappa Cross (not shown on the 1:50,000 map), the remains of a wayside cross, probably monastic.

Press on from Nappa Cross to reach a signpost at a pronounced east–west track, and turn right on this for Stockdale Lane. Easy walking ensues, taking a lovely route through undulating limestone hills with Rye Loaf Hill coming into view.

Keep following the track through gated enclosures until a left turn immediately after a gate, leaving the track, leads to another gate in a wall corner (SD868638). The ascent of Rye Loaf Hill features as part of this walk, but can be omitted. The gate gives into the large upland expanse rising to the hill summit. Through the gate stay wall-side to the obvious high point ahead, and there turn through 90° to cross a shallow valley and gain the course of a collapsed wall. Follow this upwards, turning southwards, and continue until it ends. Then simply ascend grassy slopes to the trig and shelter-cairn on the summit of **Rye Loaf Hill**, a gritstone intruder amid so much limestone. Return to the gate by the outward route.

Now resume the main track, which is clear throughout, and leads above **Stockdale Farm**, just after which the track reaches a surfaced lane. Follow the lane until it makes a pronounced bend to the left (an escape route to Settle, should it be needed), and here turn through the right-hand one of two gates. Then follow a wall-side path that leads on through more gates below the cliffs of Attermire Scar, with Langcliffe Scar beyond, and enters the Langcliffe and Attermire Local Nature

Nappa Cross

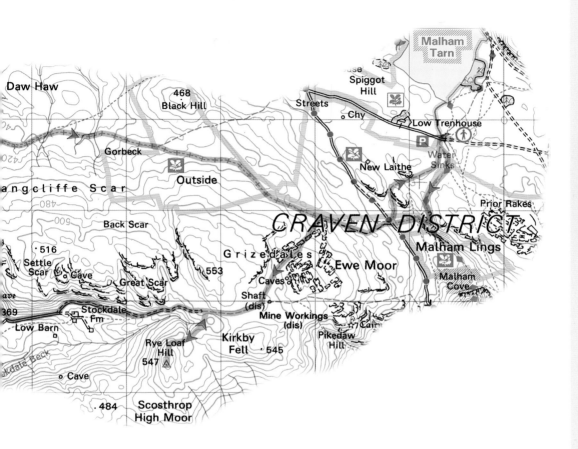

Reserve. The scars are in an area designated as a Site of Special Scientific Interest (SSSI) because of the classic Carboniferous limestone geology, which demonstrates the most complete sequence of Dinatian strata in the Craven area.

Between Attermire Scar and Langcliffe Scar a clear valley rises northwards. This is the way to go, ascending beside a wall through a narrow gorge that gradually opens up and brings **Victoria Cave** into view ahead. Keep following the obvious path to reach the base of the cave.

Victoria Cave, a Scheduled Monument and SSSI, was created by acidified water as it dissolved the limestone deposits. Within the cave's clay deposits, scientists found an extensive record of climate change over thousands of years.

The cave has also yielded evidence of the presence of hippopotamus, rhinoceros, elephant and hyena, which roamed this area during the Upper Pleistocene interglacial (130,000–120,000 years ago), when the climate was much warmer than today. It seems likely that hyena used the cave as a den into which scavenged bones were dragged. There is no evidence of human activity during this period.

After the last Ice Age the cave was used by brown bear. In among the animal bones of reindeer was found an 11,000-year-old antler harpoon point, the first evidence of people in the Yorkshire Dales.

Today's entrance to the cave is artificial, having been cut out of the cliff for ease of access when the importance of the discoveries was recognised. The natural opening, first entered in modern times in 1837, the year of Queen Victoria's accession (hence the name), was a small fissure high on the left.

Press on beyond the cave, and eventually reach the western end of the BOAT used in the early stages of the walk. Turn right onto this, passing more, smaller caves (**Jubilee Cave**) on the way. Now the track swings eastwards and starts a long, gently undulating 4.5km (almost 3 mile) traverse of limestone moorlands to return to the signpost turning point for Nappa Cross. There is little appeal in the bleak moorland landscapes to the south, but northwards is quite another matter, with far-reaching views of rolling hills in the northern reaches of the Yorkshire Dales National Park. From the signpost, retrace the outward route down to Langscar Gate.

Here, cross a cattle grid and immediately leave the road, following an initially grassy track heading for Lang Scar and Dean Scar (not named on the 1:50,000 map). A stony path leads up between the two to a wall-gap, from which a broad grassy path strikes across limestone towards low-lying Locks Scar, passing a signpost and continuing round the shoulder of a low hill before descending to rejoin the Pennine Way near **Water Sinks**. Only a few minutes now remain to complete the walk.

The view from, and entrance to, Victoria Cave

Pen-y-ghent and Plover Hill

A s you approach Pen-y-ghent from the direction of Settle, suddenly a huge bulk of a mountain looms ahead, looking nothing like the distinctive two-tiered prow viewed from Horton-in-Ribblesdale. It is an awesome moment, especially when you realise that's where you're going. The hill is the lowest of the Yorkshire 'Three Peaks', but is the only one to entertain the Pennine Way. There are two customary lines of ascent, both starting in Horton, but few walkers bother to extend their walk northwards to Plover Hill. Although this does extend the day considerably, it leads walkers into the often bleak but peaceful landscapes of Foxup Moor.

The Route

Leave the car park and turn right, walking as far as the turning on the left where the Pennine Way reaches Horton. Turn into the walled lane, but at the first bend turn right along a wide track that soon reaches and passes a farm and then pops out onto a lane in a quiet part of the village. Cross a nearby footbridge and turn left along a narrow lane that curves round towards **Brackenbottom**. Leave the lane, just before Keeper's Cottage, at a sign for Pen-y-Ghent summit. Cross to a narrow gate, and then start climbing beside a wall that guides up through the limestone landscape of Brackenbottom Scar.

The ongoing ascent is straightforward, if intermittently damp underfoot, but the path is clear throughout and leads to a wall crossing immediately south of the formidable tiered profile of Pen-y-ghent.

↑ Pen-y-ghent from Giggleswick

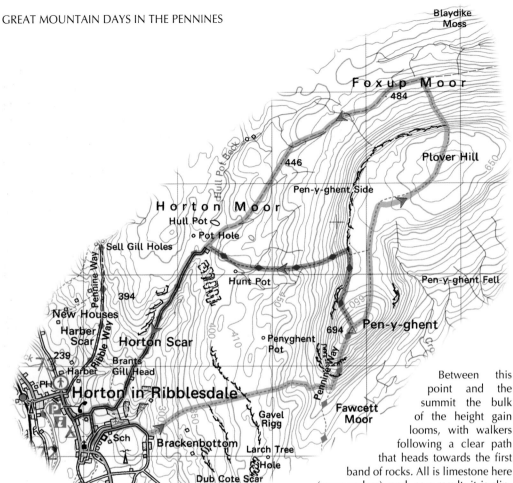

ROUTE INFORMATION

Distance	13.5km (8½ miles)
Height gain	560m (1835ft)
Time	4–5hrs
Grade	demanding
Start point	Horton-in-Ribblesdale SD808726

Getting there
National Park car park (pay and display) and information centre, Horton-in-Ribblesdale

Maps
Ordnance Survey OL2 (Yorkshire Dales: Southern and Western areas)

After-walk refreshment
Pubs and café in Horton

Between this point and the summit the bulk of the height gain looms, with walkers following a clear path that heads towards the first band of rocks. All is limestone here (more or less), and, as a result, it is slippery when wet. The way up is never in doubt, and it's a case of using whatever combination of hands, feet and teeth best suits the task ahead. Gradually, however, height is gained, and suddenly only a gently rising path remains to the trig pillar on the summit.

There are differing opinions about the origins of the name of **Pen-y-ghent**, but it must derive from the Celtic and date from a time when Brigantian tribes were forced into what were then remote and inhospitable regions by Roman and Teutonic settlers. It makes sense for the name to mean the 'hill of the wind', since *ghent* is very close to the Welsh word *gwynt* (meaning 'wind'). To suggest that it might be derived from *cant*, meaning 'rim', and therefore mean the 'hill of the border country' is rather less convincing, since there are higher and bigger summits nearby that would have a greater claim to that title.

Pen-y-ghent from Horton Scar Lane

Cross the wall at the summit and bear right, sticking close by the wall and following a path signed for Plover Hill.

Anyone wanting a **direct return** to Horton should bear away from the summit wall at this point, following a broad and clear path that eases downwards in the form of the Pennine Way and steadily descends to a fell gate at the head of Horton Scar Lane.

The walk to the remote outlier of Plover Hill is easy enough, although occasionally plagued by intermittent and unavoidable peat bogs, and crosses an intervening wall at a ladder-stile. In spite of ample bog, the summit of **Plover Hill**, a little away from the walls, does boast a sizeable cairn, and rocky outcrops are found to ring the summit of the hill, providing the wherewithal for the cairn and the impressive walls.

Continue northwards as a clear path leads down gently at first and then much more steeply to intercept a bridleway (SD846761) that runs across the moors here from the hamlet of Foxup. Turn left, following a trail to Swarth Gill Gate (SD838757) and then continuing alongside a wall. The ongoing route leads close to **Hull Pot**, one of the remarkable highlights of this moorland landscape.

Hull Pot

Hull Pot, a splendid and quite unexpected feature, is a rather large hole in the landscape – about 18m (60ft) wide and deep, and 91m (300ft) long. After prolonged rain the waterfall into the Pot is remarkable, but most of the time the waters of Hull Pot Beck simply seep underground, causing a brief resurgence at the base of the Pot cliffs and then disappearing again. The Pot is essentially a collapsed cave and is claimed to be Britain's biggest natural hole.

Press on beyond Hull Pot and before long reach a fell gate giving onto Horton Scar Lane. Now all that remains is to follow the lane about 2.4km (1½ miles) back to **Horton**, with fine forward views to Pendle Hill and to the west of Ingleborough.

Fountains Fell

*F*ountains Fell is a perfect example of how appearances can be deceptive. From the shores of
Malham Tarn it appears as a long whaleback ridge offering little walking prospect other than a
tiring slog to its summit. The reality, however, is much more appealing, since the long ridge it sends
southwards to Knowe Fell is much less boggy than might be imagined, and the climb by the Pennine
Way is arguably the gentlest ascent section of the entire route. Even so, this walk is an extended
excursion into upland moorland.

The Route

Set off along any of the paths that lead northwards
towards Malham Tarn, gradually bearing right to
pass a woodland and soon gain a broad gravel track.
Pass through a gate into the National Trust's Malham
Tarn National Nature Reserve and simply follow the
ongoing track to **Malham Tarn House**, today a field
study centre, sheltered in a cooling belt of trees.

At an altitude of 377m (1237ft), **Malham Tarn** is
England's highest freshwater lake and the highest
marl lake in Britain, lying within a classic limestone
landscape, an internationally important wetland
site and a National Nature Reserve. Although surrounded by so much limestone, which normally
contributes to water disappearing underground,

↑ *The summit of Knowe Fell, looking north to Fountains Fell*

ROUTE INFORMATION

Distance	19.2km (12 miles)
Height gain	400m (1310ft)
Time	6hrs
Grade	demanding
Start point	Malham Tarn SD894658

Getting there
Malham Tarn car park. Roadside parking space to the east of the road before reaching Tennant Gill Farm (for a shorter walk).

Map
Ordnance Survey OL2 (Yorkshire Dales: Southern and Western areas)

After-walk refreshment
Pubs and cafés in Malham and Settle

Malham Tarn sits in a bowl of impermeable Silurian slate, bordered by raised peat bog. For the botanist there is much of interest here – from a wide range of damp-loving plants, such as cranberry, bog rosemary, cross-leaved heath and bog asphodel, to the plants that love limestone, including the mountain pansy, eyebright and bird's-eye primrose.

The scenery around Malham Tarn has been the inspiration of many, including John Ruskin and Charles Kingsley, who wrote part of *The Water Babies* and *A Fairy Tale for a Land Baby* while staying at Malham Tarn House as a guest of millionaire Walter Morrison. Charles Darwin, too, found the unrivalled setting conducive to his studies.

There has been human activity at Malham Tarn since the Mesolithic era (12,000–7000 years BP), when the shores of the lake were used for camping during hunting trips for deer and wild cattle. During the Bronze and Iron Ages, the area was settled by farmers for grazing. The only Roman presence in the area was a marching camp on Malham Moor. During medieval times the land was owned by the monasteries and used for grazing. A survey undertaken in 1539, at the time of the dissolution of Fountains Abbey, records the presence of a farmstead on the northern shore of lake.

On the track to Malham Tarn House

Malham Tarn

Enter the grounds of Malham Tarn House and then follow the lane continuing westwards beyond it, gently descending. On leaving the nature reserve, turn right at a signpost (SD888673) for Tennant Gill. A delightful interlude ensues as the Pennine Way crosses easy pastured enclosures to another signpost at a wall corner. Here, descend to a through-stile beside a gate and, over this, bear immediately right (not up the vehicle track) over a low rise and continue on to reach the road not far from the access to Tennant Gill Farm. The distance travelled thus far will be reversed at the end of the walk, and this point reached via the nearby bridleway.

Now go down the track to **Tennant Gill Farm**, and on reaching the farm the Pennine Way swings around it and then climbs a sloping pasture to a through-stile beside a gate. Over this, bear immediately left for a short distance to a signpost, from where the route starts to rise easily as a green track alongside a collapsed wall onto the Middle Fell slopes of the much bulkier Fountains Fell. Further on, the Way traverses moorland to a gate, beyond which a gravel path, more or less continuous, leads on, eventually to arrive at a tall cairn on the northern edge of Fountains Fell. (Here the Pennine Way takes its leave, plunging steeply down to Rainscar and the waiting Pen-y-ghent.)

The top of Fountains Fell has seen much mining activity in the past, and there are open shafts that

On the northern summit of Fountains Fell

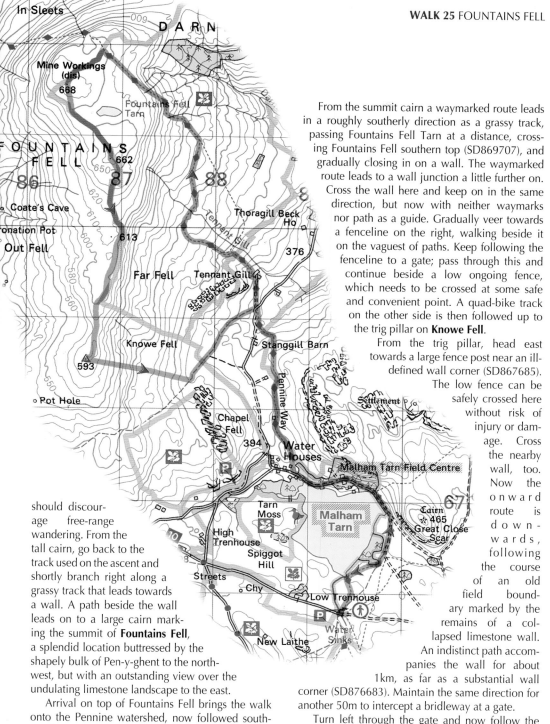

From the summit cairn a waymarked route leads in a roughly southerly direction as a grassy track, passing Fountains Fell Tarn at a distance, crossing Fountains Fell southern top (SD869707), and gradually closing in on a wall. The waymarked route leads to a wall junction a little further on. Cross the wall here and keep on in the same direction, but now with neither waymarks nor path as a guide. Gradually veer towards a fenceline on the right, walking beside it on the vaguest of paths. Keep following the fenceline to a gate; pass through this and continue beside a low ongoing fence, which needs to be crossed at some safe and convenient point. A quad-bike track on the other side is then followed up to the trig pillar on **Knowe Fell**.

From the trig pillar, head east towards a large fence post near an ill-defined wall corner (SD867685). The low fence can be safely crossed here without risk of injury or damage. Cross the nearby wall, too. Now the onward route is downwards, following the course of an old field boundary marked by the remains of a collapsed limestone wall. An indistinct path accompanies the wall for about 1km, as far as a substantial wall corner (SD876683). Maintain the same direction for another 50m to intercept a bridleway at a gate.

Turn left through the gate and now follow the bridleway across a number of gated pastures until it finally leads back to the road not far from the entrance to **Tennant Gill Farm**. Now simply retrace the outward route.

should discourage free-range wandering. From the tall cairn, go back to the track used on the ascent and shortly branch right along a grassy track that leads towards a wall. A path beside the wall leads on to a large cairn marking the summit of **Fountains Fell**, a splendid location buttressed by the shapely bulk of Pen-y-ghent to the northwest, but with an outstanding view over the undulating limestone landscape to the east.

Arrival on top of Fountains Fell brings the walk onto the Pennine watershed, now followed southwards to Knowe Fell. In spring and early summer these peaty fells, rising high above the limestone below, are filled with the sound of skylark, curlew and the piping calls of golden plover.

Janet's Foss, Gordale Scar and Malham Cove

*W*hatever the time of year, you are unlikely to have this walk entirely to yourself. It is by no means a lengthy walk, but a full circuit is best allocated a complete day – so captivating is the scenery and the way its changes unfold, and so relaxing is the air, that you will not want to hasten by. The rockwork is fascinating, drawing geology students from far and wide, while botanists will have many an excuse to linger across the limestone pavement above Malham Cove.

The Route

Leave the car park and follow the road for a short distance towards the village centre. Keep an eye open for a small footbridge across the beck on the right, and use it to gain and follow a broad path downstream.

The origins of **Malham** go back 1300 years to a simple settlement around a village green. About 400 years later, the village was cut in two when the beck became the boundary between lands owned by Fountains Abbey and Bolton Priory. Henry VIII's dissolution of the monasteries, however, brought new prosperity, replacing old wooden houses by stone buildings that still form the core of the village today.

↑ *Malham Cove*

ROUTE INFORMATION

Distance	11.5km (7 miles)
Height gain	285m (935ft)
Time	4hrs
Grade	moderately demanding (with a little awkward scrambling)
Start point	Malham SD899627

Getting there

National Park car park (pay and display) and information centre, Malham

Maps

Ordnance Survey OL10 (Yorkshire Dales: Southern area)

After-walk refreshment

Pubs and cafés in Malham

A gate gives access to a meadow, and the path, a brief section of the Pennine Way, keeps to its edge beside the stream. Shortly, pass through a gate not far from an old stone barn, and here change direction, passing the barn. A substantial path leads through more gates to a small woodland flanking Gordale Beck, in spring permeated by the strong garlicky smell of wild ransoms, which flower from April to June and especially thrive in damp woodlands.

The head of this shallow gorge is taken by a waterfall, **Janet's Foss**. Here white water tumbles 5m (16ft) into a crystal plunge pool, where once local farmers used to wash their sheep. The lip of the falls is formed by a bank of tufa about 4m (13ft) wide.

Tufa is similar to stalagmite in that it too is calcium carbonate precipitated from lime-saturated water. Unlike stalagmite, tufa is formed in a surface stream where algae grow and cause precipitation by altering the chemistry of the water. Along Gordale Beck there are many spots where tufa is found – some are inactive, but some, as at Janet's Foss, are still forming. Tufa is most evident at the Foss where it projects over a rock ledge to create the cave behind the falls where a legendary fairy queen, Janet, once lived. There is something mesmeric about this shaded spot, as if indeed the fairies have cast a spell to charm all who pass by.

Janet's Foss

Beside the falls a narrow gully climbs to a path and a metalled road. Turn right along the road and follow it for a short distance, the towering cliffs of **Gordale Scar** now suddenly appearing ahead. At a gate, enter beckside pastureland (often used as a camp site) and take a path into the very jaws of the chasm. Arguments still rumble quietly as to how the unique rock architecture of Gordale Scar came into being, some proposing that it once formed an enormous cavern which collapsed, leaving only its walls standing, but there is little real doubt that it was cut by retreating meltwater flowing from Ice Age glaciers.

The path into the gorge gives no indication of what awaits around a sharp corner, for here the walls close in dramatically – 50m (164ft) high and with barely 15m (49ft) separating them at one point, severely overhanging at their base, and vertical at their easiest angle. Higher still, more crags and scars continue upwards to the plateau surface almost 100m (328ft) above the beck. Hidden from external view, a fine waterfall gushes through an eyehole in a thin wall of limestone, pauses in its downward flight

in a natural amphitheatre, and spills splendidly to the broad base of the chasm floor. Close by the eyehole falls, which are actively depositing tufa on a bank below, a larger bank of inactive tufa, to the left, marks the site of an earlier waterfall. This was active until 250–300 years ago, when the beck suddenly discovered its new route through the eyehole.

Many walkers elect to retreat from this point to find an alternative route to Malham Cove, but it is possible (in all but spate conditions) to splash through the shallows to reach the base of a prominent buttress of banded and inactive tufa dividing the falls. Improbable though it may seem, this offers an entertaining scramble to the sanctuary of the upper gorge, safely reached damp of foot but not of spirit. Plans were once afoot to construct a staircase up the falls, and this would have tamed the scramble; getting onto the rock is the most awkward part.

Once above the falls, a steep stepped path awaits, rising to meet a good path that climbs easily away from the gorge. With the benefit of elevation, the watercourse can clearly be recognised as a meltwater channel with rocky walls. The path,

Gordale Scar

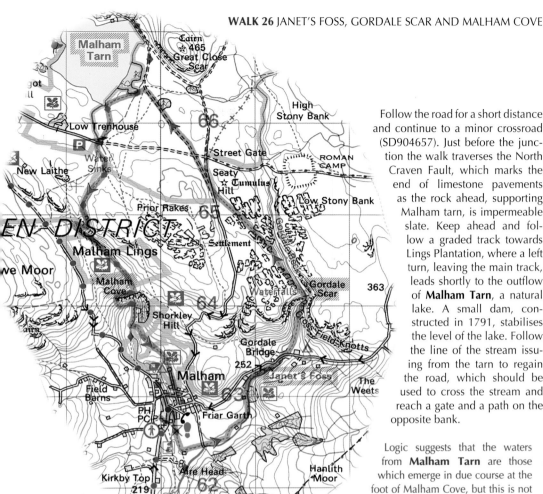

Follow the road for a short distance and continue to a minor crossroad (SD904657). Just before the junction the walk traverses the North Craven Fault, which marks the end of limestone pavements as the rock ahead, supporting Malham tarn, is impermeable slate. Keep ahead and follow a graded track towards Lings Plantation, where a left turn, leaving the main track, leads shortly to the outflow of **Malham Tarn**, a natural lake. A small dam, constructed in 1791, stabilises the level of the lake. Follow the line of the stream issuing from the tarn to regain the road, which should be used to cross the stream and reach a gate and a path on the opposite bank.

Logic suggests that the waters from **Malham Tarn** are those which emerge in due course at the foot of Malham Cove, but this is not so. Tests were first carried out in the 1870s, and again 100 years later, which demonstrate that the waters of Malham Tarn issue at Aire Head Springs, 700m south of Malham village. For this reason Malham became famous as one of the places where it was shown that underground streams are capable of crossing over one another independently in a complex system of limestone hydrology.

The water from Malham Tarn disappears sullenly into stream-bed debris, and from this spot, called **Water Sinks**, follow a path into a deepening dry valley until it curves sharply to avoid a dry waterfall, Comb Scar. Here the path doubles about to gain a stile at the head of a tributary gully that gives easy access to the floor of Watlowes, which about 14,000 years ago carried a powerful meltwater river. In those distant times the limestone was still frozen, of course, and prevented the water sinking underground as it does today.

absorbed now by a rich green fescue turf, broadens and presses on to reach a surfaced road (this would make a speedy retreat to Malham should the need arise).

The **limestone pavement**, both here and on the section leading to Malham Cove, will be irresistible to the botanist as the range of plant life is remarkable. The fissures between the blocks (clints) of limestone are called grykes, and in them, protected from sun and the attentions of sheep, a rich variety of woodland and cliff-face species of plant exists. Hart's tongue fern is but one of a dozen ferns growing side by side with herb robert, wood sorrel, dog's mercury and, in a few secluded spots, baneberry. The turfed areas, too, have a wealth of flora – violets, fairy flax, bedstraws and bird's foot trefoil.

Ahead now lies the very lip of **Malham Cove**, and this approach is infinitely more dramatic and awe-inspiring than the walk from the village. No one can fail to be impressed by the landscape, which is nothing short of spectacular, and justifies its popularity on that score alone. The last few strides to the lip of the cove are over limestone pavement once more, with only the distant views to suggest there might be an abrupt drop ahead. Walkers with a good head for heights can approach the very edge for an aerial perspective of people some 80m (262ft) below; those without should stay well away. Everyone should bear in mind that limestone is very slippery when wet, and not much better when dry.

To the right, the limestone pavement is crossed to a gate at the top of a staircase descending to the valley floor. Here a left turn leads to the base of the cliff, from where the sheer verticality of the cove can be appreciated. In the centre, where a small dry valley cuts in, the height of the wall is 70m (230ft), topped on either side by another 10m (33ft) of outcropping. The span of the cove is 200m (656ft), with grassy ledges reaching in from the edges but never quite meeting in the middle. Malham Beck, the infant River Aire, here issues from a small pool at the foot of the cliff.

So rich is this region in its diverse interests that even the short distance back to the village demands attention. Across the scree slopes on the east side of the cove are to be found the tall blue flowers of Jacob's ladder – here abundant, but nationally rare and not to be picked or trampled. Also rare is a small tree, almost wholly confined to limestone crags, the rock whitebeam, whose delicate silvery leaves catch the eye.

Along the path away from the cove watch for a clapper bridge on the left crossing the stream to a gate. From the gate climb diagonally right to a small plateau of fescue turf and continue ascending gently to a good path that works its way back to **Malham** by a succession of narrow walled lanes, reaching the village close by the green and the humped packhorse bridge. Alternatively, the main path out of the cove also leads back to the village.

Limestone pavement above Malham Cove

Buckden Pike

T he climb to Buckden Pike is a popular walk throughout the year, not least for its extensive
views and its dominant position at the head of Wharfedale. It is the fourth highest peak in
the southern Dales behind Whernside, Ingleborough and Great Whernside, but ahead of Pen-y-
ghent. As a Marilyn summit, it comes within the radar of the peak-bagging fraternity, but it makes
a satisfying excursion without such distinction. This walk takes the principal route to the summit,
but then continues southwards towards Cam Head and a broad track leading down to the village of
Starbotton, and from there the Dales Way returns the walk to Buckden.

Buckden, which means 'the valley of the bucks',
has been the abode of deer since medieval times
and is part of an ancient forest (in the sense of a
hunting domain for the nobility, rather than a place
where trees grow). The setting is magnificent, with
the village hemmed in on all sides by limestone fells.

The Route

Leave the car park at its northern end, through
a gate giving into the National Trust's Upper
Wharfedale Estate, a vast area of 6100 acres and
an attractive landscape of grey limestone crags,
drystone walls and vernacular buildings offset by

↑ *Upper Wharfedale*

139

ROUTE INFORMATION

Distance   14.3km (9 miles)
Height gain   522m (1715ft)
Time   5hrs
Grade   demanding
Start point   Buckden SD942773

Getting there
Buckden village car park (pay and display; toilets)

Maps
Ordnance Survey OL30 (Yorkshire Dales: Northern and Central areas)

After-walk refreshment
Pubs in Buckden, Hubberholme, Starbotton and Kettlewell

lush green pastures, flower-rich meadows, wooded slopes and moorland. For the archaeologist there are a number of prehistoric field patterns and the remains of old lead mines, while the botanist will find that the landscape is favoured by ox-eye daisy, yellow rattle, betony, knapweed, sedges, self-heal and orchids. Almost immediately, the track starts to rise as it climbs through **Rakes Wood** and below low outcrops of limestone.

Today, the slopes of Buckden Pike witness the tread only of walkers and sheep, but between the 16th and 19th centuries the western slopes in particular were an industrial landscape. High on the slopes, the remains of Buckden Gavel lead mine and Buckden High Smelt Mill can still be seen, although it is now more than 130 years since the workings were abandoned.

After passing through Rakes Wood, the track becomes more open and rises to a gate, where the gradient eases. Walk on a short distance further to

Primroses

Ascending through Rakes Wood

another gate and here follow a branching path for Buckden Pike as it leaves the main track (which heads for the hamlet of Cray).

The ongoing path is clear throughout and cuts diagonally across a number of walled pastures before reaching a line of low limestone crags. Press on through a gate gap and climb easily to another gate in the intake wall. Beyond, a constructed path,

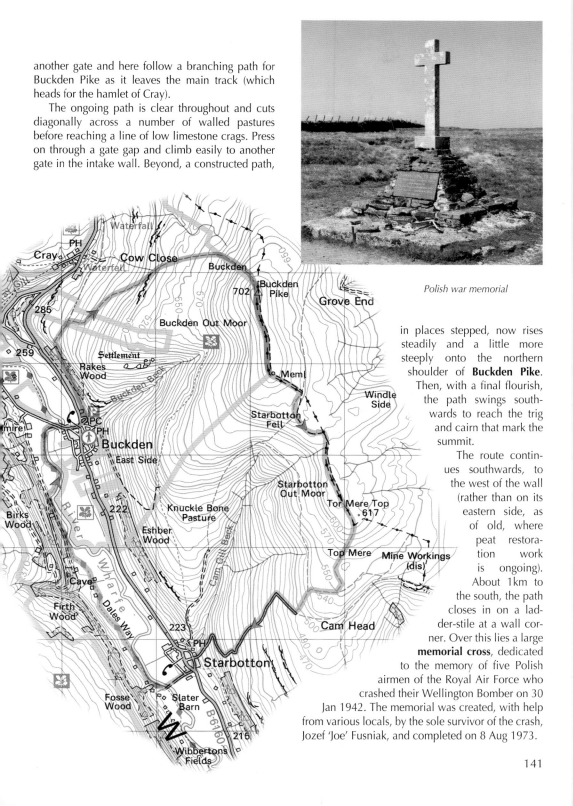

Polish war memorial

in places stepped, now rises steadily and a little more steeply onto the northern shoulder of **Buckden Pike**. Then, with a final flourish, the path swings southwards to reach the trig and cairn that mark the summit.

The route continues southwards, to the west of the wall (rather than on its eastern side, as of old, where peat restoration work is ongoing). About 1km to the south, the path closes in on a ladder-stile at a wall corner. Over this lies a large **memorial cross**, dedicated to the memory of five Polish airmen of the Royal Air Force who crashed their Wellington Bomber on 30 Jan 1942. The memorial was created, with help from various locals, by the sole survivor of the crash, Jozef 'Joe' Fusniak, and completed on 8 Aug 1973.

Boundary stone

From the memorial take a path that heads south-east parallel with the wall and changes direction a few times as it heads for **Tor Mere Top**. Continue following the wall as it crosses Starbotton Peat Ground and later intercepts an east–west track as it passes through walls, ultimately to gain a walled track, Starbotton Cam Road, which speeds walkers downwards in zigzags to the village of **Starbotton**. Bear left on entering the village to emerge onto the B6160, not far from a walled path that leads down to cross the River Wharfe and then join the Dales Way.

The compact collection of 17th- and 18th-century cottages in **Starbotton** is a legacy of the mining eras. More than once the village has felt the force of Cam Gill Beck, which tried to wash it away, the worst and most destructive occasion being in 1686 as a fearful storm turned the beck into a raging torrent.

The route along the Dales Way is clear enough, waymarked intermittently and located at varying distances from the river. In the end, however, it returns to the riverbank as it approaches **Buckden**, joining the Hubberholme road at Wharfe Bridge.

More than 200 years ago, when **Wharfe Bridge** was only half its present width, it became known as 'Election Bridge' after a prospective Member of Parliament promised to have a new bridge built if the local populace voted for him. At Buckden, they got their new bridge, but only at the expense of Hubberholme, which found funds for a new bridge there diverted to the needs of Buckden residents.

From the bridge, simply turn right and walk up to the village car park to complete the walk.

Great Whernside

*T*he long ridge of Great Whernside rises as an eastern barrier to the moors of Nidderdale, its summit visible from the streets of Kettlewell below. The name 'Whernside' is from the Old English cweorn-side, meaning 'the hill from which millstones came', and a few still scatter the Wharfedale slopes of the mountain among a rash of gritstone boulders. Yet there are many places on this looping walk where doubts arise as to whether there is any rock underfoot at all. But rock there is: gritstone on the mountain and limestone on the descent. The walk offers an alternative, and slightly longer, return route via the village of Starbotton.

Kettlewell, a former lead-mining village, is a study in grey and green, protected north, east and west by high fells. Even in winter it is noticeably warmer than neighbouring villages. 'The charm of Kettlewell is abiding,' wrote Frederic William Moorman (1872–1918), professor of English Language and Literature at Leeds University. 'The village seems the peculiar abode of peace and quiet beauty... the limestone terraces, with the fringes of hazel and rowan coppices, give to the district a characteristic beauty.' Moorman's life was cut tragically short in a drowning accident – he was succeeded at Leeds by JRR Tolkien – but his studies of Yorkshire bring an authority to his description that is every bit as valid today as it was almost a century ago.

↑ *The summit of Great Whernside, looking west to Yorkshire's Three Peaks*

Looking towards Great Whernside above Dowber Gill Beck

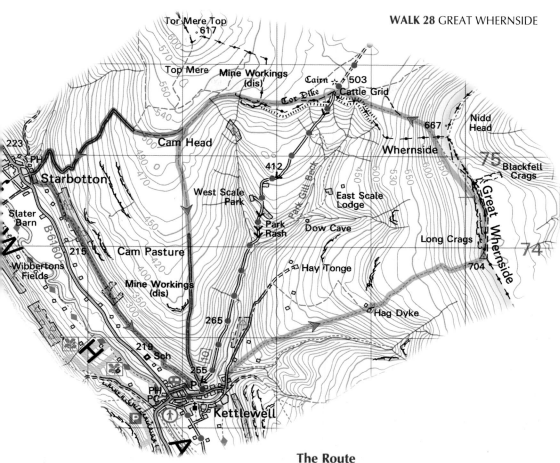

ROUTE INFORMATION

Distance 13.2km (8¼ miles); alternative finish 14.5km (9 miles)
Height gain 505m (1655ft); alternative finish 563m (1847ft)
Time 5–6hrs
Grade strenuous
Start point Kettlewell SD968723

Getting there
Car park (pay and display; toilets) near Wharfe Bridge, Kettlewell

Maps
Ordnance Survey OL30 (Yorkshire Dales: Northern and Central areas)

After-walk refreshment
Pubs and cafés in Kettlewell

The Route
Leave the car park, turning left to cross the bridge spanning the combined Dowber Gill and Cam Gill becks, and then turn right in front of the Bluebell Hotel. Follow the course of the beck, and at a road junction (post office and village stores on the corner) keep forward along the minor road to Leyburn. In a short distance, as the gradient increases and the Leyburn road swings left, leave it by going forward into a descending lane, passing an old Methodist chapel to arrive at a track junction.

Turn left and follow the track to a small bridge, and just over this turn right (signed for Hag Dyke and Providence Pot), walking tightly between a wall and Dowber Gill Beck to a stile on the left. Now the first stage of ascent begins, following a clear grassy course, upfield, through a number of pastures to reach a wall-gap, with a gated gap-stile to the right. From here, more tracks (take the middle one) rise to a signpost, where the gradient levels for a while as Great Whernside now ranges across the skyline ahead.

From the signpost, an easy path leads on to the buildings at **Hag Dyke**, today a Scout hostel, established in 1947, but formerly the highest farm in

145

Wharfedale – if not the whole of Yorkshire. Pass to the right of the building and then left through a field gate to resume the ascent – it passes through a down-spill of boulders, above which a wide boggy plateau awaits. Once across this, a final climb through more gritstone leads to the cluster of rocks on the top of which is perched a trig pillar marking the summit of **Great Whernside**. The summit lies amid a huge plateau running off north and south, with excellent views in all directions, notably to Yorkshire's Three Peaks, Fountains Fell and Darnbrook Fell, and south-west to Pendle Hill.

Leave the summit heading north and keep fairly close to the western edge of the plateau to locate a yellow-topped waymark pole (SE002742), which marks the start of a sketchy waymarked path extending northwards below the rim of rocks and gradually descending to a stile in a wall. The actual path lies a little further west than that shown on maps.

Between the stile and the Coverhead Pass the conditions underfoot call for caution; although the route is clear enough, the ground is muddy and wet at the best of times, and the Coverdale road comes as something of a relief.

Cross close to a cattle grid and press on along a broad green path that follows the course of **Tor Dike**, an earthwork with ditch and rampart constructed in the limestone. Tor Dike was built by Iron Age tribes, about 1900 years ago, as a defence against invading Romans.

Eventually, the broad green track reduces to a narrow trod, but maintains a course roughly parallel with a wall on the left before passing through a gate and on to a signpost on **Starbotton Road** (SD970753). The route here swings southwards (left, signed for Kettlewell) and follows a steadily, and occasionally steeply, descending route back to **Kettlewell**, where it rejoins the Leyburn Road. Turn right to retrace the outward route to the Wharfe Bridge.

Alternative finish From the signpost on Starbotton road, a longer walk can be accomplished by taking the right fork for Starbotton and following a clear route that feeds into a walled descent to the village. On entering the village, turn left to locate a footpath running parallel with the B6160 that leads all the way back to Kettlewell.

Heading north towards Coverhead Pass

Cracoe Fell and Thorpe Fell

*T*he great swathe of Barden Moor is hugely popular as a breeding ground for curlew, grouse, lapwing and black-headed gull, any of which may take a dislike to intruders during the breeding season. For this reason, dogs are not allowed on this walk. But the moor is not the only focus of this circuit. After a long and easy walk in, the route takes to a delightful gritstone ridge above the villages of Rylstone and Cracoe before taking to heather moorland expanses to visit the mound of Thorpe Fell. The walking is nowhere unduly difficult, and is for the most part on clear paths and tracks.

The Route

From the parking area take to the obvious stony track, a bridleway, that heads west onto the bilberry and heather moorland, and walk easily across the headwaters of numerous gills feeding Lower Barden Reservoir below. From here until the bridleway is left for the ascent of Rylstone Fell, there is little opportunity for confusion; the route is clear, broad and direct, and a pleasure to walk.

At a track junction near the top of **Hutchen Gill** (SE023561) keep right, climbing through a line of grouse butts. At the next track junction near a signpost (SE007571) bear left, soon passing another signpost and then bringing Cracoe Fell into view. **Brown Bank** is a gentle rise, but it deflects the waters to the west rather than into the reservoir catchment. At another junction (SD997571) branch right at a

↑ *Rylstone Cross*

The view northwards from Rylstone Fell to Cracoe Fell

ROUTE INFORMATION

Distance	18.5km (11½ miles)
Height gain	368m (1205ft)
Time	6½hrs
Grade	demanding
Start point	Barden Moor SE037556

Getting there
Roadside parking area south of Lower Barden Reservoir, just west of the cattle grid along the Barden–Embsay road (and another a little further on)

Maps
Ordnance Survey OL2 (Yorkshire Dales: Southern and Western areas)

After-walk refreshment
Pubs in Embsay

The way continues as a rough stony path through heather. Keep following it until eventually it reaches a wall. Here, finally leave the bridleway and turn upwards, to the right of the wall, following a gently rising path through gritstone boulders to the cross on **Rylstone Fell**. The present cross, erected in 1995, replaces a wooden one erected in 1885 to commemorate the 1815 Treaty of Paris that ended the Napoleonic Wars. Rylstone village, in the valley below, has even greater notoriety as the home of the original 'Calendar Girls', about whom a popular film was made.

A ladder-stile gives access to the cross, but from here continue to the right of the wall across an undulating and attractive landscape to the war memorial on **Cracoe Fell**, the highest point of the circuit. In some mountain tables, Thorpe Fell (506m) is shown as being higher than Cracoe Fell and is listed as

signpost, after which the route descends gently, having now left the stony vehicle track that has been followed this far.

a Marilyn. But recent measurements show that **Watt Crag**, on which the memorial stands, is actually 508m, making Cracoe Fell the Marilyn. Until the records are corrected, walkers are going to have to visit both summits – which is exactly what this walk does.

The onward route from Cracoe Fell remains to the right of the wall, at least as far as a line of grouse butts.

Alternative route Walkers not wanting to visit Thorpe Fell should continue alongside the wall a little further to reach the end of a broad track that leads across the northern slopes of the fell to a pair of isolated buildings at the site of an old mine.

Those bound for Thorpe Fell continue across heather moorland. A short distance beyond the grouse butts, opposite a gate and ladder-stile, where the heather relaxes its grip, leave the wallside path and strike roughly eastwards. There is no prominent path, but the remains of a long-disused track, now overgrown and not easily found, does serve as a guide. An interim objective is a solitary boundary stone at SE003595. From it an indistinct but continuous path threads a way through heather all the way to the damaged trig pillar on **Thorpe Fell**.

149

The low-lying rocks that lie across the top of Thorpe Fell are part of a fascinating **geology** in this area. Much of the Yorkshire Dales is formed from limestone. Between Cracoe and Burnsall are a series of relatively low limestone hills known as the Cracoe Reef Knolls, notably Kail, Elbolton, Stebden, Skelterton and Butter Haw hills. They are the geological remnants of an ancient coral reef which formed in a shallow prehistoric sea many millions of years ago. The rocks on Cracoe Fell, however, are gritstone embedded with small smooth, rounded pebbles. The smoothness and shape of the pebbles confirms that at some stage they were sea-washed and later became embedded in the silt that developed into the gritstone we see today, formed during the Namurian age (326–313 million years ago).

From the trig on Thorpe Fell, the way lies through trackless heather. Any direction between north and north-east will suffice, but as soon as an isolated mine building comes into view (SE015599) that should become the target. Once reached, pass around it and another smaller building, now once more on a broad track that leads through a former coal-mining area that served the Duke of Devonshire's cupola smelt mill in Wharfedale.

Follow the track eastwards, and shortly, when the track divides, bear right towards an isolated chimney – the remains of a boiler house and chimney connected with the coal mines. Walk down past this, and when the track next divides, just above a small reservoir, turn right and pass the reservoir. Continue following the track across the moor eventually to reach the corner of **Upper Barden Reservoir**. Here, just before reaching the dam wall, double back to the left on a broad service track. Follow this high above Barden Beck, remaining on the most prominent track until, shortly after crossing a stone bridge, it runs on to a cattle grid at a wall-gap.

Now leave the service track and descend on a Permissive Path to the sluices at **Lower Barden Reservoir**. Cross a small dam and footbridge, and then join a broad track once more, turning left. The track comes out to meet a surfaced lane near **Broad Park House**. Turn right and walk up to the Barden–Embsay road to complete the walk.

The summit of Thorpe Fell

Elslack Moor and Pinhaw Beacon

*P*inhaw Beacon is a surprisingly delightful height above the concealed valley of Lothersdale to the south and Airedale to the east. Its mantle of heather in August and September is a sharp contrast both to the greenness of the farmlands below and the harsher tussocks and reeds of Elslack Moor from which it rises. As a true warning beacon of old, it enjoys a fine panorama and rightly holds a place along the Pennine Way.

The Route

Set off from **Thornton** down Old Road, strolling easily along a narrow lane. Pass beneath a disused bridge (alternative parking here), and bear right along the continuing lane for **Brown House Farm**. Before reaching the farm, the lane passes bridge abutments that are all that remain of a railway line that once linked Colne and Skipton.

On reaching the farm pass initially through the farmyard, but on the other side quit the surfaced lane

by passing left over a step-stile into the bottom of a sloping pasture. Turn up into the pasture, moving away from a fence towards an isolated ash tree, from which the route continues across the field to a simple footbridge spanning a tributary of Brown House Beck. Beyond this, pass through a kissing-gate and then immediately turn right alongside a ditch, climbing steadily above a stream gully. Gradually, the path moves away from the gully to a gap-stile near a

↑ *Craven farmland below Pinhaw Beacon*   151

'Gradually, the path moves away from the gully to a gap-stile near a field gate.'

ROUTE INFORMATION

Distance	13km (8 miles)
Height gain	342m (1120ft)
Time	4hrs
Grade	moderate
Start point	Thornton-in-Craven SS907485

Getting there
Limited roadside parking on Old Road, Thornton-in-Craven, or either side of bridge at SD912486

Maps
Ordnance Survey OL21 (South Pennines)

After-walk refreshment
Pubs in Earby

field gate. Through the gate, swing right to rejoin the gully, walking up beside it to where it can be crossed by a narrow footbridge.

Once over the bridge, turn left beside a wall; some of the route from this point onward is on boardwalks, which can be slippery when wet. Continue upwards to a gated through-stile, shortly after which the gradient finally eases as the trig on Pinhaw Beacon comes into view. Press on beside a wall to tackle a high ladder-stile, just after which the road joins Clogger Lane, which it follows up to a T-junction.

Cross the road and go forward through a gate onto a continuing track that leads unerringly to the summit of **Pinhaw Beacon**. The view, as might be expected, is superb, reaching to the north over Malham Cove to Fountains Fell and the more distant Ingleborough, while to the south lie Boulsworth Hill, the Brontë Moors and the moors north of Hebden Bridge.

Leave the summit heading east along a clear path through heather and soon reach a path junction where an inset slab at ground level reminded walkers in pre-Access Land days to keep to the Pennine Way. The route does indeed remain on the Pennine Way, but just north of this junction a path leads on for about 200m to a spot marked as Robert Wilson's grave (SD947473).

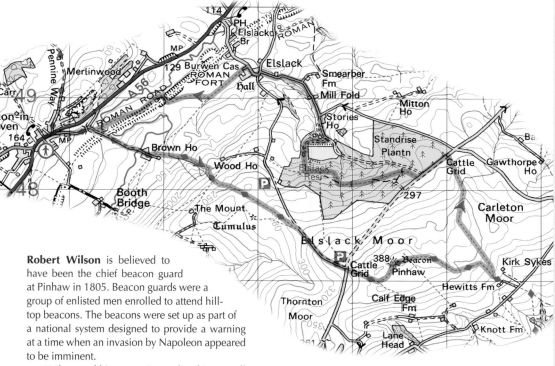

Robert Wilson is believed to have been the chief beacon guard at Pinhaw in 1805. Beacon guards were a group of enlisted men enrolled to attend hilltop beacons. The beacons were set up as part of a national system designed to provide a warning at a time when an invasion by Napoleon appeared to be imminent.

Wilson and his two assistants lived in a small hut about 30m from the beacon. During the winter of 1804–1805, severe weather trapped the men in their hut. Provisions started to run out, so Robert Wilson volunteered to try and reach Moor Side Farm to replenish them. Despite pleas from his helpers to wait until the weather broke he set off, but was never to be seen alive again. His body was discovered a short time later a mere 150m from the safety of his shelter. A stone was erected on the spot where he was found, but whether this is his actual burial place is uncertain. The inscription, faded but still legible, reads

Here was found dead the
Body of Robert Wilson, one
of the Beacon Guards, who
Died Jan 29th, 1805, aged
69 years

Back on the Pennine Way, the path winds down over Little Pinhaw to a wall corner (SD952471). Walk alongside the wall, with the way now paved. When the wall changes direction, go with it towards

Kirk Sykes Farm, just above which the route passes through a gated gap at a wall junction. From this point the continuation over nearby Ransable Hill lies through a wall-gap just 40m to the east. Those 40m, however, are neither Access Land nor a right of way; the latter continues southwards for about 100m before returning northwards to reach the wall-gap.

Once through the wall-gap, simply follow the wall closely over Ransable Hill and across the moors.

On the summit of Pinhaw Beacon

Finally descend to reach a road at a through-stile and cattle grid on the edge of **Standrise Plantation**, which here is far less wooded than maps suggest. Turn left and walk along the road and continue to the edge of woodland. Ignore the prominent access track on the right, and walk a little further to a sign-post marking a path into the plantation.

The path follows a pleasant route, weaving through the trees on a bed of pine underfoot. When it intercepts a broad forest trail, turn left and walk up to a junction, where the trail swings to the right and starts to descend. Although footpaths are shown on maps through the forest, walkers are asked to stay on the broad trails. Follow this trail until it reaches another clear junction (SD935482) at a waymark. Here branch right and descend to cross a ladder-stile at the edge of **Elslack Reservoir**.

Follow the track as it continues descending to cross the overflow from the reservoir, and follow the broad track around the northern side of the reservoir. Just before the reservoir lodge the track swings left, eventually to join Moor Lane. There, turn left and follow the lane into **Elslack**, a charming hamlet of stone-built cottages around a small green. Ignore branching lanes and pass through the village until,

just after a long barn (17th century), the road can be left for a signed footpath. The path leads through the farmyard adjoining **Elslack Hall**, which is probably 16th century with later additions and alterations. It is now a Grade II listed building.

Follow a farm track away from Elslack and walk as far as a metal gate on the right (SD925490). Through the gate go diagonally over the top of the pasture and descend to a step-stile at the end of a wall. In the ensuing field, strike diagonally across the middle, drifting gradually towards a wall on the right. On the far side, pass through a gate and go forward parallel with the trackbed of a **disused railway**. This used to run through the Roman site at nearby Burwen Castle, which would once have been a-bustle with the activities of legionnaires marching between Ilkley and Ribchester forts. After only 100m turn right through a metal gate, crossing the old track and then swinging left near a field barn.

Follow a narrow path at a field edge, but later move away from the field boundary to continue along a defined boundary. On the far side, screened by trees, a footbridge spans Thornton Beck. Over this, a lovely shaded path leads out to meet the lane used at the start of the walk. Turn right to walk into **Thornton**.

Elslack Reservoir

Rombalds Moor and Ilkley Moor

T his, the most easterly of the walks, explores the upland delights of Rombalds Moor, which here, due south of Ilkley, goes by the more popular name of Ilkley Moor (the subject of the renowned 'Yorkshire national anthem', On Ilka Moor baht 'at). The walk in the lower reaches is a delightful amble along the escarpment above the town, and it later heads upwards into sometimes boggy terrain, large sections of which are paved these days. When the route intercepts the Dales Way Link, it finds a joyous and rapid descent back to Ilkley, with walkers all the way facing north into the glaciated maw of Wharfedale, beyond the bulk of Beamsley Beacon.

The Route

Leave the car park at Darwin Gardens and continue up Wells Road. The Gardens commemorate the naturalist Charles Darwin, who came to Ilkley to take the spa waters in 1859 for health reasons. Soon pass the rather imposing former hotel, Ilkley Hydro; its water pump house stands on the other side of Wells Road. When the road divides at Westwood Lodge bear left,

ascending. As the road levels and approaches an upper car park leave it by branching right at a footpath sign, over a bridge spanning Spicey Gill, and then go forward on a broad grassy path.

The path runs parallel with the boundary wall of residential properties, and on reaching a group of three benches just before a bridge at the top of

ROUTE INFORMATION

Distance	11.5km (7 miles)
Height gain	295m (970ft)
Time	4hrs
Grade	moderately demanding
Start point	Ilkley SE117471

Getting there
Darwin Gardens Millennium Green car park,
Wells Road, Ilkley

Maps
Ordnance Survey 297 (Lower Wharfedale and
Washburn valley)

After-walk refreshment
Pubs, cafés and restaurants in Ilkley; café at
White Wells

The Swastika Stone, Woodhouse Crag, Ilkley

Heber's Ghyll leave the main track and branch left.
Climb above the stream to intercept a broad gravel
path leading right towards a field gate in a wall.
Beyond the gate, the path continues to the conspic-
uous fenced enclosure in which lies the so-called
Swastika Stone.

Located on Woodhouse Crag, the **Swastika Stone**
has a double outline of a swastika, with ten 'cup
marks' fitting within five curved arms. The design
is unique in Britain and may be of Italian origin,
dating from about 2500 years ago. It is similar in
design to the Italian Camunian rose, the name
given to a particular symbol represented among
the rock carvings of Val Camonica. There are, in
fact, another two swastikas, one more pronounced
than the other, just a metre away: the clearer one
is a Victorian copy of the original. Although the
design of the Swastika Stone is unique, there are
said to be over 250 stones on the moors above
bearing the more familiar cup and rings marks that
are a form of prehistoric art.

Continue beyond the Swastika Stone, over a
through-stile and across a narrow walled enclosure
before continuing alongside a wall, maintaining the
same direction. The ongoing path leads to a narrow
gap in a wall corner, after which the path leads on
through a collapsed wall, and then on further across
the bottom edge of the rough upland pasture that

makes up **Addingham High Moor**. Press on along
the moorland-edge path and pass through a narrow
metal gate, continuing through heather and bracken.
At the third metal gate turn immediately left, leaving
the main path, and walk up beside a wall on the left,
following the course of a narrow but continuous path
onto **Long Ridge End**. On reaching a ladder-stile over
the wall, dash off to the right to visit the trig pillar on
Long Ridge End, and from it walk briefly through low
heather and then in a south-easterly direction (left)
beside a wall to another ladder-stile in a wall corner.

Over the stile, keep forward alongside the
boundary wall of **High Moor Plantation**. In places
the going is wet underfoot and calls for a little cast-
ing about to circumvent the more persistent puddles.
But gradually the path returns to the wall and follows
it up a final short climb to the group of rocks known
as **West Buck Stones**.

At this point another wall runs off in an easterly
direction, but the path to **East Buck Stones** is more
enticing, and the rocks themselves boast enough
nooks and crannies to evade most winds. After that,
simply continue following a moderately squelchy
path to **Whetstone Gate**, where surfaced Ilkley
Road, arriving from the south, meets unsurfaced
Keighley Road, coming from the direction of Ilkley.

From the road crossing, keep forward initially on a
gravel path that passes the enclosed television masts
nearby. Later the path becomes paved and leads
out across what is now truly Ilkley Moor. The paved
route, constructed under the auspices of the Pennine
Prospects Watershed Landscape Project, leads unerringly across a peaty plateau to the white-painted trig

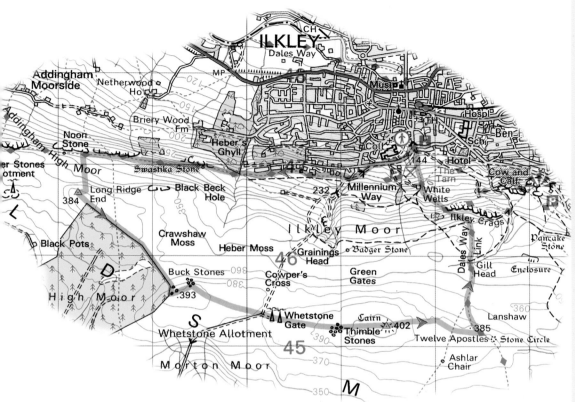

East Buck Stones

Heading out across White Crag Moss

Looking down on Ilkley from above Ilkley Crags

that marks the highest point of **Ilkley Moor**. There is a fine view northwards over Ilkley to Beamsley Beacon and the conspicuous puff balls that locate the Menwith Hill RAF station, which provides communications and intelligence support services to the United Kingdom and America.

After the trig pillar the paving ends, and a typical peaty path leads on over White Crag Moss eventually to intercept another paved route near Lanshaw Lad (SE125451). Here turn northwards, having joined the so-called Dales Way Link. A clear path rambles down the gentle moorland slopes to the top of **Ilkley Crags**, where it is deflected steeply down to the left to continue as before. A short way further on, the buildings at **White Wells** come as something of a surprise.

For over 300 years these 'Spaw Baths', known today as **White Wells**, have looked down over Ilkley. It is said, probably wishfully, that they are Britain's first 'Hydropathic Spa for the Cold Water Cure' that Victorian visitors took in quantity. What is known is that the spa water from here was used by the Middleton family of Middleton Lodge to supply a small bath-house with a deep circular plunge bath, which they built in 1699.

Today, White Wells houses a modest café, but one with an unrivalled view. Modern visitors can still use the plunge bath (bring your own costume and towel). New Year's Day is the most popular for this activity, with usually over 100 visitors taking the plunge throughout the day. Anyone contemplating such a venture need only check from the outskirts of Ilkley whether the White Wells flags are flying: if so, the place is open.

Pass directly in front of the café and locate a descending path on the left, initially down steps, and then head through bracken to the edge of **Ilkley** at Wells Road, just a cattle grid away from the car park.

SOUTH PENNINES

Brontë Bridge (Walk 34)

SOUTH PENNINES

Pressing against the northern reaches of the Dark Peak lie the industrially tormented moors of the South Pennines, where man's hand on the landscape has been as certain as the landscape's own forces upon man. For here, just as the land made possible the mills and factories, and fabricated the social history of the place, so too did it cultivate its customs, relationships and attitudes.

The South Pennines are a great swathe of harsh moors where the lovely orange and gold crystals of millstone grit have oxidised to a black that makes your eyes hurt and portrays, falsely, a land of darkness and dirt even on the brightest day. Few peaks in the South Pennines are remote from the great conurbations of Lancashire and Yorkshire, from where arose the pioneers of mining, weaving and spinning, for everywhere they are traversed by moorland roads and riven by sylvan deans and cloughs carved long ago by ice. And it is this very accessibility that has long provided the people of the South Pennines with high, refreshing oases from the turmoil and hardships of industrial life.

The protected South Pennines Heritage Area lies between the major city regions of Leeds and Manchester to the east and west and the Yorkshire Dales and Peak National Parks to the north and south. Seven million people live within an hour's drive of this area, which offers outstanding opportunities for healthy living and the enjoyment of internationally important wildlife and heritage.

The landscape is one of stark contrasts – vast tracts of open moorland dissected by steep wooded valleys, with the areas in between softened by a patchwork of hamlets and fields. The landscape today is a combined result of geology and human endeavour – enabling the visitor to trace the history of the South Pennines from the Ice Age to the Industrial Revolution.

It was here, among the rolling moors, that man began his quest for freedom to roam, long before the more vaunted efforts of those in the Peak, as admirably explained in Harvey Taylor's *A Claim on the Countryside* (see Appendix 2).

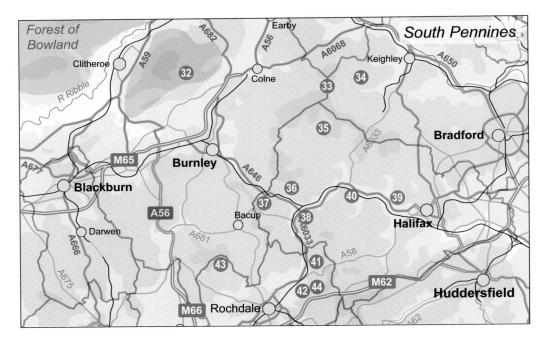

Pendle Hill

*P*endle Hill dominates the surrounding countryside and, once described as a living creature stretched in sleep, has long aroused great affection among the people of Lancashire. One 17th-century parson, Richard James, observed that Pendle stands 'rownd cop, survaiying all ye wilde moor lands', and although from the valley it seems to have a fine ridge it is actually flat-topped. Nevertheless, it is a fine shapely hill, of which it was claimed that its 'broad, round, smooth mass is better than the roughest, craggiest, shaggiest, most sharply-splintered mountain of them all'. In truth, Pendle Hill is a well-padded hill covered in grass and ling with barely a tree in sight on its vast summit plateau. It is nothing like as high as it was once thought to be and, although steep-sided, is easy of access and gentle on the legs.

The Route

Leave the car park by crossing to a footpath around the edge of a grassed play area behind the toilet block and follow the path out to the village road. Walk on to pass the Barley Mow, and at Meadow Bank Farm (on the left) leave the road for a signed footpath beside a stream that leads to a kissing-gate giving into a small pasture. Cross to a footbridge and then go left along a lane, passing close by a large house. Just after this an enclosed footpath, part of the Pendle Way, leads from a metal kissing-gate around **Ings End** and by a clearly defined route to Brown House.

Pass through another gate and briefly walk a track to **Ing Head Farm**, and there turn left through another gate onto a path beside a wall. Shortly,

ROUTE INFORMATION

Distance	10km (6¼ miles)
Height gain	455m (1490ft)
Time	3–4hrs
Grade	moderately demanding
Start point	Barley SD824404

Getting there
Substantial car park (honesty box; toilets, refreshments and information centre) at the southern end of Barley

Maps
Ordnance Survey OL21 (South Pennines)

After-walk refreshment
Café at car park; pub and restaurant in Barley

pass through the wall and continue with the path, which climbs gently to enter rough grazing, then cross to a gate. Walk up the edge of the next field to **Pendle House**. Pass through a gate in the intake wall and turn right, passing the farm, and soon bear left to a gate giving onto a footpath at the base of the long paved ramp soaring up to Pendle Hill's '**Big End**'. Plod up the ramp, finally reaching the edge of the escarpment, close by a wall. Turn abruptly left here and walk up to the trig pillar that marks the summit of **Pendle Hill**.

The view from the summit is predictably immense, reaching north to the Three Peaks of Yorkshire, east to the Pennine watershed along the dumpy heights of Boulsworth Hill and Black Hameldon, and south-east through the Cliviger Gorge towards Todmorden. To the west, the view takes in the Lancashire coastal plain, with the distant Blackpool Tower.

The **Pendle landscape and its human history** truly fascinate. South-west of the hill is the village of Sabden, famous for its connection with the Lancashire or Pendle Witches, about whom Harrison Ainsworth wrote in his novel *The Lancashire Witches*, and Robert Neill in *Mist over Pendle*. Sabden was industrialised by the Cobdens, who began in business as cotton manufacturers in the 1820s. Later, the village had a touch of light fantasy woven into its fabric, as if to set off the grimness of its industry, by claiming to be the only village to possess its own treacle mine. Old handloom-weavers, it is said, used to weave a biscuit known as parkin using oatmeal as the warp and treacle as the weft!

Looking down to Pendle House farm and distant Barley

A short distance east of Barley is the village of Roughlee, where the Nutters lived. They were locally an important family, and a sensation was caused when Alice Nutter, a wealthy and refined woman, was denounced as a witch. She was put on trial in the company of the disreputable Demdike and Chattox families, and was so unlike them in manner and means that it is thought she may have died to protect her Catholic friends. The famous trial of the Pendle Witches occurred in 1612, and while the families were accused of being in league with the Devil, the greater likelihood is that they were simply two quarrelsome families who contrived their own downfall, at an especially sensitive time in England's history, by hurling accusations of evil practice at each other.

Set slightly to one side from the main thrust of the Pennines, it is the sheer bulk of Pendle Hill which commands attention and respect – 'lying like a leviathan basking in the sunshine' (*The Lancashire Witches*), it does indeed often give the impression that one day it will rouse itself and lumber off to pastures anew.

Coming to the end of Boar Clough at the end of Upper Ogden

Leave the top of Pendle following a clear and broad path parallel with the escarpment. Walk as far as the second of two huge mounds of stones, just after which the path divides. Bear half-right here, and the path then follows a clear line across **Barley Moor** and down into Boar Clough. Follow a good path down, finally through bracken to intercept Ogden Clough. At the foot of Boar Clough, turn left and head out of the valley on a path that leads to a gate at the edge of **Upper Ogden Reservoir**.

163

Turn right across the dam of the reservoir to a stile giving onto a clear grassy path rising onto Driver Height. Keep an eye open for a step-stile on the left, by which rough grazing beyond is crossed towards the edge of **Fell Wood**. At the far end of the plantation, maintain the same direction until, after a gated stile, the rough pasture ahead starts to fall away. The path cuts diagonally across this to a mid-field waymark, which links with others to show the way down to a narrow gate that gives into an enclosed path leading down to the village road at Newchurch-in-Pendle.

Cross into Jinny Lane, the Roughlee road, and just after the last house pass through a gated stile on the left, then cross to woodland. In the woodland, take the higher of two paths, which leads through to a pleasant stroll beside a wall alongside Heys Lane Plantation.

Prominent in view along this final section (and earlier parts) of the walk is a conspicuous tower. This is Stansfield Tower, also known as **Blacko Tower**. It was built around 1890 by a local grocer, Jonathan Stansfield, who thought he would be able to see into Ribblesdale from the top, but was proven wrong. He shrugged off the disappointment saying, 'I've never drunk nor smoked in my life so am making this as my hobby.' A rather different legend says that he was trying to see his girlfriend in Gisburn... another forlorn hope.

At a wall corner, cross a double stile and then continue once more beside the wall, now on the right. The path leads down to intercept a broad walled track. Turn left and follow the track above Boothman Wood and out to reach the road at **Barley Green**. Turn right and walk down to the car park at the edge of **Barley** to complete the walk.

The path intercepts a walled track

Boulsworth Hill

*T*he chance to admire the extensive view from the summit of Boulsworth Hill was a long time coming. Access campaigns in the 1950s, led by Tom Stephenson (born not that far away in Chorley), were unsuccessful, but efforts were renewed in the 1990s by a new generation of walkers and led to a concessionary route being established up and down from the Lancashire side. Only with the passing of access legislation (CROW Act 2000) did this mound of acidic grass and gritstone boulders, almost defining the boundary between Lancashire and Yorkshire, become wholly accessible.

The Route

From the car park, walk towards **Wycoller** using a pathway parallel with the road, and take a moment to examine the ageing examples of vaccary field boundary stones passed on the way.

On entering **Wycoller** it is evident that this is a village of some antiquity. Indeed, the settlement can be traced back more than 3000 years. Later, in keeping with Anglo-Saxon tradition, the village

was named after the prominent tree in the area, the alder (*wyc-alr*). For centuries this was very much an agricultural settlement, until in the 18th century the manufacture of woollens became the more important industry.

Evidence of a thriving packhorse trade comes in the form of the rather lop-sided, double-arched bridge spanning the village stream; this alone is believed to be more than 800 years old, and its

↑ Looking across from the lower slopes of Boulsworth Hill to Pendle Hill

Double-arched bridge, Wycoller

ROUTE INFORMATION

Distance	13km (8 miles)
Height gain	413m (1355ft)
Time	5hrs
Grade	moderately demanding
Start point	Wycoller SD926395

Getting there
Wycoller village car park

Maps
Ordnance Survey OL21 (South Pennines)

After-walk refreshment
Tearoom in Wycoller; pub in Trawden

purpose is linked with paved sections of pack-horse trails on the moors above. Nearby is a comparative youngster as bridges go – a clapper bridge dating from the 18th century also spans the beck.

Use either of the bridges to cross the stream and soon reach the ruins of **Wycoller Hall**, built by the Hartley family in the 16th century and thought to have inspired Ferndean Manor in Charlotte Brontë's *Jane Eyre*. Press on past a barn conversion, now used as a visitor centre, and soon reach yet another ancient bridge, the oldest by far. This clam bridge, a simple slab of rock precariously balanced on streamside rocks, is of such age that it is now a Scheduled Ancient Monument.

Keep following the streamside track as far as **Parson Lee Farm**, and there branch left onto a narrow path that continues beside the stream. Pass through a gate and continue with the path as it now climbs gently, once more becoming a broad track. It crosses rough pasture to a gate and stile at a junction with a broad track used by the Pendle Way and Brontë Way.

Turn right along the track, but immediately keep right beside a wall to reach a gate, from which a grassy path strikes out across the moorland to enter a long walled section, ending shortly after a gate. Maintain the same direction, passing below **Brink Ends Farm**, and press on to reach Turnhole Clough, spanned by a modern bridge.

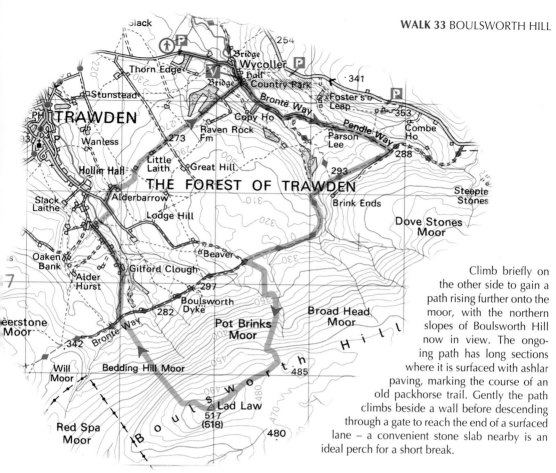

Climb briefly on the other side to gain a path rising further onto the moor, with the northern slopes of Boulsworth Hill now in view. The ongoing path has long sections where it is surfaced with ashlar paving, marking the course of an old packhorse trail. Gently the path climbs beside a wall before descending through a gate to reach the end of a surfaced lane – a convenient stone slab nearby is an ideal perch for a short break.

Reaching the summit of Boulsworth Hill (Lad Law)

The Abbot Stone at the start of the descent from Boulsworth Hill

Boulsworth Hill now rises to the east, a long, low spread of peaty moorland. Directly opposite the stone slab a clear track runs towards the hill, curving initially left to gain the top of a low ridge and leading on to the first of two gates. Go through this, continue to the second, and from this follow a well-defined track rising easily onto the slopes of **Pot Brinks Moor**. The track eventually eases onto the broad ridge of the hill near groups of gritstone boulders that have acquired the names Great and Little Saucer Stones.

Once the summit ridge of **Boulsworth Hill** is gained it is easy to appreciate why this apparently unspectacular peak has been included in the guide. The view is as good as any in the Pennines, served by the fact that Boulsworth Hill, in spite of its modest height – 517m (1696ft) – is the highest in the Southern Pennines. For good measure, it also lies along the Pennine watershed, and when the route of the Pennine Way was being contemplating the hill was for a time considered for inclusion, leading the Way down to Wycoller. But that

was not to be; the Pennine Way now passes some distance to the east. Even so, the hill remains a popular and worthwhile ascent.

The summit, marked by a trig pillar, goes by the name Lad Law, a reference to one of the many gritstone boulders here that, it was said, were a place of Druidic sacrifice. The claim was that *llad* was a Celtic word, meaning 'to kill or slaughter', while *law* is a Saxon word for hill. Today, we know that both 'lad' and 'law' are simply words for boundary markers.

Lending another note of macabre folklore to the place is the tale that a skeleton was once found here leaning against the rocks – that of a man who had lost his way and wandered the moors until he was exhausted, choosing this spot to lie down and die. It is said that the rocks bore the imprint of his body for many years. If so, they are gone now.

Long-distance walkers will be interested to know that Lad Law is one of the Six Trigs Walk developed by Andrew Bibby, starting and finishing at Hebden Bridge and taking in the circle of trig pillars across the moors to the north. Ranged along this arc are six of the Ordnance Survey's trig points: at Bride Stones (SD932268, Walk 38), Black Hameldon (SD913291, Walk 36), Boulsworth Hill (SD930357), Stanbury Moor (SD978357, Walk 34), High Brown Knoll (SE009303) and Crow Hill Nook (SE014278, both Walk 39), a circuit of around 42km (26 miles).

From **Lad Law** trig, head in a roughly westerly direction targeting a waymark pole that begins the long line of descent following what was one of the original concessionary routes onto Boulsworth Hill. This leads unerringly down, passing the conspicuous Abbot Stone, crossing a stile and continuing on across boggy ground eventually to intercept the track of the packhorse trail, used earlier in the walk, near the top of **Will Moor Clough**.

At the track turn left, but after about 40m, at a gate and through-stile, pass into the adjacent pasture and follow a path along the top edge of the clough. Shortly, the path drops into the clough, crossing the stream by a narrow footbridge, from which the route climbs, right, to a step-stile near **Gilford Clough Farm** and cottage. Keep to the right of the farmhouse and pass between outbuildings to emerge onto a surfaced lane. Turn right and follow the lane until it curves into a pronounced dip. Without crossing the stream, turn right through a metal gate and follow a broad path down past a barn and, at the bottom, over a stone bridge. Climb immediately left above the ravine and cross to a stile and gate in a field corner, from where the route runs up the edge of a pasture to another lane. Here, cross a stile and walk for a little over 100m to a signposted access lane on the right leading up to **Alderbarrow Farm**.

Pass around the farm, and just behind it go onto a broad track, still climbing, until it levels and runs on to reach **Little Laithe Farm**. On reaching the farm, pass through two metal gates on the right, and then pass in front of the farmhouse to follow a wet route across fields to Germany Farm. Keep to the left of the farm, and on the other side join its access lane. When this bends distinctly to the left, leave it by going forward across a succession of fields and alongside either a fence or a wall. This leads to **Raven Rock Farm**, where a stile gives into the top corner of a mature plantation.

Now go forward beside a wall, descending all the while along the edge of the plantation until the path joins a surfaced lane that leads, left, down into **Wycoller**, reaching the village at the clapper bridge. Now simply turn left and return to the car park.

Packhorse bridge, Wycoller

Delf Hill and Stanbury Moor

*T*he appellation 'Brontë Moors' is given to a great swathe of ground west of Haworth, setting for
Emily Brontë's only novel, Wuthering Heights, and a geographical fiction more correctly known
as Stanbury Moor and Haworth Moor. Within the folds of this austere but inspiring landscape lie the
ruins of many farms, long since abandoned to the elements, among them Top Withins, which may
have been the inspiration for the fictional Wuthering Heights farmhouse.

The Route

A desire for intimacy with the story of the Brontë
family brings hordes of visitors to Haworth, prompt-
ing a start to this walk away from the clamour and
a route that takes a most tranquil approach to Top
Withins, the so-called Wuthering Heights. The principal objective, however, is an infrequently visited
summit of modest dimensions and character, and a
gathering of ancient stones.

Set off by walking up through **Stanbury** village,
a linear span of stone cottages heavy with age. On
the far side of the village, bear left into Back Lane
(signed for Brontë Waterfall and Upper Heights).
Amble up the lane to take the first turning on the
right (for Buckley Green and Ponden Kirk). Easy
walking ensues, and at the clutch of cottages at
Buckley Green the track bears right, dropping easily
to more cottages. Here, pass through a kissing-gate
on the right and follow a sunken path (signed for the
Pennine Way and Brontë Way) that leads down to
the dam of **Ponden Reservoir**.

↑ *Heading down to Brontë Bridge*

ROUTE INFORMATION

Distance	11km (7 miles)
Height gain	365m (1195ft)
Time	4+hrs
Grade	moderately demanding
Start point	Stanbury SE013371

Getting there
A long strip of roadside parking to the east of Stanbury

Maps
Ordnance Survey OL21 (South Pennines)

After-walk refreshment
Pubs in Stanbury and Haworth

Turn left and follow the lane around the reservoir, climbing eventually to pass Ponden Hall, a listed Elizabethan farmhouse with a Georgian extension, popularly (but probably fancifully) believed to have been the inspiration for Thrushcross Grange in *Wuthering Heights*. Remain on the ascending track beyond Ponden Hall, and climb to a track junction about 200m further on. Here, turn left (for Ponden Kirk), climbing still further to reach Height Laithe Farm. Pass the farm, striding along a gravel track towards Upper Ponden Farm. At the approach to the farm cross a cattle grid and a step-stile ahead giving onto the Walshaw and Lancashire Moor.

Go forward along the ensuing track to a finger-post and turn left onto a narrow field path (signed for Ponden Clough) that leads across to the edge of Upper Ponden Farm. At another signpost bear right beside a wall on your left and later go beyond the wall, following a broad and clear path onto Bracken Hill and around the rim of **Ponden Clough**, with Delf Hill and the Alcomden Stones now discernible on the skyline ahead.

The path swings round the thumb of Ponden Clough, crosses an inflowing stream and wanders on at the edge of heather to a small gritstone platform overlooking the clough. This is Ponden Kirk, also linked to the Brontës as the likely inspiration for

Ponden Reservoir

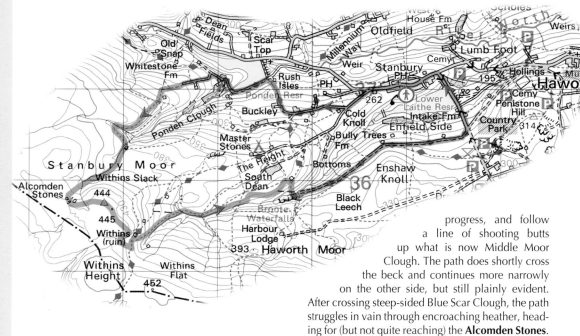

Penistone Crags; a group of tumbledown sheepfolds nearby offers the only protection hereabouts against inclement weather.

A short distance further on, the path arrives directly above a footbridge spanning Ponden Clough Beck. Ignore this, and instead keep heading up the main clough, with intermittent boardwalks aiding progress, and follow a line of shooting butts up what is now Middle Moor Clough. The path does shortly cross the beck and continues more narrowly on the other side, but still plainly evident. After crossing steep-sided Blue Scar Clough, the path struggles in vain through encroaching heather, heading for (but not quite reaching) the **Alcomden Stones**. A short stretch of pathless heather-bashing ensues until the shelter and the spectacular setting of the stones is reached.

This is a beautifully remote and tranquil spot on the edge of a massive tract of open moorland, possibly the largest such area in the South Pennines. To the west rises the hulk of Boulsworth Hill, while to

Alcomden Stones near the summit of Delf Hill

Top Withens

Top Withens plaque

the south-west the edge of Widdop Reservoir can be picked out. This is the land of the moorland birds – red grouse, curlew, golden plover, wheatear, skylark and passing raven – and a place of near perfect silence.

From the Alcomden Stones, a clear path threads a way through the heather and gradually swings in a north-westerly direction, bound for the trig pillar that marks the top of Delf Hill. There is little hereabouts, save heather, views and solitude; in season, the first of these puts on a spectacular display. As mountains go, Delf Hill has few noble characteristics, but it is a spot that many will appreciate, offering views of great arcs of moorland that form the Yorkshire Dales and the valley-hemmed southern Pennines.

From the trig, take the path striking south-east (aim for a distant wind farm); it wanders gently through the heather and grassy moorland until suddenly the ruin of **Top Withins Farm** appears directly below.

The earliest record of the name **Top Withins** ('Withens' in some spellings) is in the 14th century, when it is named simply as Withins; some time in the 17th century it becomes Withens. There are no known records that support a Brontë connection to Top Withins, but it has been passed down locally that the ruins are the inspiration for the celebrated Wuthering Heights farmhouse. The farm was last occupied in 1926, a final outpost of human endeavour in what must have been a difficult landscape.

At Top Withens the Pennine Way is joined, and many a weary leg must take a rest among these celebrated ruins. Here turn left, descending the Pennine Way, but only as far as a fingerpost. From this a path descends stone steps on the right, lower down becoming a more level and wider path following the course of Sladen Beck. Stay along the path to a ladder-stile and continue on to pass through a gap-stile at a wall corner, beyond which lie the scattered remains of walls and buildings. Keep an eye open for a steeper descent on the right to a kissing-gate just above Brontë Bridge.

Over the bridge, turn left and follow a delightful wide track that, after a little ascent, levels and takes a splendid course, gently descending all the while, across the northern flank of **Enshaw Knoll**. After a mile or so of easy walking, with the quarry remains of Penistone Hill Country Park drawing nearer ahead, the track runs out to a road junction. Turn left and descend steeply to cross the dam of **Lower Laithe Reservoir**. A brief climb on the other side, and a turn left at a T-junction, lead back to the eastern end of **Stanbury**.

Wadsworth Moor

A splendid dale, Walshaw Dean, leads onto Withins Height, from where a long moorland tramp heads across the highest ground to join an old packhorse trail at the top of the valley down to Hebden Bridge before concluding with a delightful stretch across Shackleton Moor. The walk explores a stark landscape, initially that of a water-gathering ground, but everywhere is true South Pennine hill country, bogs and all!

The Route

The early stages of this walk are straightforward, easing steadily up the Pennine Way past the Walshaw Dean Reservoirs to the wide moorland ridge above. Much of the route crosses the South Pennines Site of Special Scientific Interest, a remarkable but austere landscape in which the most ecologically important feature is upland bog. The far-reaching views, however, make the entire walk a pleasure.

Leave the parking area and immediately take to a signed path (for Walshaw Dean) that climbs briefly to join a reservoir service road. On drawing level with **Walshaw Dean Lower Reservoir** abandon the service road and descend to cross the reservoir's dam. On the other side, follow the Pennine Way as it turns left (north-east) beside the water's edge. Press on to reach the dam of the **middle reservoir** on the edge of Walshaw and Lancashire Moor, and here take to the lower of two paths, crossing a metal bridge to walk along a raised embankment between the reservoir and a water channel. (The Pennine Way takes the higher route here, but both routes combine further on.)

↑ *Walshaw Dean Middle Reservoir*

ROUTE INFORMATION

Distance	17.5km (11 miles)
Height gain	325m (1065ft)
Time	5–6hrs
Grade	moderately demanding
Start point	Widdop SD947323

Getting there
Roadside parking area at Pennine Way crossing point, Widdop

Maps
Ordnance Survey OL21 (South Pennines)

After-walk refreshment
Pack Horse pub, Blake Dean; pubs and cafés in Hebden Bridge

Follow the watercourse until the accompanying path comes out to meet a broad track (the higher route carrying the Pennine Way). Here, ignore the turning for Upper Walshaw and keep forward through a field gate for **Top Withins**. A short way further on, leave the service track and branch right.

Now simply follow the gently rising, often paved, Pennine Way up Black Clough, which is nothing like as dire as its name suggests.

Just before the highest point of the ascent, in an area largely devoid of helpful landmarks, keep an eye open for a grassy trod branching on the right (SD980347) out onto **Middle Moor**, soon passing a boundary stone. The ongoing path (2.75km/1¾ miles) begins with South Pennine bog at its most

Boundary stone on the high moorland crossing

Approaching the top of the Pennine Way; keep an eye open here for a branching path

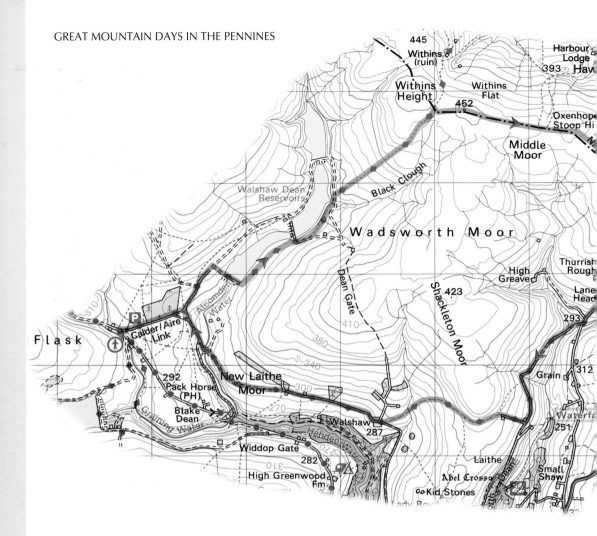

unrelenting, and the path at times is more a theory than a practical reality; expect much dodging about. Navigation across this section in poor visibility requires care and precision, or a GPS device, since it is impossible to cross in a straight line.

Eventually, however, the path does improve as it passes a boundary stone on **Oxenhope Stoop Hill** and heads towards a wall corner. Ignore branching paths and a stile on the left and move on, keeping to the right of a wall, initially on a firm grassy path. Although the early promise of a dryshod passage is not fulfilled, neither is it unremittingly bad. It's just typically Pennine, known as 'The Waste', and such difficulties as there are come and go quickly, leading on directly to a stile in a wall giving onto a broad stony track at a spot known locally as Top of Stairs – because it is at the top of Stairs Lane. At this point the route joins the Calder–Aire Link, a recent route intended to improve access to the Pennine Bridleway.

Now, in complete contrast to what has gone before, turn right to follow what is an ancient packhorse route leading down into Crimsworth Dean, with the distinctive figure of Stoodley Pike directly ahead, beyond Hebden Bridge. The track is easy walking and starts to descend as it passes Thurrish Farm, where it becomes a surfaced lane, descending steeply for a while. At the bottom of the descent, leave the lane by branching right with the Calder–Aire Link onto a vehicle track that soon crosses Paddock Beck, amid an improving pastoral landscape, and rises easily beyond.

Keep on to reach the derelict Nook Farm and there turn right, ascending through a gate and passing Coppy Farm to reach a higher track at another gate. Turn left and follow the ongoing stony track parallel with a wall. On reaching a signpost at

Crossing Paddock Beck

another gate, turn through the gate and then immediately right, walking to the left of a wall that leads the route down past Horodiddle Farm to **Walshaw**.

Keep ahead through the cluster of farm buildings at Walshaw and exit on a broad walled track that leads across the slopes of **New Laithe Moor**, eventually descending to a neat bridge spanning **Alcombe Water**. Beyond, a little more climbing is needed to rejoin the outward route at the edge of a small plantation. Turn left, over a cattle grid, and then retrace the outward route.

The pastoral landscape of Crimsworth Dean

177

Worsthorne Moor
and Black Hameldon

*T*here is a satisfaction about this circuit of Worsthorne Moor that is hard to resist, one founded on clear tracks, easy gradients and lush valleys. Alas, all that ends when the Pennine watershed is reached near the Gorple Stones, for the crossing of Black Hameldon is on pure blanket bog, and the descent to the Long Causeway road is a test for the sturdiest of legs. A visit after prolonged rain is not advised.

The Route

From the car park pass through the nearby gate onto a clear path across rough grazing, walking directly towards the distant Pendle Hill. The path gradually leads down into Shedden Clough, where there is a rash of limestone workings known as 'hushings'.

Trees among Shedden Clough hushings

↑ *Looking back to the Gorple Stones from Hare Stones*

ROUTE INFORMATION

Distance	13km (8 miles)
Height gain	300m (985ft)
Time	5hrs
Grade	moderately demanding
Start point	Long Causeway SD894289

Getting there
Maidens Cross car park, Long Causeway

Maps
Ordnance Survey OL21 (South Pennines)

After-walk refreshment
Pubs in Mereclough and Walk Mill

Shedden Clough **limestone hushings** are the remains of an opencast mining industry that produced lime for local agriculture as a fertiliser. Licences were granted to businessman and landowners to control the water supplies and to opencast the slopes of the valleys. Evidence yet to be encountered on the walk demonstrates that they did so enthusiastically for a time. This created problems for local people, who suffered for generations from an interrupted water supply, often polluted with soil and clay. As a result, it is said that the town of Burnley obtained its name from *burn*, meaning 'brown', and *lea* or *ley*, meaning 'water'; hence 'Burnley' means 'brown water'. More likely, the name is derived from *brun lea*, meaning 'the meadow by the River Brun'.

The descending path shortly meets the Pennine Bridleway and descends further into Shedden Clough; the route remains with the Pennine Bridleway for some time. Lower down, the track swings to the right between walls. Continue down to cross a stream by a footbridge and then walk beside a wall. When the path reaches a substantial bridge, keep right on the Pennine Bridleway for Hurstwood Reservoir.

The track follows an easy course across rough pasture, arriving first at **Cant Clough Reservoir**. Cross the dam, and on the far side pass through a gate and stay on the Pennine Bridleway, climbing briefly between low hills of hushing spoil, a bizarre landscape.

On reaching the edge of **Hurstwood Reservoir**, keep right on the track for Worsthorne. Beyond the end of the reservoir, the route continues with the Pennine Bridleway, still a broad track, easing up onto the moors and climbing to intercept Gorple Road, here part of the Burnley Way. Turn right,

Hurstwood Reservoir

following the obvious track steadily higher onto the moors, with the mass of Black Hameldon becoming ever more distinctive along the skyline ahead.

The track rises steadily to a gate near a fence corner, close by the Gorple Stones, which overlook Gorple Upper Reservoir. Through the gate, now leave the Pennine Bridleway and turn right, descending beside a fence towards a distant group of rocks known as the Hare Stones, and now having joined the course of the Pennine watershed and the boundary between Lancashire and West Yorkshire.

Continue past the Hare Stones and then close in on a step-stile across a fence, near a solitary shooting butt. Cross the fence here and then locate a narrow path running parallel with the fence, but at about 10m distance. The path ascends steadily, and higher up feeds into a shallow peat grough. Continue walking up the centre of the grough to emerge not far from the watershed fenceline, and with the fence continue to plod on across heather moorland. As the ground levels, so boggy ground appears.

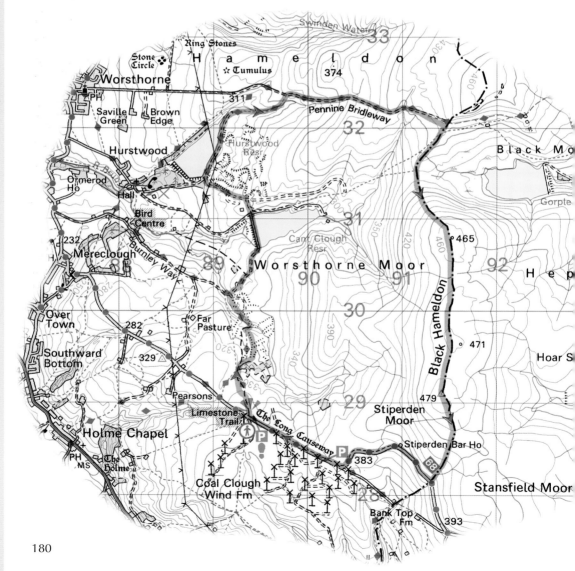

Hare Stones

There is no issue of route finding; the fence is a certain guide all the way to Hoof Stones Height, the summit of **Black Hameldon**, although avoiding the worst excesses of waterlogged ground can involve trying detours. (After prolonged rain, this can be trial by quagmire, but at other times, when the peat is firm, it is most pleasant walking, with a fine sense of open spaces and with the path, continuous throughout if occasionally a little uncertain, leading slowly onwards to the trig pillar that marks the highest point.) From the summit, the view takes in Ingleborough and Pen-y-ghent in the Yorkshire Dales, Pendle Hill and the Forest of Bowland, Blackpool Tower and, in the opposite direction, Stoodley Pike.

The next section, down to the Long Causeway, is the most problematical of the entire walk. Leave the summit in roughly a south-easterly direction, attempting to find and follow an indistinct path that parallels the watershed and county boundary down to the road at SD913282. An alternative is to descend rough heather moorland, aiming for a step-stile at SD910285; the final 30m of this choice are particularly boggy and trying. Both routes present difficult terrain, about which the only good thing is their brevity. Expect a short bout of hard work – a whole grade more difficult than the rest of the walk.

Once the road is reached, turn right and follow it back to the Maidens Cross car park, a maximum distance of 2.3km (1½ miles).

Thieveley Pike and Cliviger Gorge

*T*here is something striking about the serrated north face of Deerplay Moor, of which Thieveley Pike is the highest point – these truncated spurs are particularly dazzling in early morning light. Geologically, this is a remarkable area. The Cliviger Gorge itself is an arresting feature, in many places of rugged countenance, and displays throughout the classic effects of its former use as a direct glacial overflow channel. Most ascents to Thieveley Pike tend to take the direct approach from Holme Chapel, but in this walk a less demanding, more circuitous way is found. The walk ends with a steep descent to the Cliviger Gorge and a few fleeting moments in West Yorkshire before it returns to Lancashire on the ascent to Black Scout on the north of the valley.

The Route

Walk back along the **A646** to the Ram Inn, and just beyond it turn left down a narrow lane that once served the now demolished Holme Chapel station. At the end of the lane, just on reaching the railway line, bear right onto a bridleway for Deer Play and shortly pass through a tunnel beneath the railway line. Turn right following a clear path to a gate, from which the path runs on towards a farm.

↑ Thieveley Pike, early morning

ROUTE INFORMATION

Distance	14.5km (9 miles)
Height gain	463m (1520ft)
Time	5hrs
Grade	demanding
Start point	Holme Chapel SD880279

Getting there
Lay-by along A646, south-east of Holme Chapel

Maps
Ordnance Survey OL21 (South Pennines)

After-walk refreshment
The Ram Inn, Holme Chapel

On reaching the farm go right, through a gate, to pass around it. Press on through a field gate, heading towards a derelict building and farm. At the farm building, bear left on the Pennine Bridleway for Deer Play, soon passing through a metal gate and onto an ascending track. Climb this and then continue up a grassy slope to a field gate. Through this turn onto a broad track and keep climbing to pass through the intake wall, just after which the track swings to the left. Here, at a waymark, leave the prominent track and branch right onto a lower track that crosses rough pasture to intercept the access track to **Cow Side Farm**.

The track runs out to meet the A671, but just before joining the road at the top of Easden Clough turn left onto a gently rising path for Lumb. Walk on up to a bridle-gate in a wall, and through this turn left and now walk alongside the wall as far as a feature known locally as the High Gate (SD860275). Here, pass left through the gate, beyond which the two walls now diverge. Stick with that on the left, which, with only a minor deviation to navigate across the upper reaches of Black Clough, now leads up onto the top of **Deerplay Moor** and the summit trig on **Thieveley Pike**. Just before reaching the trig a stile crosses a fence, but use this only if intending to visit the trig, since another stile just beyond the trig leads back over the fence and on along the Burnley Way.

Derelict farm, Pennine bridleway

Thieveley Pike is an ancient beacon that was used as part of a chain in times of national emergency – Pendle Hill to the north and Blackstone Edge to the south are its near neighbours. What strikes most about Thieveley Pike is the vast landscape that gently undulates into the hazy distance as orange-brown hills punctuated by the bold darkness of gritstone. It's impossible not to notice the wind farm along the southern edge of Stiperden Moor to the north, and closer acquaintance will be made later in the walk. Beyond these huge white sails lie the folds of Worsthorne Moor, Black Hameldon and Boulsworth Hill, into which are tucked some of the many reservoirs for which this area is especially renowned.

Water flowing south from Thieveley Pike is another feature, not least because somewhere among the many springs here rises the River Irwell, which flows on to mighty things before reaching the sea. That, and the east-flowing Calder to the north, puts Thieveley Pike on the Pennine watershed.

Resuming the Burnley Way, a wide grassy path through an ocean of reeds and tussocks is a sure guide to a gate and stile. Maintain the same direction beyond the stile, but when the wall changes direction keep ahead following a narrow trod out onto the expanse of **Heald Moor**. At a waymark, the path swings to the north-east and begins the long and steady descent to the valley. On the way it crosses a wall at a stile, just beyond which a broad farm access track is met. Turn left and follow this all the way down to the valley, in the process entering West Yorkshire on the edge of **Portsmouth**.

Turn right along the A646, pass the Roebuck Inn, and a short way further on turn into Station Parade on a footpath for Kebs Road. Cross the railway line and go forward into an ascending grass-centred track, still on the Burnley Way. At the top of the lane at Monkroyd, cross a stile and then climb the steep shoulder above to a waymark. Keep following the

The summit of Thieveley Pike

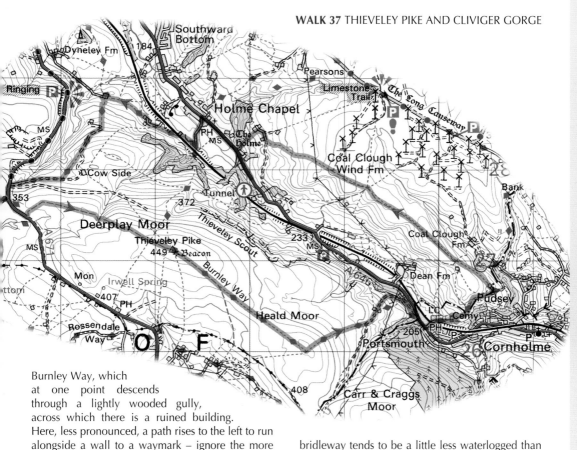

Burnley Way, which at one point descends through a lightly wooded gully, across which there is a ruined building. Here, less pronounced, a path rises to the left to run alongside a wall to a waymark – ignore the more prominent lower track.

Follow the Burnley Way over the shoulder of a hill, then descend a broad track to Brown Birks Farm. Here, leave the Way, keeping instead to the left of the farm to continue along a vehicle track parallel with a wall. A long trek now ensues along the top of Black Scout, with a bridleway on one side of a wall and a footpath on the other. Away to the north, the wind farm looms more closely now. The

bridleway tends to be a little less waterlogged than the footpath. Press on along this ridge, with far-reaching views to the north and the bulk of Deerplay Moor and Thieveley Pike to the south.

On drawing level with an electricity sub-station, cross a stile on the left and walk down beside a wall, letting waymarks take the route onwards when the wall changes direction. Keep an eye open for a waymark that directs the path across a stream on the right, after which, parallel with the stream, it runs down beside a wall to reach an access lane. Turn right and walk towards buildings, using a strange stile to pass an automated gate. On reaching the first building on the left, turn onto a grassy path down its flank to a stile. Descend the ensuing pasture, keeping to the right of a wall, and at the bottom pass into a belt of woodland, through which the path leads down, almost to the valley road. Move briefly to the right to round a building and reach the road, there turning left to return to the lay-by at the start.

Heading across Heald Moor

185

Bride Stones Moor

*T*he moorland heights above the Calder valley have long been popular, a place of gritstone
boulders and lush farmland criss-crossed with myriad ancient tracks and pathways. Numerous
rashes of scattered boulders are a feature of this walk, which climbs easily to one particular group,
known as the Bride Stones. The walk itself is not especially time-consuming, being the shortest walk
in this guide, but it leads into a fascinating landscape that is both a pleasure to dawdle across and a
fine introduction to walking in the South Pennines.

The Route

Start from the car park in **Lydgate** on the A646, heading in a north-westerly direction (away from Todmorden) and walking as far as Stoney Royd Lane (signed for the Calderdale Way). Here, turn right and follow the lane beyond houses and soon pass beneath an arched railway tunnel. Approaching Stannally Farm, the lane steepens; it continues steeply above the farm and then above the edge of Kitson Wood, a deeply cleft wooded ravine.

Press on up the lane, enclosed throughout, to a top gate giving onto the edge of heather and bracken moorland at a waymark post. Here, follow the track to the right, which offers a fine retrospective view of the castle-like Orchan Rocks, to be encountered later in the walk. Follow the path up to pass a farm and, a little higher, to join another track. Turn right and press on through a gate and along more walled track. When the wall ends, keep forward across

↑ *On the summit of Bride Stones Moor*

Distance	10km (6¼ miles)
Height gain	360m (1180ft)
Time	3–4hrs
Grade	moderate
Start point	Lydgate SD929250

Getting there
Large car park opposite the Hare and Hounds pub, Lydgate, and another near the leisure centre

Maps
Ordnance Survey OL21 (South Pennines)

After-walk refreshment
Pub at start; pubs and cafés in Todmorden

reedy moorland, following an ashlar block path. This type of paving is generally accepted as indicative of the course of packhorse trails.

Cross to a gate at a wall corner, and here immediately turn left onto an ascending path that rises above the Whirlaw Stones. At the top of a brief rise

This stony faced character stands beside the track below Windy Harbour

Typical moorland landscape above the Calder valley

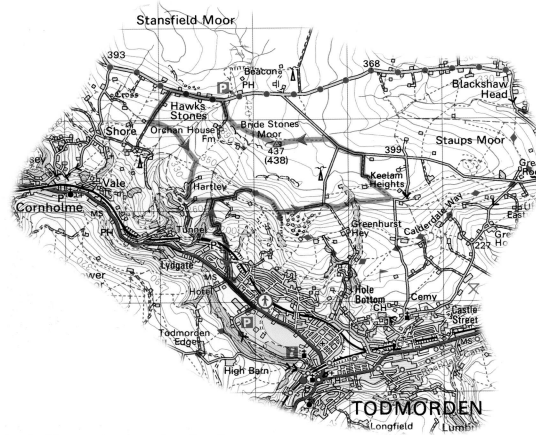

Stoodley Pike comes into view, as the path continues as a grassy track across Whirlaw Common to a gate giving onto another enclosed track. At a road junction, below Windy Harbour, a strange stony faced character is encountered loitering beside the track.

Press on, maintaining the same direction as the track takes a lovely course high on the valley side, passing shortly through another narrow and wooded ravine and then running on towards a surfaced lane. Just before reaching the lane turn left at a waymark, going through a narrow gate and along a grassy path that strikes upfield to reach a collapsed wall. Walk parallel with the wall for a while, shortly passing to the right of a walled field boundary, which leads up to a short section of enclosed track. At its end, turn right and walk out to Eastwood Road, a narrow lane.

Turn left and walk as far as a kissing-gate on the left (SD938268), giving onto **Bride Stones Moor**, the highest point of which, a trig pillar, is now in sight, perched atop a group of gritstone boulders. Follow a grassy path across the moor to the trig, taking time to explore the gritstone display.

The **Bride Stones** form part of a moorland with fine panoramic views across the South Pennines, notably north to Boulsworth Hill (Walk 33), north-west to Black Hameldon (Walk 36), south-east to Stoodley Pike (Walk 40) and Langfield Common (Walk 41), and west across the over-deepened Cliviger Gorge to Thieveley Pike (Walk 37).

The rock type here is known as Lower Kinderscout Grit, which outcrops as much as 5m high, forming a well-defined rock face or edge. The gritstone has been weathered and eroded into unusual-shaped blocks, among which is a 4m-high pedestal rock. For the geologist, there are many sedimentary structures along this edge, including cross bedding, joint patterns, honeycomb weathering and graded bedding, all of which demonstrate the coarse nature of Kinderscout Grit, which forms the distinctive moorland landscape of Upper Calderdale.

First encounter with the Bride Stones

Old sign, Sagar Lane Farm

Continue across the top of Bride Stones Moor, diverting from the path at leisure to explore the many more boulders and edges that lie to the west. The path leads down to a stile/gate giving onto a gravel track, followed out to the Hebden Bridge road. Turn left and walk for about 550m, as far as a bridleway turning on the left (SD921273) for Sagar Lane Farm. Go down a broad track to pass the farm and continue

beyond through an enclosed path rich in spring and summer with wild flowers.

At a track junction (SD919270) turn left for Cross Stone, the bridleway now enclosed between tumbledown walls. Press on to cross Redmire Water and go as far as a turning on the right (SD924265). Here leave the track by turning through a pair of old gate pillars to continue down a track leading to Orchan Rocks. Just below the rocks, a wall-gap beside a gate gives onto a wall-side path leading down to **Lower Hartley Farm**. Turn right through a gate to pass the farm. Just after the farm buildings go left through another narrow gate to pass in front of the farm and then alongside a wall towards Kitson Wood. The wooded ravine is accessed by a gated wall-gap in a corner. Cross the ravine, and a few strides later rejoin the outward route. Turn right, descending, and return to the start of the walk.

Luddenden Dean and Midgeley Moor

*L*uddenden Dean is a collective name for a group of pastures, woodlands, farmsteads and hamlets probing northwards as a lush green wedge into the gently undulating Warley and Midgeley moors. The route traces the course of a couple of catchwater drains linked by Warley Moor Reservoir, a popular spot for yachting. Slight deviations in the second half of the walk visit minor tops, one of which calls for a little heather-bashing. The whole is a delightful circuit – as perfect in winter as on a warm summer's day.

The Route

A stile at the bottom of the car park gives onto a broad descending track above a campsite, leading to a bridge spanning Luddenden Brook. Over the bridge turn right, and immediately take the higher of two paths ascending through woodland. At a junction turn sharply left, climbing on the Calderdale Way. Ignore a flight of steps on the right, and keep ahead to climb gently through broad-leaved woodland join a path beside a wall above hay meadows.

As the ascent eases, the route reaches the end of a level track beside a wall. Follow this, and at its far end climb around an isolated house, The Hullet. Shortly afterwards, intercept surfaced Heys Lane. Turn right briefly and then left, leaving the lane for a bridleway which continues the climb. Eventually the climbing eases, passing Upper Green Edge Farm. Below, to the left, the Luddenden valley is especially pleasing, a lush green finger probing into the moors.

↑ *Luddendean Dean*

ROUTE INFORMATION

Distance	15km (9¼ miles)
Height gain	385m (1265ft)
Time	5hrs
Grade	moderately demanding
Start point	Booth SE037278

Getting there
Jerusalem Farm car park, Booth

Maps
Ordnance Survey OL21 (South Pennines)

After-walk refreshment
Pubs in Luddenden village, Mytholmroyd and
Hebden Bridge

Later the route joins a surfaced lane that leads on to
a collection of buildings at Height Edge.

Among these buildings stands an ornate Gothic
arch, part of the estate belonging to **Castle Carr
House**, a castellated mansion built in 1852 for
Captain Joseph Priestley Edwards of Fixby, who
died in an accident before it was completed. The
house, which was so grand it even had its own
gas works, was occupied for only 20 years, following which it became ruinous and was demolished
in the 1960s, leaving only the gatehouse to tell of
former times.

Just before the arch, take the through-stile on the
right to gain a grassy path for Fly Flatts. The path
climbs easily onto **Warley Moor** and runs up to intercept a seemingly derelict catchwater drain. Here,
turn left following the course of the drain around
Too To Hill, a minor elevation at the edge of the
moor. The drain ends at a group of settlement tanks,
but from here a narrow path presses on, contouring
across the moor and still following a drainage ditch,
although shortly this, too, comes to an end.

The route now runs on as a narrow grassy path
towards the head of the valley. The path is continuous throughout and leads on to intercept a
reservoir service track. Turn right along this to the
edge of **Warley Moor Reservoir**. When the track
reaches a T-junction near a valve house, walk
around the building and climb up onto the reservoir embankment.

Approaching Warley Moor Reservoir

The view, especially south-westwards, is inspirational, a scene of gently undulating moorland reaching beyond prominent Stoodley Pike to the northern edges of the Peak District. Across the valley Midgeley Moor awaits, and is reached by continuing along the embankment to its far end. There, turn through a gate and join a path alongside a concrete catchwater drain. Now simply stride out alongside the drain for the next 2.4km (1½ miles) as far as a path junction at SE014301, by a bridge over the drain and a marker pole. The route here bears left, but this is an opportunity to extend the walk a little (700m each way) by taking the right-hand path and following this up, past a marker stone, to the trig pillar on **High Brown Knoll**. This is no Matterhorn, but it is the highest point of the walk. Return to the bridge and path junction.

Turn down the path, descending heather moorland. Follow this as it runs down into a dip at SE016293. On leaving the dip, look for an indistinct grassy path on the right that picks a way through heather, becoming less and less clear until in the end a short bout of heather-bashing is called for – a line of shooting butts is a rough guide.

Eventually, intercept a clear path running north–south. Turn left along this, climbing easily onto Crow Hill, with fine views out across the Calder valley. When the path forks at SE016285, keep right along a fine trod that skims through the heather and leads directly to the trig pillar on **Crow Hill**.

From the trig, take the most pronounced of the radiating paths, targeting Stoodley Pike. The path soon frees itself from the heather and descends steeply to a stile at a wall corner, where the Calderdale Way is rejoined. Turn left, walking beside the wall, and when the path divides take the lower option, which later turns the end of the wall

Standing stone on High Brown Knoll

and starts to descend. The ongoing path continues to follow the Calderdale Way, which is clearly way-marked across moorland pasture. Above an intake wall and fence at SE024271 keep left, still following the Calderdale Way, which here runs alongside the intake wall.

Continue above the intake, which gradually changes direction, heading roughly northwards beside a fence and then a wall. Eventually the path closes in on a narrow lane on the right, and finally joins it as the fence reaches a wall and gate/stile (or at an earlier step-stile). Turn left down the lane, descending, now with much of the day's walk up the valley gloriously opening up to the front and left.

Follow the lane down, and after a right-hand bend turn sharply left into Dry Carr Lane. Keep following the lane down until a signpost on the left is reached for Jerusalem Farm. Here the choice is either to leave the lane at this point and follow a woodland footpath down to rejoin the outward route at the bridge over Luddenden Brook; or, easier, to simply continue down the lane to reach the entrance to the farm to complete the walk.

Retrospective view of Crow Hill from the Calderdale Way

Stoodley Pike

*A*lthough the Pennine Way chooses not to visit Hebden Bridge, passing by the town to the west, the presence of Stoodley Pike and a wealth of moorland pastures and complex network of paths ensures that Hebden receives its share of visiting walkers. This walk follows a good section of the Pennine Way over the high ground before it descends through the splendid Pennine village of Lumbutts to return to Hebden along the towpath of the Rochdale Canal.

Hebden Bridge is a traditional mill town snugly accommodated in the confines of the Calder valley – a busy community, proud of its heritage and of the friendly welcome it extends to visitors. Any preconception that here is nothing more than the stark grimness of an industrial past is soon dispelled. Modern-day Hebden is full of bright shops, cafés, restaurants and pubs, and has an amazing architectural heritage, too.

The Route

Leave the town centre car park and cross the main road into Holme Street, walking past the Hebden Bridge Little Theatre and the post office. At the end of the street turn up onto the towpath of the Rochdale Canal. On the other side turn right, and shortly go left over the River Calder to ascend a flight of steps. At the top, turn right and walk out to join a back road, there going left over

↑ *Stoodley Pike*

ROUTE INFORMATION

Distance	15.5km (9½ miles)
Height gain	405m (1330ft)
Time	4–5hrs
Grade	demanding
Start point	Hebden Bridge SD992272

Getting there

Town centre car park (pay and display, max 4hrs), Hebden Bridge

Maps

Ordnance Survey OL21 (South Pennines)

After-walk refreshment

Pubs, cafés, tearooms in Hebden Bridge

Break free of the woodland to a view of hillside pastures, and climb past Wood Top Farm. Continue up the lane behind the farm, and then up a cobbled continuation. At the top of the climb, at a T-junction (with farm buildings off to the right), bear left over a cattle grid onto a rough track towards a farm. At the turning into the farm, keep forward through a metal gate, now climbing an enclosed track. At the top, pass through a gate and turn right onto a footpath beside a fence that leads to a stile and bridle-gate giving on to a walled track. This leads up a track junction with Kilnshaw Lane.

Keep left towards Erringden Grange, and soon Stoodley Pike monument comes into view ahead. At the next lane junction, keep forward towards **Erringden Grange** and Kilnshaw Farm. Kilnshaw Lane is mostly level and easy walking, passing scattered farmsteads, and offers improving views along the Calder valley to Todmorden and the distant Cliviger Gorge.

Go all the way to Swillington Farm, then just beyond it pass through a gate in the intake wall and press on to a signpost at the junction with the Pennine Way. Turn left, following the Way onto the moors

a railway bridge into Palace House Road. Follow the road through a residential area, and after passing the railway station, to which the road gradually descends, swing right onto a rising concrete lane into woodland.

The Rochdale Canal at Hebden Bridge

Close-up of Stoodley Pike

From the Pike, take to a clear path south along the edge of Higher Moor and follow this through low-lying gritstone boulders until eventually it descends to a large and prominent stone pillar at Withens Gate, which marks the start of the descent. But before hastening in that direction, it is worth diverting along a level track running in a south-easterly

beneath a prominent outcropping of gritstone known as the Doe Stones. The path is in part gravelled and climbs to pass through walls, after which it leads directly to **Stoodley Pike**, and the opportunity to take a break and admire the austere Pennine landscape that rolls away as far as you can see.

After more than 20 years of warfare against Revolutionary – and (from 1799) Napoleonic – France, Napoleon's exile to Elba in 1814 prompted the construction of a monument to peace on **Stoodley Pike**. Unfortunately, Napoleon escaped and returned to France in March 1815, overthrew the restored monarchy, and began his reign of a 'Hundred Days'. Work on the monument to peace was halted, but completed shortly after Napoleon's defeat at Waterloo (18 June 1815).

In 1854 the monument collapsed, and the present tower, solid, soot-blackened and with few outstanding features save its internal staircase to a balcony, was built two years later. It stands about 38m (125ft) tall and is one of the best-known landmarks in the Pennines.

direction for about 250m to a gate in a wall, just beyond which stands the Te Deum Laudamus stone.

The **Te Deum Laudamus** stone is inscribed with a cross, the initials ID, and the Latin words 'Te Deum Laudamus', which translate as 'We praise Thee, O Lord'. The stone has long been regarded as sacred, and coffins were rested here during long journeys along the packhorse route between Cragg Vale and Mankinholes in the Pennines. It was probably used as a marker or guide stone, of which there are many throughout the Pennines.

Te Deum Laudamus stone

Marker stone at Withens Gate

The path out to the stone is partially surfaced with ashlar blocks, typical of those used elsewhere in the Pennines along packhorse trails, such as the one onto Blackstone Edge and on Stanage Edge in Derbyshire. From Withens Gate, where the Pennine Way is now left, a paved path descends in a westerly direction towards the hamlet of Mankinholes. Follow the path down to a wall corner, with two gates nearby. Here, turn through the right-hand gate and walk a wide walled track to **Mankinholes**.

Press on through the village, and after passing the Old Sunday School bear left, leaving the road for the Pennine Bridleway, now another ashlar-paved track between walls that leads down to the hamlet of Lumbutts, close by the Top Brink Inn (formerly the Dog and Partridge). Here, turn immediately right around Brink Top cottage to gain a walled path between houses that leads to a hand-gate giving into the bottom of a sloping pasture. Keep forward beside walls to a wall-gap, something of a squeeze-stile between two ancient gateposts and a triangular standing stone.

Through the gap turn half-right onto a grassy path, following the Calder Way Link Path. At a wall, the path starts to descend towards **Lumbutts**. Continue following the descending track, which leads down to a lane. Here turn right and follow the lane down to reach the **Rochdale Canal**. Across the bridge, descend steep steps to gain the towpath, and now simply follow the towpath all the way back to **Hebden Bridge**, a distance of 5km (3 miles).

Descending the walled lane to Mankinholes

Langfield Common

*L*angfield Common is the name of a large swathe of moorland rising to the east of the Todmorden–Littleborough valley. There are many individually named moors here, all of them valuable contributors to the climatic well-being of the planet by their absorption of unwanted carbon gases into the peat. This circuit of the moors, and the reservoirs they contain, is the easiest walk in the book, being virtually flat and on good tracks or paths throughout. What it offers, apart from suitability for a lazy day, is an intimate acquaintance with the blanket bog that sits astride the Pennine watershed.

The Route

The walk begins along a stretch of the Pennine Way, which here runs northwards from Blackstone Edge. What becomes immediately evident is that this is a precious environment – reservoir land used to feed the Rochdale Canal in the valley below, as well as the people of Rochdale – and it is rare to find the reservoirs visited on this walk anything other than full.

Some find this austere landscape dreary and uninteresting, but it provides an elevated view of things and far-reaching views, regardless of whether you view it as the roof of Lancashire or the roof of Yorkshire. Blanket bog does prevail, yet this environment is interesting in itself now that its function in capturing and retaining carbon gases is better understood than of old.

↑ *Crossing Turley Holes Moss (Stoodley Pike in the distance)*

199

Rain Rock, inscribed with a poem by Simon Armitage

ROUTE INFORMATION

Distance	15km (9¼ miles)
Height gain	92m (300ft)
Time	4hrs
Grade	moderate
Start point	near The White House pub SD969179

Getting there
Car park adjoining the A58, just west of The White House pub

Maps
Ordnance Survey OL21 (South Pennines)

After-walk refreshment
Pub at start; pubs and cafés in Littleborough and Todmorden

Walk up past **The White House** to a metal gate giving onto the Pennine Way, where a level service track runs below the dam of **Blackstone Edge Reservoir**. The whole area is part of the Turley Holes and Higher House Moor project site managed by 'Moors for the Future', which covers 665 ha of Site of Special Scientific Interest (SSSI) blanket bog. The fluffy white heads of cottongrass – a sedge that manages to grow in boggy conditions – are evident throughout most of the year and used to be collected to stuff pillows.

As the track leads on, accompanied by a man-made drainage ditch to one side, it reaches a conspicuous pile of gritstone outcrops on the right. Into the base of this, a poem – 'Rain', by Simon Armitage – has been carved:

Be glad of these freshwater tears, each pearled droplet some salty old sea-bullet air lifted out of the waves, then laundered and sieved, recast as a soft bead and returned.

And no matter how much it strafes or sheets, it is no mean feat to catch one raindrop clean in the mouth, to take one drop on the tongue, tasting cloud pollen, grain of the heavens, raw sky.

Let it teem, up here where the front of the mind distils the brunt of the world.

Continue a short way further along the track, and when it divides at a signpost (SD962194), just before reaching overhead powerlines, turn right onto the 'Reservoir Circuit' for White Holme and follow a broad track around **White Holme Reservoir**. At the southern edge of the reservoir, the track divides again. Here, keep left alongside the reservoir and then pass along the north-eastern dam to reach **White Holme Drain**, and turn right along this. At a small sluice a gate is encountered, and beyond this point the broad track deteriorates into a narrow path, but remains constant throughout. To the right (east) the land falls steadily into Turvin Clough, beyond which it rises again to the low hill of Manshead End.

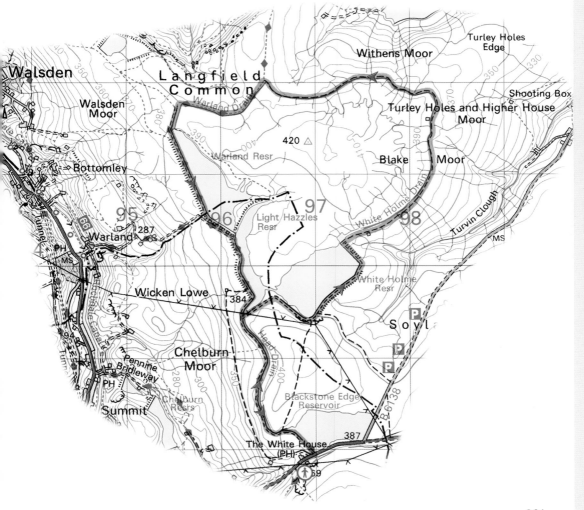

Interior of derelict cottage

As Stoodley Pike eases into view, so the path changes direction to reach the Cloven Stone (SD981219), a convenient place to take a break. A little way further on, the remains of a small cottage are equally suited to having a rest.

For a while, just beyond the cottage, the going is less accommodating until a gate is reached and the route enters an area where peat regeneration is being carried out. New fences have been erected here to allow vegetation to grow and to reduce sheep grazing. After the gate, a culverted stream is encountered (contained in concrete pipes) and followed until it ends. Now, press on to another gate directly north of the obvious Holder Stones on the moor to the south (not named on the 1:50,000 map).

Eventually, the ongoing path emerges through another gate to meet up again with the Pennine Way. Turn left and follow this along **Warland Drain**, which flows into Warland Reservoir, on the way joining the Todmorden Centenary Way. Easy walking on a broad track leads back to the point where earlier in the walk the route divided to head for White Holme Reservoir. From this point simply retrace the outward route.

Warland Reservoir

Blackstone Edge

*U*p here is the top of the world – 'the Andes of England', as Daniel Defoe called it. Sandwiched between the Peak District National Park and the Aire Gap, this vast moorland rises easily from the industrial valleys of East Lancashire. The ridge of Blackstone Edge forms the boundary between Yorkshire and Lancashire, and this ascent to it from the shores of Hollingworth Lake is a joy at any time of year – a moorland walk of no great difficulty, historically interesting and a firm favourite since Victorian times. In spite of a covering of peat and gritstone, the going, even along the summit ridge where the Pennine Way is joined, is nowhere strenuous, and there is only one short stretch not on a footpath of one kind or another.

The Route

The ascent of Blackstone Edge has been popular since Victorian times. Yet with only two accounts to go on – of Celia Fiennes (who came in 1698 and found Blackstone Edge to be 'a dismal high precipice') and Daniel Defoe (who in 1724 found the character of the country so awe-inspiring – 'the most desolate, wild and abandoned country in all England' – that it made the horses uneasy and frightened the dog) – it is a wonder that anyone ever ventured this way again. But theirs is only one side of the story, for mild spring days and the summer sun, aired by gentle breezes, create a different scene, one of

↑ Blackstone Edge forms the skyline above Lydgate farmland

ROUTE INFORMATION

Distance   15km (9¼ miles)
Height gain   335m (1100ft)
Time   5hrs
Grade   demanding
Start point   Hollingworth Lake SD940153

Getting there
Visitor centre car park, Hollingworth Lake, near Littleborough

Maps
Ordnance Survey OL21 (South Pennines)

After-walk refreshment
Café in Hollingworth Lake visitor centre; pubs and cafés in Littleborough

uninterrupted views reaching as far as north Wales, of long, leg-swinging days tramping the moors, of peaceful, sheltered corners, and the trill of curlew.

Hollingworth Lake was constructed in 1801 as a reservoir to keep the levels of the Rochdale Canal topped up. To the Victorians it was a source of pleasure and entertainment, of steamboat rides, dancing, merrymaking and drinking. In terms of popularity not a lot has changed, and most weekends will find the lake and its environs thronged with visitors.

Beyond the visitor centre car park, follow a broad track north-eastwards beneath **Cleggswood Hill**. When the track veers right, leave it by going left onto a path (waymarked) along the edge of light woodland, not far from a dipping pond. Cross a narrow footbridge and continue with the stream until a minor road is reached near Lane Foot Farm. A neat wooded valley runs left here to the Littleborough suburb of Ealees, and another, less immediately obvious, to the right of the great prow of hill directly ahead. To reach it, proceed left alongside the stream for a short distance, just as far as a flight of steps on the right that climb towards the farm before veering across the lower spine of the ridge into the adjacent valley. Another wooden bridge spans the valley

Heading up the Roman road onto Blackstone Edge

stream. This narrow valley and its nearby counter-part are quiet now, sylvan glades, but were at one time busy with coal mining. Mining was made easy by the presence of coal seams at very shallow depth, often reaching the surface and accessible simply by digging into the hillside, using techniques known locally as 'light holes' or 'breast eas'.

At the top edge of the woodland, cross to a gate giving onto the edge of a golf course. Through the gate, follow a path ahead across the course, which soon becomes a broad track along the edge of one of the fairways. Especially visible now, Blackstone Edge rises like a distant castle wall, fretting along the distant skyline. Once beyond the golf course, go left to a metalled roadway leading north to the row of cottages at **Lydgate**.

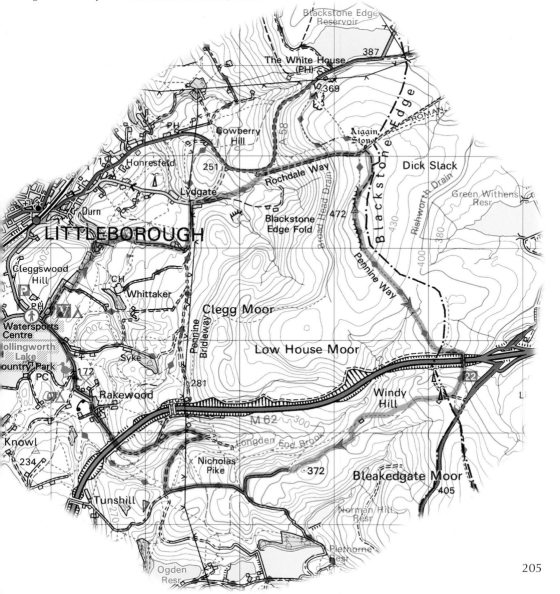

The **Lydgate cottages** were built by Sir Alfred Law of Durn and Lydgate Mills, who was MP for the High Peak Division of Derbyshire. Nearby Lydgate Mill was a typical early example of a cotton mill, built where it could make most effective use of water from Red Brook for power. The mill's 'tenterground' was on the south-facing hillock on the other side of the stream. Here woollen cloth was stretched on hooks to dry and bleach in the sun – hence the expression 'on tenterhooks'.

At Lydgate, turn right just before reaching the main road, passing in front of the cottages, to gain an undulating path beside a wall that leads to within a few strides of the **A58**.

Here the walk sets about the steepest part of the walk, following a line of controversy. On maps, the line is marked as a 'Roman road' – but is it?

That the **trans-Pennine road** over Blackstone Edge was a medieval packhorse route is not in question: in 1286 there was a complaint to the Sowerby Constables which mentions the route being used to carry salt. Similarly, in 1291 Richard de Radeclive and Hugh Elland were granted permission to levy custom for two years on goods for sale carried over 'Blacksteynegge'.

The earliest suggestion that this route might be of Roman origin was made by William Stukely in 1725, with numerous subsequent opinions supporting or rejecting this claim. The point of controversy lies in the way the road is paved. Sometimes referred to as 'Dhoul's Pavement', a corruption of 'Devil's Pavement', it is some 5.5m (18ft) wide, with kerbs, and a fine example of ashlar paving. Down the centre of the road is a shallow trough either cut or worn in the stones. Many theories have been advanced as to its purpose, the most commonly accepted being that the trough acted as a guide for vehicles descending the incline, which in places is quite steep, achieving a gradient of 25 per cent (or 1 in 4).

The road is in many respects Roman in construction, and could have formed part of a route from Manchester (Mancunium) to York (Eboracum) or Ilkley (Olicana). Not far away was found the silver arm of a statue of Victory, to which was attached a silver plate inscribed with a dedication to Valerius Rufus of the Sixth

The Aiggin Stone, a medieval travellers' waymark

Legion, which accompanied Hadrian into Britain and was stationed in Northumbria, at York and at Ribchester. So, the balance of probability suggests Roman antecedents, but no one really knows.

At the high point of the road, the Pennine Way crosses on its way north over Chelburn Moor to the White Horse Inn on the Halifax road. At this juncture stands a prominent stone, the **Aiggin Stone** (pronounced 'ay-jin'), inscribed with a Latin cross and the initials 'IT'. While this could be a Roman navvy's autograph, it is more likely to be the handiwork of one of the 19th- and 20th-century vandals whose names are etched into numerous road blocks, and especially on the summit rocks all along Blackstone Edge – Timothy Iveson (1826), Abraham Rhodes (1838) and Loft Lads (1864), to name but a few.

At the Aiggin Stone, leave the cross-ridge route and turn right over a low stile to traverse an area of peat and gritstone towards the top of **Blackstone Edge**. The summit trig is perched atop a massive gritstone boulder and is awkward to attain.

All the summit rocks here are excellent vantage points from which to survey the bracken-clad hillside rolling gently towards the intake fields and distant Hollingworth Lake.

Several of the boulders display fine examples of splash erosion and chemical weathering in the form of bowl-shaped hollows or pot-holes. The largest outcrop has, inevitably, attracted a name, and is known as 'Robin Hood's Bed'. The name of **Robin Hood** occurs quite frequently throughout the southern Pennines and the Peak, formerly a vast tract of land stretching from here to the East Midlands, the medieval hunting forest of Sherwood.

Robin Hood is not a name invented to adorn a legend, for he was almost certainly a Yorkshireman who died and is buried at Kirklees Priory, near Brighouse; Maid Marion came from Wakefield, and Little John is buried at Hathersage. After 600 years, fact and legend have become inseparable, and who would want to destroy the myth? Nevertheless, Robin Hood was an outlaw of a kind common in years past – a moss trooper, perhaps, who would have found these Pennine fastnesses ideal easily defended bases for foraging and marauding expeditions... taking only from the rich and giving to the poor, of course.

From the summit of Blackstone Edge, the Pennine Way slips easily towards the trans-pennine motorway (M62) and the distant radio masts on Windy Hill. Continue in this direction and ultimately cross the splendid bridge carrying the Way high above the **motorway**. On the other side stay on the Pennine Way a short distance further until it is possible to branch right to pass between the two radio masts. A broad track sets off across **Windy Hill**, now heading roughly in a south-westerly direction. The route is undulating, clear and follows fences and walls to be guided in due course into the end of a walled track.

Follow the track to a junction (SD960133) where it meets the Pennine Bridleway, which here is also part of the Rochdale Way. Turn right, following a walled track (known as Tunshill Lane) to another obvious junction (SD952133). Here turn right, through a gate, and take a broad track as it descends northwards across the shoulder of **Nicholas Pike**. The track swings into an easterly direction before reaching another junction.

Now turn left and walk down past an isolated cottage, through a gate, and then remain on the Pennine Bridleway to be guided beneath the **motorway** to meet the end of a surfaced lane near Schofield Hall. All that remains now is to follow the lane, which emerges at the southern edge of **Hollingworth Lake**, and then continue on to the visitor centre car park.

The summit of Blackstone Edge

Rooley Moor and Cowpe Lowe

*W*ind turbines are an ever-present feature of this walk, but – other than visually – they do nothing to detract from the quality of the walk. These moors, not far from Rochdale, have always attracted industry, although it is little in evidence these days. The track across the upper section of Rooley Moor, above the Spodden valley, has for generations been known as the 'Cotton Road' or 'Cotton Famine Road', and visitors will be surprised to encounter a substantial Victorian cobbled road. The moors, although predominantly peat bog and heather, are nowhere oppressive, and rise gently to a maximum height of 474m (1555ft) at oddly named Top of Leach.

Scout Moor Wind Farm, above Rochdale, is the largest onshore wind farm in England, and was built for Peel Wind Power Ltd. It produces enough electricity to serve the average needs of 40,000 homes. A protest group was formed to resist the proposed construction, and attracted support from the botanist and environmental campaigner David Bellamy. Despite the opposition, planning permission was granted in 2005, and construction began in 2007. Although work on the project was hampered by harsh weather, difficult terrain and previous mining activity, the wind farm was officially opened in 2008.

↑ *Heading for Cowpe Lowe*

ROUTE INFORMATION

Distance 20km (12½ miles)
Height gain 492m (1615ft)
Time 6–7hrs
Grade strenuous
Start point Ashworth Moor Reservoir
SD831158

Getting there
Roadside parking on A680 at Ashworth Moor Reservoir

Maps
Ordnance Survey OL21 (South Pennines)

After-walk refreshment
Owd Betts pub at start; pubs in Edenfield and Rochdale

The Route
Cross the road and take the signposted track onto Ashworth Moor. Shortly, when the path intercepts another, turn left towards the wind turbines. A short distance further on, when the path divides at a low post, keep right, climbing onto the bilberry- and

heather-covered moorlands. Soon Knowl Hill comes into view, a distinctive profile recognisable from many parts of the South Pennines.

Just before reaching a couple of stiles spanning a fence, a path doubles back on the right and crosses the course of an old track to join a path on the other side. Turn left along this and follow it to a gate, beyond which a clear path leads up onto **Knowl Hill**, topped by a trig pillar, a low stone shelter and the remains of a viewpoint indicator.

From the trig, head east, targeting the southern-most of the wind turbines and following a narrow grassy path. The path passes close by the base of the wind turbine and continues across the moor, gradually closing in on a high wall. Beyond this the ground falls dramatically into the valley of Naden Brook, today occupied by reservoirs.

Just as the ground drops steeply, the wall is crossed at an awkward through-stile. Continue then on a narrow path that skims along the top of the hill slope, high above the reservoirs. Cross a stile at a wall corner and continue, still above the steep drop, following waymarked poles that denote the Rochdale Way. Press on to a bridle-gate, after which a broad grassy track descends to **Greenbooth Reservoir**.

Knowl Hill

Through a lower gate, go forward between a couple of trees and then turn left to join a track now heading back up the valley, below the steep slopes just crossed. On reaching Naden Middle Reservoir, turn right to cross its **dam**, and on the other side take the broad service track through a gate and rising steadily out of the valley. At the top of the climb, cross a cattle grid and keep forward on a broad track, continuing past the end of a surfaced lane. About 150m further on, as the track divides, branch left (SD862162) onto a stony track onto **Rooley Moor**.

When the track next divides, before reaching overhead powerlines, branch left, following a track that comes out to intercept the Pennine Bridleway, which becomes a companion for the next hour or more. As far as the moorland high point, known as Top of Leach, the road, still cobbled in stretches, is known as the Cotton Famine Road.

It is claimed that the **Cotton Famine Road** was built in the 1860s to alleviate unemployment caused by the Union blockade of Confederate ports during the American Civil War. The blockade led to shortages of raw cotton supplies to Lancashire, at that time the world's leading

On Rooley Moor, with Knowl Hill in the distance

producer of finished cotton goods. Although supplies of cotton from India and Egypt continued, the deficit caused by the lack of American supplies was described at the time as a 'famine'. Such a description must have been agonising for the numerous Irish migrants who had sought sanctuary in the mill towns of Lancashire as a result of the Potato Famine in Ireland in the 1840s and 1850s. They had swapped the blighted fields of Ireland for struggling Lancashire mills.

Rochdale district had a mixed economy, with wool and fustian textile production in addition to cotton. However, there remained significant hardship for many in the town as a result of the American Civil War. As the Battle of Gettysberg raged in July 1863, the Rochdale (Poor Law) Union minutes recorded almost 20,000 families in receipt of 'outdoor relief' – an oblique reference to the widespread poverty and starvation that was occurring. In those days before the welfare state, Rochdale, like many other Lancashire districts, organised its own Cotton Famine Relief Fund.

211

In spite of all these tempting links, maps from the 1850s show ditches along the line of the Cotton Famine Road, suggesting that it is probably an unfinished road from Saddleworth.

The track continues on along the upper moorland. Shortly after passing a brightly coloured signpost at the head of a mountain-bike trail, leave the main track and bear left to the trig and comfy shelter on Top of Leach (not named on the 1:50,000 map). This also goes by the name Hail Storm Hill and is a Marilyn. From here, take a gently descending grassy path heading westwards towards a clear escarpment edge, with Cowpe Lowe now coming into view in the far distance.

The path gradually leads down to **Cragg Quarry**, an old site now given to a number of mountain-bike trails, one of which runs through the lower part of the quarry and soon appears as a level and direct route across the moorland edge.

Continue along the track until, finally, it passes through a bridle-gate and continues beyond towards Cowpe Lowe. At a track junction (SD829203), keep right at a fork on the Pennine Bridleway. (Anyone not wishing to continue to Cowpe Lowe should keep left at this junction and descend to a lower track near an old gatepost, there turning left to take the ongoing route.)

At the next junction, at a Pennine Bridleway signpost, take to a narrow path, the middle one of three, that runs along the top of a narrow embankment. Follow this just as far as a clear path ascending steeply to a collapsed wall on the edge of **Cowpe Lowe**, with the summit trig just a short distance away. The view from here notably includes the Peel Monument on Holcombe Moor, Winter Hill and distant Darwen Tower.

Return to the Pennine Bridleway sign and branch right onto the lower of two paths, crossing to an old gate pillar (the shortened route joins here). Go forward on a broad track beside a dilapidated wall, which later joins a more substantial track rising across the moors. When this track divides, take the higher option, which soon leads to Foe Edge Farm, visited by

the Lancashire dialect writer Edwin Waugh, who came here in the 1860s to convalesce.

Press on beyond a stile, and a short way further on reach Waugh's Well, a welcome resting point on a warm day, issuing clear and refreshing spring water. Gradually the path winds up through the narrowing ravine of Scout Moor Brook. The ascent is pleasant and gradual, and ends just beyond a couple of ancient gate pillars. Now keep forward to cross a wind-farm service road and go ahead onto a long, descending stony track.

Walk for almost 1.6km (1 mile), as far as a tall ladder-stile on the left (SD824177); cross this and keep to the right, descending a large enclosed pasture. At the bottom, at a gate, turn left, keeping to the left of a fence and later a wall, and passing through a brief damp, pathless passage of tussock and reed. At the end of the wall, a stile gives onto a flight of steps leading down to cross Cheesden Brook. On the other side, continue beside a collapsed wall heading for the site of Paradise Farm, marked by a solitary tree.

Press on to the reach the ruins of another farm building, and from there walk up the sloping grassy path across the side of Tom Hill. The path then continues alongside a tumbledown wall and leads down to a ladder-stile spanning a wall above Cheesden Fold Farm. Beyond this a gently rising path cuts across a hill slope in the direction of **Ashworth Moor Reservoir** and the conclusion of the walk.

Waugh's Well on Foe Edge

White Hill and Piethorne Clough

*P*iethorne Clough, to the east of Milnrow, holds a number of reservoirs created to supply the developing towns between Rochdale and Oldham. High above the clough, to the east, rises the comparatively insignificant White Hill, which nonetheless hosts the Pennine Way and the Pennine watershed, and provides extensive views over Lancashire and Yorkshire. Making use of the Pennine Bridleway, the walk begins at Hollingworth Lake and wanders up into the folds of numerous small hills that work effectively to combat the sight and sound of the M62 motorway. Once White Hill is gained, a fine return is made first across a corner of the Marsden Moor Estate and then down to the reservoirs.

The Route

There is nothing to suggest to high-speed motorists on the nearby M62 that to the south lies a convoluted landscape of cloughs, deans and reservoirs, once very much geared to industry, which, while still providing a water-supply service, is now a splendid landscape amid which walkers, cyclists and horse riders can roam in peace and quiet. This walk makes the most of the area, using sections of the Pennine Bridleway as well as the Pennine Way itself, rising first to a high point on White Hill before picking a way through the numerous waterways. For good measure, the highest section also follows the Pennine watershed.

↑ Retrospective view on the approach to Windy Hill

ROUTE INFORMATION

Distance   21km (13 miles)
Height gain   430m (1410ft)
Time   5–6hrs
Grade   demanding
Start point   Hollingworth Lake SD940153

Getting there
Visitor centre car park, Hollingworth Lake, near Littleborough

Maps
Ordnance Survey OL21 (South Pennines)

After-walk refreshment
Café in Hollingworth Lake visitor centre; pubs and cafés in Littleborough

Begin by leaving the visitor centre car park and walk out to the road, turning left beside the lake, and following the surfaced lane to the hamlet of **Rakewood**. At Schofield Hall Road, keep forward

and press on to pass beneath the **motorway**, then continue beyond on a broad track above **Longden End Brook**. Keep following the track, and just beyond a gate near an isolated cottage and bridge bear right, rising gently. After about 200m, swing right with the Pennine Bridleway, following a clear track as it climbs to a junction (with Tunshill Lane: not named on 1:50,000 maps). Here, turn left and walk up a walled lane until it divides at a signpost (SD960133). Here, leave the Pennine Bridleway by branching left onto another walled track for Windy Hill.

When the walled track ends, go forward, ascending a low shoulder. The ongoing path levels briefly as it runs on beside a tumbledown wall, but then starts to descend to take to a path passing to the south of **Windy Hill**, and finally rises as a narrow trod to reach the compound housing a large radio mast.

On passing the main radio mast, bear right and head out towards the A672, but before reaching it join an obvious path, the southbound Pennine Way. Cross the A-road (occasional mobile refreshment van here) and, through a gate, follow a clear route up to the trig pillar on **White Hill**. In spite of

its evident prominence in relation to the surrounding landscapes, White Hill has no distinction other than as a superb viewpoint – one from which the view extends northwards to and beyond Stoodley Pike, and south to Standedge and the Wessenden and Saddleworth moors.

Press on across the top of White Hill and later, at a stile and fence, enter the National Trust's Marsden Moor Estate, here a small corner of a much larger estate of 2429 ha (5685 acres) based on the town of Marsden to the east. The manor of Marsden originally belonged to the crown and formed part of the Honour of Pontefract, which was granted to William the Conqueror in 1067. The estate supports large numbers of moorland birds such as the golden plover, red grouse, curlew and twite, and is designated a Site of Special Scientific Interest.

The ongoing path eventually leads down to reach the

Approaching Windy Hill

A640. Here turn right, descending and using the roadside verge to evade passing traffic. Walk only as far as a gate and stile on the right (a Restricted Byway) giving onto a broad track. Walk this and then, from a signpost at a track junction, continue forward to **Readycon Dean Reservoir** (signed for Piethorne Reservoir). Follow the track around the reservoir, across its dam, and then out to the **A672**.

Turn left and walk parallel with the A-road for a short distance to leave it at a sign for the Ram's Head Inn. Cross a short section of enclosed pasture to a gate, and there turn right on a broad track. At a nearby track junction, keep forward through another gate, now with Piethorne Reservoir in sight, along with a distant view of Winter Hill in the West Pennine moors.

Follow a descending track to a junction to the east of **Piethorne Reservoir** (SD970125) and there turn left, now following a broad reservoir service track that soon crosses the dam of a small reservoir and then leads on, running to the south of Piethorne, Kitcliffe and Ogden reservoirs. Along the way the track becomes a surfaced lane, and this leads on to a ramp on the right (SD952122) leading up to the dam of **Ogden Reservoir**.

On the far side of the reservoir, the path climbs steps to reach a track at a woodland edge. Turn right (north) and follow this above the edge of the reservoir. Pass through a gate, and then about 50m beyond it, where a pipe crosses a shallow gully, descend to the right and climb a short distance to intercept a horizontal path. Turn left and parallel the path, which is overgrown, but which leads to the ruins of Rachole Farm, and here branch right, ascending on a broad track that rises to intercept a higher track. Keep left along this and follow it to the junction with Tunshill Lane, passed earlier in the walk.

Now go forward through a gate, as if retracing the outward route, but within 150m leave the main track and branch left on a path to a stile. The path beyond crosses the flank of Tunshill Hill and Castle Hill, and gradually descends to pass beneath the **motorway**. When the ongoing path divides after the motorway, take a lower path on the right, above the edge of playing fields. At a junction, turn right to pass through a wall onto the playing fields. The right of way actually crosses the playing pitches, but it is more courteous to keep to the edge of the fields, following the boundary round to a gap giving onto a narrow path. Follow this to the right to emerge on the outward route near Schofield Hall. Now simply turn left and retrace the outward route.

DARK PEAK

Rough-cut millstones below Crow Chin (Walk 50)

DARK PEAK

Influenced by a fascinating geological structure, the Peak District is divided into the High (or Dark) Peak and the Low (or White) Peak because the former is predominantly fashioned from gritstone and the latter from limestone. The old name for the district is Peakland, or 'Peaclond', as it appeared in the Anglo-Saxon Chronicle for 924, and means 'the land of the hill dwellers'. In those times of early history, the district lay on the northern edge of the Kingdom of Mercia, and those who lived here were called 'Pecsaetna', meaning 'hill dwellers'.

Being the most southerly region of the Pennines, the Peak District was the first to attract the attention of early travellers, many arriving, even in the 17th century, to see 'the Wonders of the Peak'. With the arrival of the railways in the 19th century, a day trip to this land, famous in court circles as a place of exile for recalcitrant wives, was within the reach of everyone who could afford the fare.

The Dark Peak lies within easy reach of millions resident in the great conurbations of Lancashire, Cheshire, Derbyshire and Yorkshire. Here gritstone predominates, and the moorland is cloaked in a rich shroud of heather and bilberry and tough, resilient grasses. But it is the ubiquitous peat and gritstone that impresses on the mind, especially on a first visit, and it takes time to appreciate the subtleties of line and shape, colour and hue, and contrasts. Often, for example, it is the very bleakness of the peaty moorland plateaux which emphasises the verdant loveliness of the valleys and fringes, giving the whole a satisfying sense of completeness. This is nowhere better exemplified than in the two walks above the Derwent valley (Walks 48 and 49) and along Stanage Edge, north of Hathersage.

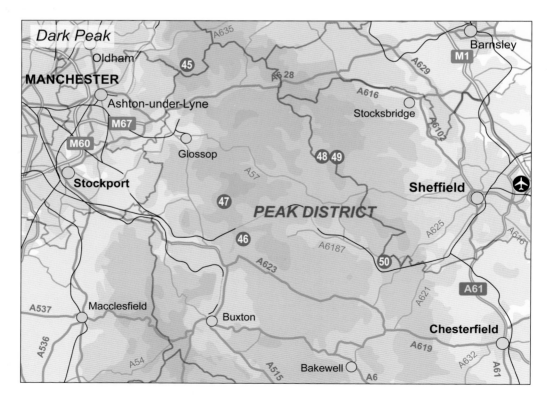

Saddleworth Edges

*M*ention the Peak District and most walkers think of dark, peaty plateaux such as are found on Kinder and Bleaklow. Yet only a short distance west, where the plateau drops abruptly to the heavily populated valleys around Mossley, Greenfield and Uppermill, is one of the most endearing walks in the whole of the Peak District. In contrast to the starkness of the plateau above, this area, dotted with reservoirs and known locally as the Saddleworth Edges, is a place of unexpected beauty in a rough-hewn sort of way and represents for the people of eastern Lancashire an entire Lake District on their own doorstep.

The Route

The reservoirs – Greenfield, Yeoman Hey and Dove Stone in particular – are immensely popular at weekends almost throughout the year, but few visitors undertake more than a stroll beside them, leaving the grand balcony above free for more energetic souls. Walkers prepared to venture this way, however, will find the recesses of Greenfield Brook and

Birchin Clough, and the walk which ensues, full of interest, with a wide range of birds – buzzard, kestrel, sparrowhawk, skylark, golden plover, wheatear and meadow pipit – for company.

From the Binn Green car park and picnic area a flight of steps leads down into a small copse of conifers and to a gate giving access to the reservoir

↑ Striding the Edge path

ROUTE INFORMATION

Distance	14km (9 miles)
Height gain	560m (1835ft)
Time	5hrs
Grade	demanding
Start point	Binn Green picnic area SE018044

Getting there
Parking at Binn Green picnic area, A635, just out of Greenfield (shown but not named on the OS map); additional parking at Dove Stone Reservoir (access at SE008040)

Maps
Ordnance Survey OL1 (The Peak District: Dark Peak area)

After-walk refreshment
Mobile refreshments kiosks at Dove Stone Reservoir car park; pubs in Greenfield

road. The route turns left here and descends to **Yeoman Hey Reservoir**, constructed in 1880 and visited 101 years later by the King of Tonga, Taufa'ahau Tupou IV. Yeoman Hey may seem a bit out of his way, but he had been in London for the wedding of Prince Charles and Lady Diana Spencer, and was invited to tour the reservoirs by a contractor who had built a wharf in Tonga some years earlier.

Follow the service track around the left (western) side of the reservoir. Above rises a conifer plantation known as Bill o'Jack's, after the former innkeeper, William Bradbury, of the Moor Cock Inn, until 1935 to be found along the Holmfirth road. He and his father, Jack, met untimely deaths in 1832 at the hands of unknown assailants and were buried at Saddleworth church.

Continue in company with the relief channel until in due course it arrives at **Greenfield Reservoir** (1903). Leaving the reservoir behind, the route enters Greenfield Brook, a place of delightful cascades frowned down upon by the dark cliffs of **Raven Stones Brow**, prominent among which is the curious tower of The Trinnacle, perhaps the most impressive feature along the Edges.

The waterfall in Birchin Clough – try to cross just below this point

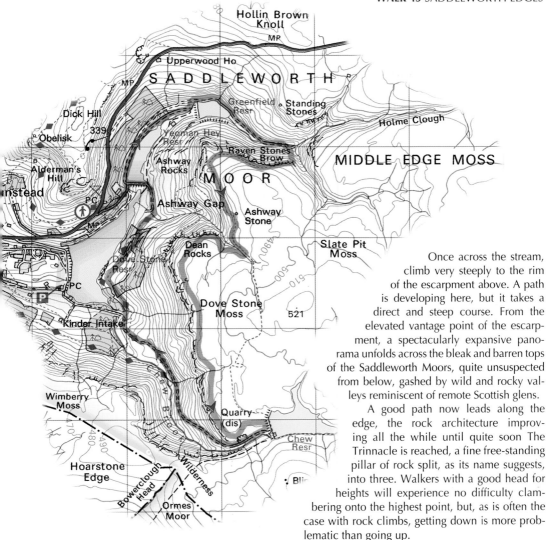

Once across the stream, climb very steeply to the rim of the escarpment above. A path is developing here, but it takes a direct and steep course. From the elevated vantage point of the escarpment, a spectacularly expansive panorama unfolds across the bleak and barren tops of the Saddleworth Moors, quite unsuspected from below, gashed by wild and rocky valleys reminiscent of remote Scottish glens.

A good path now leads along the edge, the rock architecture improving all the while until quite soon The Trinnacle is reached, a fine free-standing pillar of rock split, as its name suggests, into three. Walkers with a good head for heights will experience no difficulty clambering onto the highest point, but, as is often the case with rock climbs, getting down is more problematic than going up.

The Trinnacle marks the true start of the edge walk, and from here a good path wanders onwards in splendid airy fashion to the next objective, the Ashway Cross, a memorial to a Member of Parliament killed in a shooting accident. But not long after leaving The Trinnacle, by way of diversion, seek out a narrow path ascending left to a large cairn, Major's Cairn (not shown on the map). Major was a dog, and with his owner spent a good deal of time wandering these moors. If the path is missed (easy to do), the cairn can be found in a matter of minutes by ascending left from the edge path through the heather at almost any point. From the cairn a good path leads down to the Ashway Cross. (**Note** The Ashway Cross is on the higher of two paths across the plateau.)

A short distance further on Greenfield Brook divides into Holme Clough (left) and Birchin Clough (right). Close by, a dark tunnel captures the waters of Birchin Clough and sends them tumbling underground to the Dove Stone Reservoir. Do not be tempted to explore!

Cross the top of the tunnel in-flow and then the stream of Birchin Clough. A brief, scrambly route over and around boulders leads into a narrowing section to a point just below a small cascade. A path does continue above this waterfall, but just below it is usually a good place to cross with reasonable ease; heavy rainfall in preceding days will call for further progress upstream before finding a crossing point.

The Trinnacle

From Ashway Cross, the path bends to cross Dovestone Clough before resuming its progress along the edge above another fine escarpment of gritstone faces. Further on yet another memorial is encountered, this time to two climbers killed in 1972 in the Dolomites, and beyond that is a quite unique dwelling, Bramley's Cot, constructed against a face of rock in a most ingenious way. In its present incomplete state it is tempting to think 'Cot' means that it was half a cottage! But there was a time when it was sufficiently complete to see service as a shooting lodge.

Bramley's Cot

Continue along the marginal path, with just a few unavoidable patches of peat to contend with, noting the obvious gully across the valley, Wilderness Gully, scene in 1963 of one of England's largest avalanches, in which two climbers were killed. The path continues along the edge until a final bout of peat-bashing leads to **Chew Reservoir**, constructed in 1912 and the highest reservoir in England.

By following the reservoir service road a speedy descent to the valley bottom may be made, where walkers will be greeted in summer by shoals of would-be adventurers gathered around the dam of **Dove Stone Reservoir** and along its shores. Cross the dam, and on the other side take to a broad path running beside the reservoir. At the far end meet the outward route; turn left up a surfaced lane to the gate giving into woodland, with the **Binn Green** car park above.

Lord's Seat and Mam Tor

*T*his walk heads along the Pennine watershed, the great geological divide between Dark and White Peak, a demarcation nowhere more graphically illustrated than in the contrast between the gritstone landscape to the north and the limestone to the south. The highlight is Rushup Edge and the fine ridge continuing eastwards from Mam Tor. The route then dips into Edale to make a start on the Pennine Way, which it follows until it turns northwards for Kinder Downfall. The result is a happy association of relaxing valley pathways and airy ridge walking.

The Route

The miners who long ago moved northwards, seeking hidden lead in the limestone bedrock of the White Peak, must have viewed the great ridge of Rushup Edge as an impassable barrier, the end of everything. Imagine their surprise if they had climbed over the wiry tussock grass to crest that long divide and seen, not a higher continuation of the white rock plains they were leaving behind, but 'a wide deep valley,

sombre and swampy, over-shadowed by huge buttresses... which look like the bastions of eternity'. For here the lands of the Peak divide – Dark and High to the north; White and Low to the south.

In the Peak, this great crest is special, one of few real ridge walks in the region, an enfolding arm sweeping protectively around the Noe valley. Within its embrace the ridge became a hidden enclave, long

ROUTE INFORMATION

Distance	18km (11¼ miles)
Height gain	555m (1820ft)
Time	5–6hrs
Grade	strenuous
Start point	Rushup Edge road SK091824

Getting there
Parking at lay-by on Rushup Edge road

Maps
Ordnance Survey OL1 (The Peak District: Dark Peak area)

After-walk refreshment
Pubs in Edale, Castleton and Chapel-en-le-Frith

ago carved by glaciers, that only gradually opened up as packhorse routes developed commerce between east and west, presaging the road and railway links that finally revealed to the outside world the cluster of sheltered communities that make up the valley.

Although the walk could just as easily be started in Edale, the option used here leads directly onto the ridge. Walk along the road for a short distance and then bear left (ignoring the earlier turning onto the Pennine Bridleway) to follow a sunken sandstone track that rises steadily onto **Rushup Edge** and reaches Access Land at a stile. Thus far the track has followed one of the oldest routes linking Edale with Chapel-en-le-Frith, but now leaves it.

A wall leads gently along Rushup Edge to the Bronze Age round barrow that marks the summit of **Lord's Seat**. The barrow is associated with the hill fort about to be encountered on Mam Tor, although there is little to tell who the 'Lord' was, a tag first attached to the summit as long ago as 1620.

From Rushup Edge, the gash of Winnats Pass is now visible to the south-east, thought to have been a submarine formation rather than the product of a collapsed cave system. As with the route through the Noe valley, Winnats for centuries saw service as an important trade route between east and west, and became the route adopted by a new turnpike road in 1750 linking Manchester and Sheffield. Barely half a century later this was superseded by a new and less severe road looping beneath the unstable cliffs of Mam Tor, which 165 years later, in 1978, destroyed parts of the road, causing traffic to revert to the time-honoured passage through Winnats.

Ascending onto Rushup Edge

Such landslips, for which parts of the Great Ridge are notorious, have also carved into Rushup Edge, and as Mam Nick is approached the ridge narrows appreciably, honing an awareness of steep descents on either sides. Just to the south of the descending ridge crest, a broad path appears. Follow this down to meet the road squeezing through Mam Nick, turn left and walk up to a gate on the right giving onto a flight of steps that lead up to the trig pillar on the top of **Mam Tor**.

Mam Tor rests on a base of Edale shales, soft, crumbly rocks formed from the mudbanks of an estuary over 300 million years ago. As a result, when these slates become wet they tend to lose cohesion and much of their bearing strength. Above the Edale slates lie layers of the sandstones and gritstones that make up the Millstone Grit series, each layer discernible by its coloration and its respective resistance to the effects of eroding winds, rain and frosts.

Commanding such a prominent position, it is hardly surprising that Mam Tor became the location of a late Bronze Age hill fort, the largest in Derbyshire. There is evidence to date it from about 1200BC, although the visible ramparts that remain today were probably made by Iron Age people who inhabited the region until the Romans made their presence felt in the first century AD.

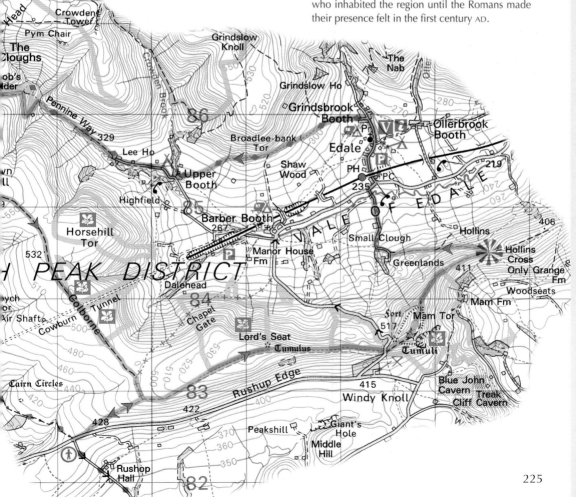

Continue on from Mam Tor, following the ridge path in splendid fashion as it dips to **Hollins Cross**, a superb viewpoint. From here, the walk changes direction and heads for Edale. From Hollins Cross a bridleway descends steeply in a westerly direction heading for **Greenlands Farm**, where it joins another bridleway that runs north to the Edale road. Turn right briefly and then left to pass the railway station and enter **Edale** itself. Stay on the lane, heading northwards to **Grindsbrook Booth**, and opposite the Old Nag's Head Inn head left along the start of the Pennine Way.

Pleasant pasturelands ease the Way on to the cluster of buildings at **Upper Booth**, from where the Pennine Way continue westwards into the enclosing folds of the upper Noe valley. Prominent gritstone outcrops, for which the Peak is renowned, dot the skyline, marking progress as the route tackles the rungs of **Jacob's Ladder**. Finally, at SK081861, the walk leaves the Pennine Way and follows a wall that zigzags roughly southwards to the trig pillar on the domed summit of **Brown Knoll**. This is the highest point of the journey, although the panorama is dominated by the higher swell of the Kinder plateau to the north, which from here appears at its highest and most mountainous, especially in winter, when the whole expanse lies buried beneath crisp and gleaming snow.

From Brown Knoll a path descends gently southeastwards for 2.5km (1½ miles) across boggy ground to meet an ancient route, **Chapel Gate** (SK098831). Turn right (south) on this for a short distance to meet the outward route at the Access Land boundary, and simply retrace the sunken sandstone gully to complete the walk.

The summit of Mam Tor

Kinder Downfall

*T*here can be few places more dramatic, more inspiring or better renowned than Kinder Downfall, the highest of the waterfalls in the Peak District. This rocky gash, where the River Kinder plunges over the lip of a massive amphitheatre of weathered gritstone, is spectacular, especially so when the river is full and the wind is from the south-west, for then the otherwise simple crossing of the river becomes something of a cold shower. This is a deceptively energetic walk, with all the uphill work coming in the early stages. After that, a huge playground of gritstone boulders heaped haphazardly is the backdrop for a splendid rim walk, gently undulating until Kinder Low is reached.

The car park at Bowden Bridge, once a small quarry, featured in the **mass trespass** on Kinder in 1932, an act documented in Harvey Taylor's seminal work *A Claim on the Countryside* and on which, even now, there are mixed views as to its efficacy. The very path along which this walk begins, from Hayfield to the Snake Inn, was itself hard-gained from local landowners as long ago as 1897 and came a year after the great right-of-way battle on Winter Hill in the West Pennine moors, one of the biggest mass trespasses in British history, but in hill-walking folklore overshadowed by the Kinder Trespass 36 years later.

↑ *On Kinder Edge*

ROUTE INFORMATION

Distance	13.5km (8½ miles)
Height gain	580m (1905ft)
Time	5hrs
Grade	demanding
Start point	Hayfield SK048869

Getting there
Bowden Bridge car park (pay and display), Hayfield

Maps
Ordnance Survey OL1 (The Peak District: Dark Peak area)

After-walk refreshment
Selection of pubs and eateries Hayfield

The Route
From the **Bowden Bridge** car park, turn left along Kinder Road and follow this to the entrance to the grounds of **Kinder Reservoir**. Here go right across a small arched bridge over the River Kinder, and only a short way further on leave the road on the left to follow the banks of the river. A few minutes of burbling water chorus leads to a second bridge, where the river is recrossed.

On the right now are the main gates to Kinder Reservoir, and just to their left pass through a small wooden gate on the right giving on to a rising stony path beside a wall, signed for White Brow. Initially uphill, this path soon reaches a small crest, from where there is a fine view over the reservoir to the distant Kinder Scout plateau, with Kinder Downfall tucked away to the left.

A short distance further on a rising track on the left is met at the end of a wall, and while this may be

Plaque at Bowden Bridge car park commemorating the Kinder Trespass

Above Kinder Downfall, looking south to Kinder Low

followed, turning right along the shelf of White Brow as it reaches higher ground, there is no real advantage in doing so, as the height gained will all be surrendered later in the walk only to be regained again.

Continue ahead instead, following a clear path around the reservoir to the foot of **William Clough**, the folds of which can now be seen ahead. Turn into William Clough, crossing and recrossing the stream many times until, near its summit (Ashop Head), the clough divides. Take the right fork and ascend steps to **Ashop Head**, where the Pennine Way is intercepted. From just below the high point of this pass,

turn right along a paved path to tackle the steepness south-east of this mini-crossroads, which leads to the rim of the Kinder plateau. What follows is a fairly dry path undulating through and around outcrops of gritstone boulders, bringing the conspicuous ravine of the Downfall ever nearer.

There are many exciting vantage points both before and after crossing the River Kinder from which to view **the Downfall**, but extreme caution is demanded of photographers and anyone seeking descents into the amphitheatre, which for the most part don't exist or are accessible only to experienced scramblers. If in doubt, stay on firm ground. Whether the Downfall puts on a show will largely depend on the extent of rainfall over preceding days, and it is not uncommon to find the River Kinder reduced to a mere trickle.

Cross the shallow river and continue by heading south through numerous gritstone boulder groups to reach the ravine of **Red Brook**. Pass around Red Brook gully and shortly reach the trig pillar on **Kinder Low**, perched high on a natural gritstone stage.

The summit of Kinder Low

From Kinder Low, continue southwards. There are larger areas of blanket peat here, and picking up the correct line might be difficult. But eventually a path does appear that leads down to a path junction by a large cairn (SK079865) above **Edale Head** and

continues as a paved path, passing to the left of Edale Rocks before descending. The main path bears left to the top of Jacob's Ladder, but there is a clear point at which to leave it and go right to join Monk's Road, an old packhorse route to the Yorkshire markets from Hayfield and the Sett valley. Turn right through a gate and face one last uphill section, climbing to the stone alcove that shelters **Edale Cross**, a boundary marker of the medieval Royal Forest of the Peak.

Continue heading west from Edale Cross, following the ancient trail and ignoring all diversions. Passing above the head of **Oaken Clough**, this trail eventually leads down to join a surfaced lane near the River Sett, where it feeds into Coldwell Clough. Follow the lane as it swings northwards, and when it climbs to the left leave it for a low-level track parallel with and to the right of the river, later rejoining the lane.

Now stay on the lane, passing **Tunstead House** set splendidly on a nearby hillside, and at the end of its access lane bear left and shortly left again to follow a surfaced lane out of the valley to return to **Bowden Bridge**.

Rowlee Pasture and Alport Castles

*T*he Derwent valley is outstandingly beautiful, and especially so when the reservoirs are full, for then they simply assume the guise of natural lakes. Most visitors spend their time around the reservoirs and along the gritstone outcrops of Derwent Edge (Walk 49). But this walk goes in the opposite direction to visit an area where landslip has created a convoluted and fantastic landscape.

Originally a farm, Fairholmes, where this walk starts, was used as a mason's yard during the construction of the **Derwent valley dams**. The reservoirs were built to supply water to Derby, Leicester, Nottingham and Sheffield, and the Derwent was used during the Second World War for training runs by the Dambusters, whose task it was to demolish the Moehne and Eder dams in the Ruhr valley in 1943. Much of the 1955 film 'The Dambusters', which depicts these events, was made on location at Derwent.

Climbing through the plantation to Lockerbrook Farm

↑ *Alport Tower*

231

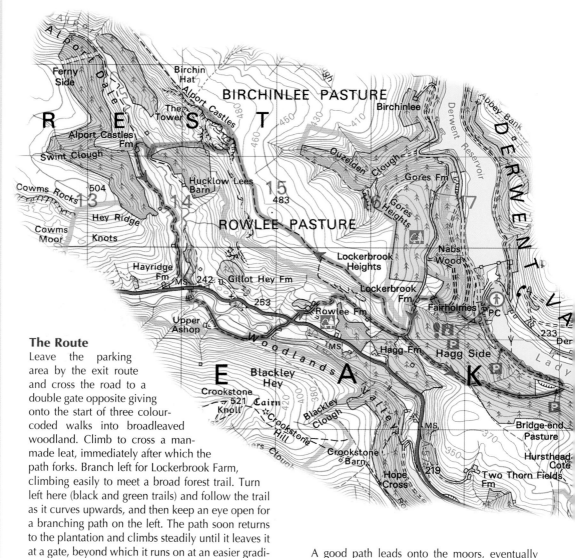

The Route

Leave the parking area by the exit route and cross the road to a double gate opposite giving onto the start of three colour-coded walks into broadleaved woodland. Climb to cross a man-made leat, immediately after which the path forks. Branch left for Lockerbrook Farm, climbing easily to meet a broad forest trail. Turn left here (black and green trails) and follow the trail as it curves upwards, and then keep an eye open for a branching path on the left. The path soon returns to the plantation and climbs steadily until it leaves it at a gate, beyond which it runs on at an easier gradient to a gate giving onto a broad stony track. Turn left here and walk down to pass **Lockerbrook Farm**, these days an outdoor centre.

Follow the track up to its highest point, close by a four-way junction (to which the route returns later). Here turn sharply right, leaving the main trail, and walk up to a ladder-stile and gate at a wall near a plantation edge. Beyond, a grassy path rises gently to a stile giving onto **Rowlee Pasture**, a good place to keep an eye open for skylark, kestrel, golden plover, short-eared owl and possibly a goshawk or merlin. To the south-west there is a fine view between the hills of Mam Tor, Back Tor and Lose Hill, which form the headwall of the Hope valley.

A good path leads onto the moors, eventually becoming paved and now providing views of the northern slopes of the Kinder plateau. As the path progresses through vast emptiness it reaches and then follows a dilapidated wall, finally reaching a point directly above a jumbled and chaotic landscape. Here a massive landslide has produced weird formations known as **Alport Castles** and a stand-alone feature, **The Tower**.

Alport Castles is arguably one of the most dramatic landscape features in the Peak District and is claimed to be the largest natural landslip in the Britain, although the Quiraing on the Isle of Skye might have something to say about that.

The paved section across Rowlee Pasture, with Alport Castles in the distance

Alport Castles and The Tower

Some 300 million years ago, this area would have been at the centre of a wide river delta that flowed into a shallow tropical sea which then covered the Peak District. The mud and sand particles carried in the river were deposited in layers, and over millions of years they were slowly compressed as layer upon layer gradually created the smooth, soft shale and coarse, hard gritstone rocks we see today.

From this craggy place, retreat along the outward route to a clear path (SK145913) descending the escarpment. Initially it drops beside a wall, crossing it twice before continuing down grassy slopes. Keep following the descending path to cross the River Alport by a footbridge, then take the path beyond up to **Alport Castles Farm**. On reaching a farm access, turn left and enjoy a leisurely stroll high above the River Alport south towards the Snake Road.

About 100m before reaching **Hayridge Farm**, leave the farm access by descending left across a sloping field to a stile in a fence corner. Then follow the path down to a stile, after which a short section alongside the River Alport leads out to the road. Cross with care into the bridleway opposite.

A track leads to a ford at the River Alsop, beyond which a broad trail rises below **Upper Ashop Farm**. The track is part of the Roman road between Bradwell and Glossop. When it divides, bear left (signed for Upper Derwent) and descend to cross Rowlee Bridge, and then walk up to cross the Snake Road again. Go up the lane to **Rowlee Farm**.

The path passes around the farm, climbs a little further and then reaches a more level passage that eventually leads back to the four-way junction reached earlier in the walk. (The shortest way back to Fairholmes is to take a signed path into woodland at this point or to retrace the outward route.)

From the path junction, turn right and soon pass through a gate/stile onto a clear track along the southern edge of **Hagg Side** plantation, which leads to a complex of gates. Here bear left, descending into the plantation and finally emerging on the Derwent valley road at the **Bridge End car park**. Turn left and walk along the roadside footpath until it becomes possible to bear right onto a path that parallels the edge of **Ladybower Reservoir**. In due course, this comes back out to the road, with Fairholmes just a short distance further on.

Back Tor and Derwent Edge

*T*his entertaining walk begins along the shores of the Derwent Reservoir, then follows the sinuous Abbey Brook to an airy moorland crossing before finishing with an easy amble beside the Ladybower Reservoir. Interest is maintained throughout; the twists and turns of the Abbey Brook divide initially, leading onward into its depths, while the moorland plateau above is littered with the weird shapes of weathered gritstone.

The Route

The eastern moors of the Peak, Howden and Derwent, while not quite reaching their highest point during this walk, fall steeply to the Derwent valley, although never quite aspire to the precipitous gritstone escarpment further east along Stanage Edge (Walk 50). They remain, nevertheless, firm favourites with walkers seeking peace or the company of like minds. During the Ice Age the highest stretches of the moors, unlike the valleys below, may never have been entirely covered by glaciers, leaving the

gritstone monoliths found today projecting above an ocean of ice, exposed to the winds and rains of a bitterly cold environment.

These lands of the Derwent were once among the most prized possessions of the monks of Welbeck Abbey, who derived their title towards the end of the 12th century, during the reign of Richard I. Sheep farming largely determined the pattern of settlements in the valleys, principally during the 13th and 14th centuries. These remained very much intact until

The twin towers of Derwent Dam

ROUTE INFORMATION

Distance	17.7km (11 miles)
Height gain	395m (1295ft)
Time	5hrs
Grade	demanding
Start point	Derwent valley SK173893

Getting there
Fairholmes car park (pay and display; toilets, refreshments, visitor centre)

Map
Ordnance Survey OL1 (The Peak District: Dark Peak area)

After-walk refreshment
Snack bar at visitor centre; Snake Pass Inn on Snake Road; pubs and cafés in Glossop, Sheffield and Hathersage

the Derwent Water Board (as it then was) drowned the valley between 1912, when the Howden Dam was built (followed by the Derwent Dam in 1916), and the end of the Second World War, when the Ladybower Reservoir was constructed.

Leave the car park and pass the visitor centre to head towards the dam along a path and then on a minor road. When the dam is full the overspill is a fascinating sight, contrasting sharply with the serene beauty of the reservoir above and the conifer-clad hillsides beyond. As the road swings southwards, leave it and take a signed path ascending left through woodland and finally connect with a broad track beside the east tower of the Derwent Dam.

The next section, a little over 2km (about 1¼ miles), calls for little expenditure of energy, ambling pleasantly beside the reservoir. There is a strong temptation to dawdle and delight here as kestrel, buzzard or the rarer goshawk patrol distant slopes.

Approaching Howden Dam, **Abbey Brook** opens up on the right. Leave the main valley track here (SK171919; signposted Bradfield and Strines) for a clear branching path. A short, sharp pull is the opener to Abbey Brook, up to a gate, just beyond which bear left when the track divides. Once beyond the initial woodland there is a keen sense of moorland promise, with a clear, broad track running on across the shoulder of **Little Howden Moor**.

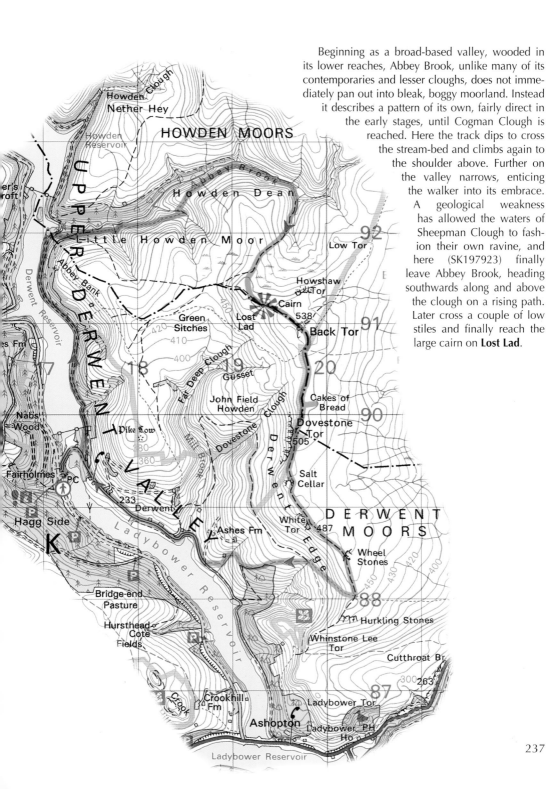

Beginning as a broad-based valley, wooded in its lower reaches, Abbey Brook, unlike many of its contemporaries and lesser cloughs, does not immediately pan out into bleak, boggy moorland. Instead it describes a pattern of its own, fairly direct in the early stages, until Cogman Clough is reached. Here the track dips to cross the stream-bed and climbs again to the shoulder above. Further on the valley narrows, enticing the walker into its embrace. A geological weakness has allowed the waters of Sheepman Clough to fashion their own ravine, and here (SK197923) finally leave Abbey Brook, heading southwards along and above the clough on a rising path. Later cross a couple of low stiles and finally reach the large cairn on **Lost Lad**.

237

Suddenly the view opens up magnificently, a virtue endorsed by the erection of a topograph on Lost Lad by the Sheffield Clarion Ramblers in memory of WH Baxby. The summit is named after a shepherd lad lost in the snow.

From it a paved path dips a little and reascends to continue to **Back Tor**, a nearby conspicuous outcrop topped by a trig pillar. The conquest of Back Tor demands a little mild scrambling, its trig pillar being splendidly placed on the very top of a fine array of weathered gritstone. This is one of the Peak's finest vantage points, a splendid accumulation of the ancient bones of the landscape. In a narrow niche, a touch of romance arouses finer feelings as you discover that Mary and Jack became engaged here on 5 March 1933.

A steady, paved descent leads on from Back Tor and intersects a path that ascends through Shireowlers Wood from the reservoir track used earlier in the day to a place known as Bradfield Gate. What remains of Bradfield Gate is just a solitary pillar.

Ahead and to the left of the path more gritstone outcrops appear, rudely fashioned by weather into forms that have become known as the **Cakes of Bread**. A little further are the rocks of **Dovestone Tor**, sibling of Back Tor, but smaller and less impressive. Nearby, yet another weatherworn sculpture, the **Salt Cellar**, requires less imagination than many named outcrops on these vast moors and gazes down on what remains of the lost community of Derwent, submerged for ever by the rising waters of Ladybower. Although the Salt Cellar is visible on

In the upper section of Abbey Clough

The Salt Cellar

the approach to it, in the immediate vicinity it seems to disappear, calling for a slight diversion.

From the Salt Cellar return to the main path and continue east of south to **White Tor** and on to yet more gritstone gargoyles, the **Wheel Stones**, fancifully thought to simulate the wild flight of a coach and horses across the moor. Continue a little further to encounter another trans-moor track, this time linking Derwent and Moscar, and turn right to follow this. The track initially descends north-west to intercept a lower path and then reaches a gate above Grainsfoot Clough. Pass through the gate, taking the path beyond, and fall gently to the edge of the wooded plantations which flank the eastern side of the Derwent valley.

Descend easily to the plantations, the drystone wall along the northern edge of the footpath having been completely rebuilt by conservation workers in 1989. Eventually cross Grindle Clough, and a short way further on pass between the ancient Grindle Barns (one bears the date 1647) to descend a steep stony path to a gate giving onto the reservoir road. Now all that remains is a simple and delightful stroll around **Mill Brook** inflow back to **Fairholmes** at the end of a walk arguably as fine as any in the Peak District.

Stanage Edge

H *overing above the Hope and Derwent valleys like a surfer's wave about to break, Stanage Edge defines the western edge of Hallam Moors as they rise from the suburbs of Sheffield and marks a distinct contrast with the lands of the Low Peak. To the south lies a pastoral landscape of walls and rolling greenness, culminating at the natural gateway to the High Peak, Hathersage, a peaceful settlement clustered around its church. On Stanage Edge wild moorland spreads northwards, rising in brooding shades to the heights of Derwent Edge, Kinder, Bleaklow and beyond.*

The Route

Many walkers bound for Stanage Edge ignore Hathersage altogether, making with indecent haste for the car parks that lie alongside the minor road linking Burbage Rocks and Bamford Edge. Such impatience brings a premature introduction to Stanage, and walkers miss the drama of seeing their objective from afar and working steadfastly through the valleys to gain it.

Stanage Edge, the longest and most impressive of all gritstone escarpments in England, has its place, rightfully, in the annals of rock-climbing history, having been explored since the late 19th century and still providing a challenge for modern climbers. But it is remarkable, too, in affording lesser mortals, those who like their feet firmly on more or less level ground, a splendid and airy walk, full of interest, easy of access, and with a fine panorama.

↑ *Stanage Edge*

ROUTE INFORMATION

Distance	19.5km (12 miles)
Height gain	500m (1640ft)
Time	5hrs
Grade	demanding
Start point	Hathersage SK232815

Getting there
Large car park (pay and display) near the fire station in the centre of Hathersage, reached by a side-road at the southern end of the village

Maps
Ordnance Survey OL1 (The Peak District: Dark Peak area)

After-walk refreshment
Pubs in Hathersage

On leaving the car park, turn left and in a short while pass through an alleyway leading on to the main road. Cross the road and enter Baulk Lane. This surfaced lane soon degenerates into a broad track, passing the village cricket green and pressing on easily across a number of meadows. Onwards the track climbs gently until, at a signpost in mid-pasture, it branches half-left and descends to a narrow gate giving onto a path, soon passing behind **Brookfield Manor**. Continue ahead to a minor road, Birley Lane. Continue right along Birley Lane to the first turning on the left, and here turn uphill on a surfaced track leading to **North Lees Hall**.

North Lees Hall, an austere edifice and Grade II listed tower house, was built in the 16th century, and from 1750 to 1882 occupied by the Eyre family. The Hall is now owned by the National Park Authority and leased as a farm; the outbuildings buildings house the remains of a chapel built in 1685, only to be sacked in 1688. The tall three-storeyed castellated tower is said to have provided the inspiration for Thornfield Hall in Charlotte Brontë's *Jane Eyre*, Charlotte having spent three weeks in Hathersage in 1845.

Pass behind the Hall and ascend a rough flight of stone steps to gain a track across a field leading to a small plantation bordering a cascading stream. There is a relaxed air about this short stretch through

North Lees Hall

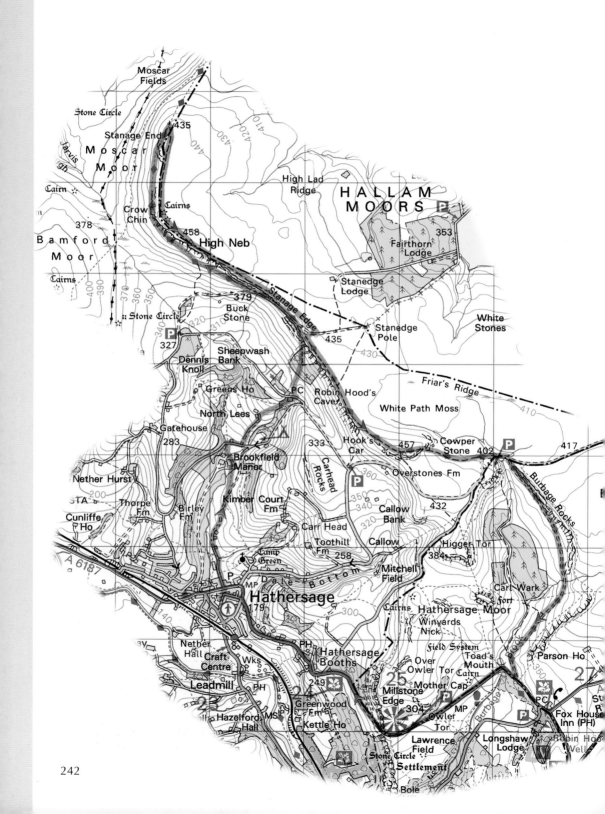

Crow Chin and Stanage Edge

the plantation; Stanage Edge, glimpsed fleetingly through the trees, is now more prominent high above, a spectacular fringe of rock decorating the skyline like an afterthought in a child's drawing.

The path emerges from the plantation onto the old turnpike road that ran from Ashopton (long since submerged under Ladybower Reservoir) to Sheffield. Here the true extent of Stanage Edge at last becomes obvious, stretching away to the right to Burbage Rocks and left to the identifiable beak of Crow Chin and High Neb. It is one enormous wall of rock, invariably festooned with the ropes and jingling paraphernalia of rock climbers.

Cross the road and ascend easily to a small copse directly beneath the rocks of the Edge. Emerge from the sparse shelter of the trees onto a path composed of gritstone blocks, now worn smooth by countless generations of feet, that ascends to the rim of the escarpment. This is known as Jacob's Ladder and is probably no more than an ancient packhorse way that has been paved. There is about it, however, a similarity with the so-called 'Roman' Steps in Cwm Bychan in the Rhinogs of Wales, and with tracks

across the moors of East Lancashire above Wycoller, further north.

Once on the escarpment edge continue north-west (left) with the path, but almost immediately throwing away all the height just gained by descending a broad track of loose stones to pass beneath the escarpment of **High Neb**. Shortly after a wall-end and stream descending from the hill slope on the right, leave the main track by branching right to cross a stile onto a narrower but clear path through bracken. This soon leads into the midst of a profusion of millstones, lying about the hillside as their makers left them – some lying flat, some half-buried, others leaning, yet more stacked as if in some ancient wheel-repair depot, one even with a smiling face. Many possess centre holes, others are blank, the odd one or two only half-finished, and here and there lie square blocks yet to be tackled. Fifty, a hundred, perhaps, lie scattered about – testimony to the end of an era.

Continue on the path through this millstone graveyard, with the prominent 'beak' of **Crow Chin** above, allegedly named by a millstone cutter who

243

Climbing through Stanage Edge crags

is said to have mistaken the protruding rock for the beak of a giant crow bearing down on him. Away from this abandoned factory, the path passes on pleasantly, in due course to meet the A57 at Moscar. But walk only as far as you wish, with the crags on the right diminishing all the while. Ascend through the crags at any time that suits to reach the rim of the escarpment a short distance north-west of the trig point on High Neb, the highest point along the Edge.

Along this section of the Edge there is a series of basins scooped out of the rock, some with curved lines rather like upturned cat's whiskers. All of them are numbered and total 100, and this numbering is the clue that they are man-made. They are in fact drinking bowls for grouse, sculpted at the beginning of the last century by gamekeepers who were paid one old penny a time for their construction to ensure the birds had a plentiful supply of water.

From **High Neb** follow the edge path on a long and splendid traverse to the highest, and at this remove quite distant, point on Stanage. The scenery, especially that formed and framed by the weathered

Grouse drinking bowl

rocks of the escarpment, is consistently splendid, and the marvellous view a generous reward for so little effort; small wonder, then, that Stanage Edge is a popular promenade. Near the top of Jacob's Ladder a Roman road, the Long Causeway, is joined leading north-west across Hallam Moors to Redmires reservoirs. Follow this but briefly to a waymark post, where the road swings left to distant Stanedge Pole.

At the waymark, leave the road and descend to a path that continues over a stile and along the line of the escarpment.

Along the way there are many places to sit and watch the antics of rock climbers. **Robin Hood's Cave**, a conspicuous balcony with a large flat roof, is worthy of exploration, and it seems quite plausible that this legendary hero might have resorted to the cave as a hideaway, although there is no evidence to support this.

Like High Neb, the highest point at the opposite end of the Edge is also marked by a trig point and forms the culmination of the long and easy crossing. Here the turnpike road climbs to meet the escarpment near Burbage Rocks. Follow the path from the trig until this road is met. Continue along it to the second bridge, where a gate gives access to the Duke of Rutland's Drive, a green and gentle

track running beneath **Burbage Rocks**, which should now be followed to its junction with the A625 at SK263806. A couple of miles of easy strolling leads back to **Hathersage**.

Optional extra Repeated faulting has added an interesting dimension to the landscape above Hathersage, providing a series of table-like hills – Higger Tor, Carl Wark and Winyards Nick. These flat-topped hills, with gently sloping concave sides, rise impressively from the moorland, and a network of paths makes them easily accessible. Walkers with energy to spare should not miss them, and can simply head for them at any point along the walk to the A625. After your exploration head west to the minor road that leads down to Hathersage Booths or cut across to the A625 near Hathersage Booths.

Striding out above Stanage Edge

APPENDIX 1
Concise walk reference and personal log

WALK		DISTANCE	HEIGHT GAIN	TIME	GRADE	WALKED
1	Thack Moor and Black Fell	18km/11¼ miles	525m/1725ft	6–7 hours	strenuous	
2	Melmerby Fell and Fiend's Fell	16.5km/10¼ miles	546m/1790ft	6 hours	demanding	
3	Cross Fell	15km/9¼ miles	683m/2240ft	5–6 hours	strenuous	
4	High Cup Nick and Backstone Edge	15.5km/9½ miles	592m/1940ft	5–6 hours	strenuous	
5	Cauldron Snout and Widdybank Fell	13km/8 miles	145m/475ft	4–5 hours	moderate	
6	High Force and Cronkley Fell	20.5km/12¾ miles	372m/1220ft	6 hours	demanding	
7	Harter Fell and Grassholme	13.5km/8½ miles	317m/1040ft	4–5 hours	moderately demanding	
8	Bowes Moor	16.7km/10½ miles	205m/675ft	5+ hours	moderately demanding	
9	Hartley Fell and Nine Standards Rigg	14.5km/9 miles	540m/1770ft	4–5 hours	demanding	
10	Lunds Fell, Hugh Seat and High Seat	16km/10 miles	535m/1755ft	6 hours	strenuous	
11	Wild Boar Fell and Swarth Fell	16.5km/10¼ miles	570m/1870ft	6+ hours	demanding	
12	Green Bell	10.5km/6½ miles	430m/1410ft	4 hours	moderately demanding	
13	The Fairmile circuit	13.8km/8½ miles	900m/2955ft	5 hours	strenuous	
14	Cautley Spout and The Calf	11.5km/7 miles	603m/1980ft	5 hours	demanding	
15	The Calf from Sedbergh	17.5km/11 miles	675m/2215ft	6+ hours	strenuous	
16	Great Shunner Fell and Lovely Seat	19.5km/12 miles	615m/2020ft	6–7 hours	strenuous	
17	Upper Swaledale and Rogan's Seat	20km/12½ miles	485m/1590ft	5–6 hours	demanding	
18	Dodd Fell Hill and Drumaldrace	20.8km/13 miles	512m/1680ft	6+ hours	strenuous	

WALK		DISTANCE	HEIGHT GAIN	TIME	GRADE	WALKED
19	Gragareth and Great Coum	13km/8 miles	435m/1425ft	4–5 hours	moderately demanding	
20	Whernside	15.2km/9½ miles	550m/1805ft	5 hours	demanding	
21	Ingleborough	17.5km/11 miles	593m/1945ft	6 hours	strenuous	
22	Giggleswick Scar	14.5km/9 miles	310m/1015ft	5 hours	moderately demanding	
23	Nappa Cross, Rye Loaf Hill and Victoria Cave	17.5km/11 miles	340m/1115ft	5–6 hours	moderately demanding	
24	Pen-y-Ghent and Plover Hill	13.3km/8½ miles	560m/1835ft	4–5 hours	demanding	
25	Fountains Fell	19.2km/12 miles	400m/1310ft	6 hours	demanding	
26	Janet's Foss, Gordale Scar and Malham Cove	11.5km/7 miles	285m/935ft	4 hours	moderately demanding	
27	Buckden Pike	14.3km/9 miles	522m/1715ft	5 hours	demanding	
28	Great Whernside	13.2km/8¼ miles	505m/1655ft	5–6 hours	strenuous	
29	Cracoe Fell and Thorpe Fell	18.5km/11½ miles	368m/1205ft	6½ hours	demanding	
30	Elslack Moor and Pinhaw Beacon	13km/8 miles	342m/1122ft	4 hours	moderate	
31	Rombalds Moor and Ilkley Moor	11.5km/7 miles	295m/970ft	4 hours	moderately demanding	
32	Pendle Hill	10km/6¼ miles	455m/1490ft	3–4 hours	moderately demanding	
33	Boulsworth Hill	13km/8 miles	413m/1355ft	5 hours	moderately demanding	
34	Delf Hill and Stanbury Moor	11km/7 miles	365m/1195ft	4+ hours	moderately demanding	

WALK		DISTANCE	HEIGHT GAIN	TIME	GRADE	WALKED
35	Wadsworth Moor	17.5km/11 miles	325m/1065ft	5–6 hours	moderately demanding	
36	Worsthorne Moor and Black Hameldon	13km/8 miles	300m/985ft	5 hours	moderately demanding	
37	Thieveley Pike and Cliviger Gorge	14.5km/9 miles	463m/1520ft	5 hours	demanding	
38	Bride Stones Moor	10km/6¼ miles	360m/1180ft	3–4 hours	moderate	
39	Luddenden Dean and Midgeley Moor	15km/9¼ miles	385m/1265ft	5 hours	moderately demanding	
40	Stoodley Pike	15.5km/9½ miles	405m/1330ft	4–5 hours	demanding	
41	Langfield Common	15km/9¼ miles	92m/300ft	4 hours	moderate	
42	Blackstone Edge	15km/9¼ miles	335m/1100ft	5 hours	demanding	
43	Rooley Moor and Cowpe Lowe	20km/12½ miles	492m/1615ft	6–7 hours	strenuous	
44	White Hill and Piethorne Clough	21km/13 miles	430m/1410ft	5–6 hours	demanding	
45	Saddleworth Edges	14km/9 miles	560m/1835ft	5 hours	demanding	
46	Lord's Seat and Mam Tor	18km/11¼ miles	555m/1820ft	5–6 hours	strenuous	
47	Kinder Downfall	13.5km/8½ miles	580m/1903ft	5 hours	demanding	
48	Rowlee Pasture and Alport Castles	15km/9¼ miles	515m/1690ft	6+ hours	demanding	
49	Back Tor and Derwent Edge	17.7km/11 miles	395m/1295ft	5 hours	demanding	
50	Stanage Edge	19.5km/12 miles	500m/1640ft	5 hours	demanding	

APPENDIX 2
Bibliography

Ainsworth, Harrison
The Lancashire Witches (London: Granada Publishing, 1980)

Alderson, James
Under Wetherfell: The Story of Hawes Parish and its People (self-published, 1980)

Bentley, John
Portrait of Wycoller (Nelson: Nelson Local History Society, 1975)

Bibby, Andrew
Backbone of England: Life and Landscape on the Pennine Watershed (London: Frances Lincoln, 2008)

Boyd, Donald and Monkhouse, Patrick
Walking in the Pennines (London: Maclehose, 1937)

Brumhead, Derek
Geology explained in the Yorkshire Dales and on the Yorkshire Coast (Newton Abbot: David and Charles, 1979)

Ffinch, Michael
Portrait of Penrith and the East Fellside (London: Robert Hale, 1985)

Gibson, Thomas
Legends and Historical Notes of North Westmoreland (London: Unwin Brothers, 1887)

Hanson, Neil
Walking through Eden: A Riverside Journey (Pavilion Books, 1990)

Hartley, Marie and Ingilby, Joan
– *The Yorkshire Dales* (London: JM Dent, 1956)
– *Life and Tradition in the Yorkshire Dales* (Otley, West Yorkshire: Smith Settle, 1997)

Hauxwell, Hannah with Barry Cockcroft
Hannah: The Complete Story (London: 1991)

Lofthouse, Jessica
Countrygoer in the Dales (London: Robert Hale, 1964)

Marsh, Terry
The Pennine Mountains (London: Hodder and Stoughton, 1989)

Mitchell, WR
High Dale Country (London: Souvenir Press, 1991)

Neill, Robert
Mist over Pendle (London: Arrow Books, 1955)

Peel, JHB
Along the Pennine Way (Newton Abbot: David and Charles, 1972)

Porteous, Crichton
Portrait of Peakland (London: Robert Hale, 1963)

Redfern, Roger
Portrait of the Pennines (London: Robert Hale, 1969)

Riley, W
The Yorkshire Pennines of the North-West (London: Herbert Jenkins, 1934)

Robinson, Trevor
Working with the Curlew (Totnes, Devon: Green Books, 2003)

Speakman, Colin
– *Walking in the Yorkshire Dales* (London: Robert Hale, 1982)
– *Portrait of North Yorkshire* (London: Robert Hale, 1986)

Stephenson, Tom
Forbidden Land: The Struggle for Access to Mountain and Moorland (Manchester: Manchester University Press, 1989)

Walker, Stephen
Nine Standards: Ancient Cairns or Modern Folly? (Kirkby Stephen: Hayloft Publishing Ltd, 2008)

Waltham, Tony
The Yorkshire Dales: Landscape and Geology (Marlborough: Crowood Press, 2007)

Wightman, Peter
Pennine Panorama (Nelson: Gerrard, 1969)

Wright, Geoffrey N
Roads and Trackways in the Yorkshire Dales (London: Guild Publishing, 1985)

Yee, Chiang
The Silent Traveller in the Yorkshire Dales (London: Methuen, 1948)

INDEX

A
Aiggin Stone 206
Alport Castles 232
American Civil War.. 210
Ancient Unicorn, The, Bowes.. 52
Ashway Cross 221

B
Back Tor... 238
Black Fell 23, 25, 27
Blacko Tower 164
Blackstone Edge 203
Boulsworth Hill 165
Bowes 52
Bramley's Cot 222
Bride Stones, The... 188
Brontë Moors... 170
Buckden 139
Buckden Pike 139
Burtersett 103

C
Cakes of Bread 238
Calf, The...82, 83, 85
Castle Carr House... 191
Cautley Spout 83
Clapham 114
Clifford, Lady Anne 64
Cotton Famine Road.. 208
Cowan Bridge... 105
Cow Green Reservoir 40
Cracoe Fell 148
Cross Fell 31
Cross Keys Inn 82

D
Darwin, Charles 155
Defoe, Daniel 203
de Morville, Hugh 66
Derwent 235
Dickens, Charles 52
Dodd Fell Hill 100, 101, 103
Dotheboys Hall 52

E
Edale Cross.. 230
Eden Benchmarks.. 65
Eden Springs... 66
Elslack Hall 154

F
Faraday, James 68
Faraday, Michael... 62
Farrer, Reginald 114
Fiend's Fell 27
Fiennes, Celia.. 203
first aid kit 20
Fountains Fell 130

G
Gaping Gill 116
Giggleswick Scar...119, 121
God's Bridge 54
Gordale Scar 136
GPS systems 15
Great Coum.. 104
Great Shunner Fell...92, 93, 95
Great Whernside 143

H
Hail Storm Hill 212
Hawes 101
Hebden Bridge 194
Helm Wind 32
High Cup Nick 38
High Way, The 65
Hollingworth Lake 204
Howgills, The.. 57
Hugh Seat.. 66
Hull Pot 129

I
Ilkley Hydro 155
Ilkley Moor... 155
Ingleborough 113
Ingleborough Hall 114

J
Jane Eyre 105
Janet's Foss.. 135

K
Kettlewell 143
Kinder Downfall 227
Kingsley, Charles... 131
Kirkcarrion 49

L
Lady Anne's Way.
    See High Way, The
Langfield Common 199
Lower Kinderscout Grit... 188
Lune valley... 78
Lydgate cottages... 206

M

Malham... 134
Malham Cove... 138
Malham Tarn.. 130, 137
Mam Tor.. 225
Maps... 15
Marilyns.. 12
Mastiles Lane.. 118
Melmerby.. 27
Middleton-in-Teesdale.. 48
Moor House–Upper Teesdale NNR 40

N

Nappa Cross.. 123
Nine Standards Rigg... 59
North Lees Hall.. 241

O

Outhgill.. 68

P

Peak District.. 218
Pendle Hill.. 161
Pennine Bridleway... 12
Pennine watershed... 12
Pennine Way.. 12
Pen-y-ghent.. 127, 129
Piethorne Clough.. 213
Pinhaw Beacon... 151

R

Renwick... 23
Ribblehead Viaduct.. 112
Robert Wilson's grave.. 152
Robin Hood.. 207
Robin Hood's Cave.. 245
Rogan's Seat.. 96, 97, 99
Roman road.. 206
Roughlee... 163
Rushup Edge... 224
Rye Loaf Hill.. 123
Rylstone.. 148

S

Sabden... 162
Saddleworth Edges.. 219
Scout Moor Wind Farm.. 208
Sedbergh.. 85
Settle.. 119
Settle–Carlisle railway... 112
Shedden Clough limestone hushings..................... 179
Six Trigs Walk.. 168
South Pennines Heritage Area............................... 160
Stanage Edge.. 240
Starbotton.. 142
Stoodley Pike... 194
Swastika Stone... 156
Swinner Gill Kirk... 97

T

Te Deum Laudamus stone...................................... 196
Thack Moor.. 23, 25, 27
Thieveley Pike.. 182
Thorpe Fell.. 147
Top Withins.. 173
Tor Dike.. 146
Trow Gill.. 115
Turley Holes and Higher House Moor.................... 200

U

Ure Head... 66

V

Victoria Cave.. 123

W

Warcop Artillery Range... 37
Watercut.. 65
Waterloo, Battle of.. 196
Whernside.. 109
White Wells.. 158
Wild Boar Fell.. 69, 71, 73
Wilderness Gully.. 222
Wycoller... 165
Wycoller Hall... 166

NOTES

MORE TO EXPLORE
RELATED CICERONE GUIDEBOOKS

Great Mountain Days series

*Great Mountain Days
in the Lake District*
Mark Richards

*Great Mountain Days
in Scotland*
Dan Bailey

*Great Mountain Days
in Snowdonia*
Terry Marsh

Walking guidebooks

High Peak Walks
Mark Richards

*Historic Walks
in North Yorkshire*
Jim Rubery

South Pennine Walks
Jack Keighley

The Lune Valley and Howgills
Dennis and Jan Kelsall

The Reivers Way
Paddy Dillon

The Ribble Way
Dennis and Jan Kelsall

The Teesdale Way
Martin Collins and Paddy Dillon

*The Yorkshire Dales
Vol 1 – South & West
Vol 2 – North & East*
Dennis and Jan Kelsall

Walking in Lancashire
Mary Welsh

Walking in Northumberland
Alan Hall

*Walking in the Forest
of Bowland and Pendle*
Terry Marsh

*Walking on the West
Pennine Moors*
Terry Marsh

Walks in the Yorkshire Dales
Jack Keighley

Cycling guidebooks

Cycling in the Peak District
Chiz Dakin

Cycling the Pennine Bridleway
Keith Bradbury

*Mountain Biking in the
Yorkshire Dales*
Ian Boydon

Other large format guides

The National Trails
Paddy Dillon

The UK's County Tops
Jonny Muir

General skills and techniques

Geocaching in the UK
Terry Marsh

Map and Compass
Pete Hawkins

*Mountain Weather:
Understanding Britain's
Mountain Weather*
David Pedgley

Outdoor Photography
Chiz Dakin and Jon Sparks

*Pocket First Aid
and Wilderness Medicine*
Jim Duff and Peter Gormly

Photo: *Heading for Rye Loaf Hill
(Walk 23)*

LISTING OF CICERONE GUIDES

**BRITISH ISLES CHALLENGES,
COLLECTIONS AND ACTIVITIES**
The End to End Trail
The Mountains of England and Wales
  1 Wales and 2 England
The National Trails
The Relative Hills of Britain
The Ridges of England, Wales and Ireland
The UK Trailwalker's Handbook
The UK's County Tops
Three Peaks, Ten Tors

MOUNTAIN LITERATURE
Unjustifiable Risk?

UK CYCLING
Border Country Cycle Routes
Cycling in the Hebrides
Cycling in the Peak District
Cycling the Pennine Bridleway
Mountain Biking in the Lake District
Mountain Biking in the Yorkshire Dales
Mountain Biking on the South Downs
The C2C Cycle Route
The End to End Cycle Route
The Lancashire Cycleway

SCOTLAND
Backpacker's Britain
  Central and Southern Scottish Highlands
  Northern Scotland
Ben Nevis and Glen Coe
Great Mountain Days in Scotland
North to the Cape
Not the West Highland Way
Scotland's Best Small Mountains
Scotland's Far West
Scotland's Mountain Ridges
Scrambles in Lochaber
The Ayrshire and Arran Coastal Paths
The Border Country
The Great Glen Way
The Isle of Mull
The Isle of Skye
The Pentland Hills
The Southern Upland Way
The Speyside Way
The West Highland Way
Walking in Scotland's Far North
Walking in the Cairngorms
Walking in the Ochils, Campsie Fells
  and Lomond Hills
Walking in Torridon
Walking Loch Lomond and the Trossachs
Walking on Harris and Lewis
Walking on Jura, Islay and Colonsay
Walking on Rum and the Small Isles
Walking on the Isle of Arran
Walking on the Orkney and Shetland Isles
Walking on Uist and Barra
Walking the Corbetts
  1 South of the Great Glen
Walking the Galloway Hills
Walking the Lowther Hills

Walking the Munros
  1 Southern, Central and
    Western Highlands
  2 Northern Highlands and
    the Cairngorms
Winter Climbs Ben Nevis and Glen Coe
Winter Climbs in the Cairngorms
World Mountain Ranges: Scotland

NORTHERN ENGLAND TRAILS
A Northern Coast to Coast Walk
Backpacker's Britain
  Northern England
Hadrian's Wall Path
The Dales Way
The Pennine Way
The Spirit of Hadrian's Wall

**NORTH EAST ENGLAND, YORKSHIRE
DALES AND PENNINES**
Historic Walks in North Yorkshire
South Pennine Walks
St Oswald's Way and St Cuthbert's Way
The Cleveland Way and the
  Yorkshire Wolds Way
The North York Moors
The Reivers Way
The Teesdale Way
The Yorkshire Dales
  North and East
  South and West
Walking in County Durham
Walking in Northumberland
Walking in the North Pennines
Walks in Dales Country
Walks in the Yorkshire Dales
Walks on the North York Moors 1 and 2

**NORTH WEST ENGLAND
AND THE ISLE OF MAN**
Historic Walks in Cheshire
Isle of Man Coastal Path
The Isle of Man
The Lune Valley and Howgills
The Ribble Way
Walking in Cumbria's Eden Valley
Walking in Lancashire
Walking in the Forest of Bowland
  and Pendle
Walking on the West Pennine Moors
Walks in Lancashire Witch Country
Walks in Ribble Country
Walks in Silverdale and Arnside
Walks in the Forest of Bowland

LAKE DISTRICT
Coniston Copper Mines
Great Mountain Days in the Lake District
Lake District Winter Climbs
Lakeland Fellranger
  The Central Fells
  The Mid-Western Fells
  The Near Eastern Fells
  The Northern Fells
  The North-Western Fells
  The Southern Fells
  The Western Fells

Roads and Tracks of the Lake District
Rocky Rambler's Wild Walks
Scrambles in the Lake District
  North and South
Short Walks in Lakeland
  1 South Lakeland
  2 North Lakeland
  3 West Lakeland
The Cumbria Coastal Way
The Cumbria Way and the
  Allerdale Ramble
Tour of the Lake District

**DERBYSHIRE, PEAK DISTRICT
AND MIDLANDS**
High Peak Walks
Scrambles in the Dark Peak
The Star Family Walks
Walking in Derbyshire
White Peak Walks
  The Northern Dales
  The Southern Dales

SOUTHERN ENGLAND
Suffolk Coast and Heaths Walks
The Cotswold Way
The North Downs Way
The Peddars Way and Norfolk Coast Path
The South Downs Way
The South West Coast Path
The Thames Path
Walking in Berkshire
Walking in Kent
Walking in Sussex
Walking in the Isles of Scilly
Walking in the New Forest
Walking in the Thames Valley
Walking on Dartmoor
Walking on Guernsey
Walking on Jersey
Walking on the Isle of Wight
Walks in the South Downs National Park

WALES AND WELSH BORDERS
Backpacker's Britain – Wales
Glyndwr's Way
Great Mountain Days in Snowdonia
Hillwalking in Snowdonia
Hillwalking in Wales
  Vols 1 and 2
Offa's Dyke Path
Ridges of Snowdonia
Scrambles in Snowdonia
The Ascent of Snowdon
Lleyn Peninsula Coastal Path
Pembrokeshire Coastal Path
The Shropshire Hills
The Wye Valley Walk
Walking in Pembrokeshire
Walking in the Forest of Dean
Walking in the South Wales Valleys
Walking on Gower
Walking on the Brecon Beacons
Welsh Winter Climbs

INTERNATIONAL CHALLENGES, COLLECTIONS AND ACTIVITIES
Canyoning
Europe's High Points
The Via Francigena
  (Canterbury to Rome): Part 1

EUROPEAN CYCLING
Cycle Touring in France
Cycle Touring in Ireland
Cycle Touring in Spain
Cycle Touring in Switzerland
Cycling in the French Alps
Cycling the Canal du Midi
Cycling the River Loire
The Danube Cycleway
The Grand Traverse of the Massif Central
The Rhine Cycle Route
The Way of St James

AFRICA
Climbing in the Moroccan Anti-Atlas
Kilimanjaro
Mountaineering in the Moroccan
  High Atlas
The High Atlas
Trekking in the Atlas Mountains
Walking in the Drakensberg

ALPS – CROSS-BORDER ROUTES
100 Hut Walks in the Alps
Across the Eastern Alps: E5
Alpine Points of View
Alpine Ski Mountaineering
  1 Western Alps
  2 Central and Eastern Alps
Chamonix to Zermatt
Snowshoeing
Tour of Mont Blanc
Tour of Monte Rosa
Tour of the Matterhorn
Trekking in the Alps
Walking in the Alps
Walks and Treks in the Maritime Alps

PYRENEES AND FRANCE/SPAIN CROSS-BORDER ROUTES
Rock Climbs in The Pyrenees
The GR10 Trail
The Mountains of Andorra
The Pyrenean Haute Route
The Pyrenees
The Way of St James
  France and Spain
Through the Spanish Pyrenees: GR11
Walks and Climbs in the Pyrenees

AUSTRIA
The Adlerweg
Trekking in Austria's Hohe Tauern
Trekking in the Stubai Alps
Trekking in the Zillertal Alps
Walking in Austria

EASTERN EUROPE
The High Tatras
The Mountains of Romania
Walking in Bulgaria's National Parks
Walking in Hungary

FRANCE
Chamonix Mountain Adventures
Ecrins National Park
GR20: Corsica
Mont Blanc Walks

Mountain Adventures in the Maurienne
The Cathar Way
The GR5 Trail
The Robert Louis Stevenson Trail
Tour of the Oisans: The GR54
Tour of the Queyras
Tour of the Vanoise
Trekking in the Vosges and Jura
Vanoise Ski Touring
Walking in Provence
Walking in the Auvergne
Walking in the Cathar Region
Walking in the Cevennes
Walking in the Dordogne
Walking in the Haute Savoie
  North and South
Walking in the Languedoc
Walking in the Tarentaise and
  Beaufortain Alps
Walking on Corsica

GERMANY
Germany's Romantic Road
Walking in the Bavarian Alps
Walking in the Harz Mountains
Walking the River Rhine Trail

HIMALAYA
Annapurna
Bhutan
Everest: A Trekker's Guide
Garhwal and Kumaon:
  A Trekker's and Visitor's Guide
Kangchenjunga: A Trekker's Guide
Langtang with Gosainkund and Helambu:
  A Trekker's Guide
Manaslu: A Trekker's Guide
The Mount Kailash Trek
Trekking in Ladakh

ICELAND AND GREENLAND
Trekking in Greenland
Walking and Trekking in Iceland

IRELAND
Irish Coastal Walks
The Irish Coast to Coast Walk
The Mountains of Ireland

ITALY
Gran Paradiso
Italy's Sibillini National Park
Shorter Walks in the Dolomites
Through the Italian Alps
Trekking in the Apennines
Trekking in the Dolomites
Via Ferratas of the Italian Dolomites:
  Vols 1 and 2
Walking in Abruzzo
Walking in Sardinia
Walking in Sicily
Walking in the Central Italian Alps
Walking in the Dolomites
Walking in Tuscany
Walking on the Amalfi Coast
Walking the Italian Lakes

MEDITERRANEAN
Jordan – Walks, Treks, Caves, Climbs
  and Canyons
The Ala Dag
The High Mountains of Crete
The Mountains of Greece
Treks and Climbs in Wadi Rum, Jordan

Walking in Malta
Western Crete

NORTH AMERICA
British Columbia
The Grand Canyon
The John Muir Trail
The Pacific Crest Trail

SOUTH AMERICA
Aconcagua and the Southern Andes
Torres del Paine

SCANDINAVIA
Walking in Norway

SLOVENIA, CROATIA AND MONTENEGRO
The Julian Alps of Slovenia
The Mountains of Montenegro
Trekking in Slovenia
Walking in Croatia
Walking in the Karavanke

SPAIN AND PORTUGAL
Costa Blanca: West
Mountain Walking in Southern Catalunya
The Mountains of Central Spain
The Northern Caminos
Trekking through Mallorca
Walking in Madeira
Walking in Mallorca
Walking in the Algarve
Walking in the Cordillera Cantabrica
Walking in the Sierra Nevada
Walking on La Gomera and El Hierro
Walking on La Palma
Walking on Tenerife
Walks and Climbs in the Picos de Europa

SWITZERLAND
Alpine Pass Route
Canyoning in the Alps
Central Switzerland
The Bernese Alps
The Swiss Alps
Tour of the Jungfrau Region
Walking in the Valais
Walking in Ticino
Walks in the Engadine

TECHNIQUES
Geocaching in the UK
Indoor Climbing
Lightweight Camping
Map and Compass
Mountain Weather
Moveable Feasts
Outdoor Photography
Polar Exploration
Rock Climbing
Sport Climbing
The Book of the Bivvy
The Hillwalker's Guide to Mountaineering
The Hillwalker's Manual

MINI GUIDES
Avalanche!
Navigating with a GPS
Navigation
Pocket First Aid and Wilderness Medicine
Snow

For full information on all our guides, and to order books and eBooks, visit our website: **www.cicerone.co.uk**.

Walking – Trekking – Mountaineering – Climbing – Cycling

Over 40 years, Cicerone have built up an outstanding collection of 300 guides, inspiring all sorts of amazing adventures.

Every guide comes from extensive exploration and research by our expert authors, all with a passion for their subjects. They are frequently praised, endorsed and used by clubs, instructors and outdoor organisations.

All our titles can now be bought as **e-books** and many as iPad and Kindle files and we will continue to make all our guides available for these and many other devices.

Our website shows any **new information** we've received since a book was published. Please do let us know if you find anything has changed, so that we can pass on the latest details. On our **website** you'll also find some great ideas and lots of information, including sample chapters, contents lists, reviews, articles and a photo gallery.

It's easy to keep in touch with what's going on at Cicerone, by getting our monthly **free e-newsletter**, which is full of offers, competitions, up-to-date information and topical articles. You can subscribe on our home page and also follow us on **Facebook** and **Twitter**, as well as our **blog**.

Cicerone – the very best guides for exploring the world.

CICERONE

2 Police Square Milnthorpe Cumbria LA7 7PY
Tel: 015395 62069 info@cicerone.co.uk
www.cicerone.co.uk